LOSING CONTROL

LOSING CONTROL

THE EMERGING THREATS TO WESTERN PROSPERITY

STEPHEN D. KING

To Show

With all best wish

from The

[signature]

YALE UNIVERSITY PRESS
NEW HAVEN AND LONDON

For information about this and other Yale University Press publications, please contact:
U.S. Office: sales.press@yale.edu   yalepress.yale.edu
Europe Office: sales@yaleup.co.uk   www.yalebooks.co.uk

Set in Minion by IDSUK (DataConnection) Ltd
Printed in Great Britain by TJ International Ltd, Padstow, Cornwall

Library of Congress Cataloging-in-Publication Data

King, Stephen D., 1963–
   Losing control : the emerging threats to western prosperity / Stephen D. King.
      p. cm.
   ISBN 978-0-300-15432-0 (cl : alk. paper) 1. Western countries—Economic conditions—21st century. 2. Western countries—Economic policy. 3. Developing countries—Economic policy. I.
Title.
   HC59.3.K56 2010
   330.9—dc22   2009052119

A catalogue record for this book is available from the British Library.
10 9 8 7 6 5 4
2014 2013 2012 2011 2010

CONTENTS

To Yvonne, Helena, Olivia and Sophie

ACKNOWLEDGEMENTS

I may have spent many days (and nights) umbilically attached to my keyboard in a quest to complete this book but I can hardly claim to have done so without the support of others who have, throughout the project, offered encouragement, advice and numerous helpful suggestions.

I would like to thank those friends and colleagues who have provided comments on the manuscript, whether in its early stages or as it approached completion. Of particular help were Richard Cookson, Ian Morris, David Bloom (all, at the time, at HSBC) and Peter Oppenheimer (at Goldman Sachs). I am also very grateful to the two anonymous academic referees who provided sage advice to a book-writing novice.

When I delivered speeches on the global economy at the Universities of Oxford and Warwick, both teachers and students encouraged me to think about some of the ideas that now find their way into the book, notably those associated with the history of globalization.

Professor Tim Besley from the London School of Economics offered useful advice on Part 1. The chapter on state capitalism benefited from a lengthy conversation with Professor Dieter Helm from New College, Oxford. The sections on monetary policy were helped by discussions over the years with policymakers, notably from the Bank of England, HM Treasury, the Federal Reserve and the European Central Bank.

My economic horizons have been expanded as a result of regular attendance at events where I have had the chance to converse with fellow economists. Of particular value have been regular meetings at the Bank for International Settlements in Basel, the Oesterreichische Kontrollbank AG (OeKB) in Vienna and the Accumulation Society in London. I have also benefited from my occasional involvement with the Business Council for Britain.

Those who offered encouragement when the book was merely a vague concept include Diane Coyle, Hamish McRae and Martin Wolf. All three know a lot more than I do about writing books and all were kind enough to steer me in the right direction.

I am enormously grateful to the people at Yale University Press. Special thanks go to Phoebe Clapham, my editor, who was dogged in her determination to turn my scribblings into a coherent final manuscript. I also offer my gratitude to Sarah Harrison and Liz Pelton, who have provided so much support on publicity. Heather Nathan has been a source of tremendous encouragement throughout with her infectious enthusiasm, which was instrumental in persuading me to pursue the project from day one.

Many people at HSBC have gone the extra mile to help me in my bid to complete the book. I am grateful to Stuart Gulliver, David Burnett and Bronwyn Curtis for encouraging me to take time off to write the bulk of the material. My colleagues in the HSBC economics team have been enormously helpful. Janet Henry, Stuart Green and Karen Ward picked up the pieces while I was away. Others travelled from far and wide to provide support in my absence, notably Qu Hongbin, Fred Neumann, Robert Prior-Wandesforde and Simon Williams. I also acknowledge the help of Pierre Goad, Jezz Farr and Fiona McClymont, who have worked closely with Yale to bring the project to fruition. I offer particular thanks to Nic Bastion, my PA, and to the University of Bath students who have provided me with statistical support.

Finally, and most importantly, I have to thank my wife, Yvonne, and my three daughters, Helena, Olivia and Sophie. Without their love, and their ongoing support, I would have made little headway. Their patience in the light of the ongoing disruption within the King household – piles of paper, towers of books, the occasional tantrum – knows no bounds. I dedicate the book to them.

PREFACE

As a teenager in the 1970s, I made a trip with a dance band to Bulgaria, a country very much in the true Soviet mould. Even to a rather naive fourteen-year-old saxophonist, the denial of economic freedoms in Bulgaria's capital, Sofia, was fairly obvious. Western goods could be purchased only in so-called 'tourist shops', using foreign currency. Not surprisingly, the black-market exchange rate was far more favourable from a British point of view than the official rate. Bulgarians regarded East German Praktica cameras as the best in the world, seemingly unaware of the growing international dominance of Japanese brands like Canon, Nikon and Pentax. And one youth was particularly keen to purchase my Levis, even though I was wearing them at the time, making me a financial offer I was almost unable to refuse. In hindsight it was obvious that the collapse of Soviet Communism would lead to a very different kind of global economy.

In 2007, I was in Shanghai for a conference. I was lucky enough to be staying at the Grand Hyatt hotel. It's located on the 53rd through to the 87th floors of the Jin Mao Tower, which at the time was the tallest building in China and, indeed, one of the tallest buildings in the world. I had been to the hotel on a number of previous occasions and each time had been mightily impressed by the views from the panoramic windows in my guest room, at least when the building wasn't enveloped in low cloud. Because the building was so high, there was no need to draw the curtains. Privacy was assured.

Stepping out of the bathroom wearing nothing other than my glasses, I was therefore surprised to see a group of Chinese construction workers staring at me through the window. They were building Shanghai's new World Financial Center, a tower that had sprung up with remarkable speed and was shortly set to rise above the Jin Mao tower. I hope none of them fell off on seeing me.

Pudong, the area of Shanghai where these and other spectacular buildings are located, used to be not much more than poor farmland on the less prosperous side of the Huangpu River. The farmers have been shifted elsewhere, sometimes forcibly. The workers and residents of Pudong, in their smart new offices and apartments, can look down upon Shanghai's past. Across the river, the Bund still sparkles at night, providing a reminder of Shanghai's colonial history. Many of its buildings were constructed by the British, the French, the Germans, the Americans and the Russians. Foreign powers erected consulates, banks and sleazy nightclubs. Those working, living or partying in the Bund, meanwhile, are now able to stare across the river and look up to Shanghai's future.

Other than the need to close curtains in tall buildings, the obvious lesson from my experiences in Sofia and Shanghai is that the world economy has fundamentally changed and, for the most part, changed for the better. The tired and arthritic communist systems of the 1970s have mostly gone, either because regimes have fallen or because they have reinvented themselves to accommodate a world of openness. The opportunities created have been truly astounding.

We are living through a new and radical form of globalization where economic prospects are changing, not just in the emerging nations but also in the Western world. However, I am not convinced we have understood the full implications.

WE'RE NOT ON OUR OWN

In my twenty-five years as a professional economist, initially as a civil servant in Whitehall but, for the most part, as an employee of a major international bank, I've spent a good deal of time looking into the future. As the emerging nations first appeared on the economic radar screen, I began to realize I could talk about the future only by delving much further into the past. I wasn't interested merely in the history incorporated into statistical models of the economy, a history which typically includes just a handful of years and therefore ignores almost all the interesting economic developments that have taken place over the last millennium. Instead, the history that mattered to me had to capture the long sweep of economic and political progress and all too frequent reversal. In recent years, as the emerging nations have taken their seats at the international table of powers and superpowers, economic and political history has become increasingly important. How else can we hope to understand the re-emergence of China and India, the growing influence of Russia and the closer integration into the world economy of nations in Latin America, the Middle East, Africa and Eastern Europe?

Through much of the twentieth century, political systems prevented economies from becoming more integrated: indeed, they pushed economies further apart. The collapse of the British Empire, the destruction associated with the First World War, the rise of nationalism, fascism and communism, the horrors of the Second World War and the stalemate of the Cold War all contributed to the destruction of economic relationships. These relationships are now rapidly being rebuilt. Changing patterns of trade and investment opportunities around the world provide compelling evidence of this shift.

Yet many people are in denial. They still tend to think in the old domestic mindsets. They are slaves to national economic data that, for the most part, include only the most recent domestic economic developments. They are slaves to a world that, in effect, crumbled as Deng Xiaoping opened up China to the global economy at the beginning of the 1980s and as the Berlin Wall collapsed in 1989.

During the 1980s, as cumbersome mainframe computers were replaced by PCs, economists began to calibrate statistically the ways in which economies operated. With reams of annual, quarterly, monthly, daily and even intra-day data at their disposal and with significant advances in computing power, they were able to build economic models linked to past reality (and, as the models became more complex, to 'expected' future reality). The mathematics employed in the construction of these models was often mind-bogglingly complex, but, at the end of the day, all the models rested on a few simple assumptions: (i) the recent past could be represented with some degree of accuracy; (ii) the future was similar to the recent past; (iii) the public understood the aims of policymakers who, in turn, delivered credible and socially desirable policies, thereby confirming the public's understanding; and (iv) economic relationships with other countries could be captured through some simple trade equations, a global interest rate and an assumed level for oil prices and the exchange rate.

These models, essentially national in nature and limited to economic experience over only a few years, performed like clockwork. The rest of the world mattered, but only in a minor way. Capital flows hardly mattered at all, in part because in the 1980s there was still a significant home bias in savings and investment flows. The models gave the impression that domestic policymakers were, for the most part, in control of their nation's economic destiny.

Those employed to run the models were happy to support this view. In the mid-1980s, when I worked at HM Treasury, many dozens of economists were employed to analyse the UK economy. There were only four monitoring developments in the rest of the world. Today, the numbers covering the rest of the world have gone up but the language remains the same: politicians in particular routinely claim their countries are subject to global 'shocks' as if the rest of the world is on another planet rather than just over the sea or across the border. Admittedly, policymakers recognized long ago that 'when America sneezes, the rest of the world catches a cold', but there was little understanding of how the global economy as a whole operated. Nation states were, apparently, economically sovereign.

Over the years, I have become more and more frustrated with this approach, in particular because of the huge expansion of global capital markets linking economies together in ways which, in the 1980s, seemed unimaginable. Savers in one part of the world can now easily invest elsewhere. In theory, their behaviour implies that capital is more efficiently allocated globally, delivering a higher level of economic well-being as a result. In practice, however, these cross-border capital flows are sometimes a source of inefficiency given that many of the biggest players are nation states that choose not to pursue commercial objectives but, instead, focus on meeting the interests of their various internal constituents: the US government is the world's biggest borrower while the Chinese, Saudis and Russians are among the world's biggest savers.

It may be that the data simply do not exist to measure, calibrate and analyse these growing interactions between the developed and emerging worlds, but that does not mean to say they can be ignored. Regrettably, as with the 2007/8 credit crunch, they too often are. Even when they are taken into account, it's often just one-way traffic. Plenty of economists spend their time trying to work out how developments in the United States affect the rest of the world. Few spend their time asking how the rest of the world and, in particular, the emerging nations affect the US. Yet, as I argue in this book, this second question needs to be asked more and more if we are to understand anything about developments in the world economy and in our own economies in the twenty-first century.

GLOBALIZATION OPENS UP THE WORLD

Openness matters. Never before has the world economy been quite so 'open' as it is today. I strongly believe this is a good thing. The number of people lifted out of poverty since the 1980s has swamped anything achieved at any time in the past, even during the heady days of the Industrial Revolution. Their improving lifestyles reflect much that is good about globalization.

To pretend, however, that globalization is automatically leading us to an economic land of milk and honey through the miracle of market forces, as is so often claimed, is foolish. Parallels are often drawn with the late nineteenth and the early twentieth centuries, when globalization last reached a peak (and, with the advent of the First World War, came to a sticky end). Yet we live in a very different, and rather paradoxical, world. We have more globalization today, in the form of much higher international trade and cross-border capital flows. A company headquartered in the US might make its profits through a subsidiary in China which, in turn, imports raw materials from Brazil. Its sales, meanwhile, may be primarily in the Middle East, while its profits will be distributed to its large numbers of European shareholders.

We also, however, have much less globalization. There has been a proliferation of nation states and, hence, legal and regulatory systems as the empires of the nineteenth and twentieth centuries have given way to self-determination, nationalism and religious sectarianism. We have a much-reduced volume of cross-border migration, at least in relation to the size of now much bigger indigenous populations.[1]

Hoards of people crossed borders, seas and oceans in the nineteenth century, through both the coercion of slavery and the search for a better life. Indeed, the US would not be the nation it is today had it not been for earlier large-scale waves of migration. The border controls we now take for granted were an invention of the twentieth century: they limit the ability of entrepreneurial workers to go in search of economic opportunities in other parts of the world.

Even if the global economic cake is bigger as a result of this latest wave of globalization, there are both winners and losers. The heightened gravitational pull of the emerging world may be reducing income inequality between nations, but it is also increasing income inequality within nations. Over the last forty years, for example, income inequality in the US has risen dramatically.[2]

The rise of the emerging nations thus creates a whole new set of challenges which, all too often, are either swept under the carpet by the supporters of globalization or, instead, distorted to suit the varying interests of xenophobes, nationalists and the anti-big business lobby.[3] Globalization has undoubtedly led to higher global incomes but, at the same time, individual nations are struggling to cope with some of its other effects: greater economic instability, heightened income inequality and financial market turmoil.

It is, of course, a comforting thought that the rest of the world is embracing the spirit of industrial innovation established in the late eighteenth and early nineteenth centuries in a newly enlightened Europe and a newly independent United States. Technologies now spread more quickly to other parts of the world, a reflection of lower transportation costs and, more recently, much lower information costs. Trade between Western and emerging nations has flourished. There are more democracies now than there used to be. Yet, as I shall argue, economic progress in the developed world did not just depend on improvements in technology or the adoption of democracy. It also depended on access to 'enabling resources' – land, raw materials, migration (and, in the past, slavery) – and the ability to rig markets. The arrival on the world economic stage of the emerging nations has the potential to undermine these sources of Western prosperity, both through the emerging nations' own demands over resources that are ultimately limited and through the heightened level of cross-border competition in a wide range of markets. The West had been economically comfortable for many years: life is now becoming distinctly uncomfortable.

Do additional enabling resources still exist? Can the world easily accommodate continued rapid economic growth without bumping into a new economic constraint? Is the replication of existing technologies across more and more nations sufficient to allow continued economic advance at a pace that people have come to expect? Can Western labour markets easily withstand the competitive onslaught coming from the rapidly improving labour markets in the emerging world?

At the very least, the West needs to consider its relative position in the world economic and political order. In the 1950s, 1960s and 1970s, the West *was* the world economy, with only Japan and South Korea threatening the old economic order. Other countries were, in economic terms, also-rans. By the 2050s and 2060s, I argue, the West will be a shadow of its former economic self, both in terms of its falling share of the global economic pie and its rapidly diminishing share of the world's ever-increasing population. How and why this process will happen, and its likely consequences – both good and bad – are the key themes of this book.

THE OUTLINE

In the following pages, I outline some of the many ways in which the developed world is in danger of losing control over its economic destiny. Part One, 'Scarcity and History', tries to place our understanding of globalization today in the context of basic economic principles and our economic past. I underline the importance of China's emergence as a growing economic superpower in the late 1970s, a development of epic importance. As China begins to throw its weight around, the West will no longer be able to take its economic progress for granted. Too often, I believe, policymakers lose sight of one of the key issues in economics, namely the idea that resources are ultimately *scarce*. They have done so because, for many years, the West has not had to face competition from others for the world's scarce resources. It does now.

Part Two, 'Broken Economic Barometers', deals with our understanding of what makes economies tick. Are standard theories of comparative advantage – which have been the mainstay of free-trade arguments over the years – still useful in explaining the trade patterns emerging today? Is the growing instability of financial markets a response to the heightened importance of the emerging nations? Why have financial market returns been so low since the 1990s despite the rapid growth of the emerging nations? Are we seeing a modern-day version of the Californian gold rush, with the vast majority of investors seeing their dreams of rising wealth continuously dashed? Part Two ends with a critique of Western monetary policy. Has the pursuit of inflation-targeting become a source of instability in a world where the prices of goods, services and capital are now increasingly being determined by developments in the emerging nations?

Part Three, 'The Return of Political Economy', examines some of the big questions confronting Western nations in the years ahead. Why is income inequality so high, particularly in the US and the UK? Why have the benefits of globalization accrued largely to the already very rich (and, thus, very lucky)? If globalization represents a triumph for market forces, why are we seeing the rise of state capitalism, a topic that crops up time and again in this book? Do we really live in a global market economy when so much economic activity is influenced by governments, either directly via high levels of public spending or indirectly through government influence on energy supplies or bond prices?

If past economic success owed much to mass migrations of people both within countries and across borders, what should we make of heightened border controls and the growth of anti-immigration politics? How will Western countries deal with the economic hole created by population ageing? Will they be forced to rethink their current resistance to large-scale immigration?

Part Four, 'Great Power Games', draws together the various strands of my thesis. Like Spain in the sixteenth century, the US is in danger of becoming a busted flush. Yes, it has the most powerful military machine in the world, but so did Spain five hundred years ago. Frankly, the US has become too dependent on the willingness of other nations to hold its dollars, in the same way that Spain depended on others to hold its silver. The more the US has borrowed from the rest of the world, the more economically powerful the rest of the world has become. In time, it's quite possible that China's renminbi will replace the dollar as the world's reserve currency.

More broadly, I examine the options open to the world's policy-makers. Reforming the international monetary system is of great importance. In my view, the peculiarities of the euro – a currency which can and does attract new members – offer a blueprint for future monetary reform. If membership of a single currency can gradually increase, it surely creates the opportunity to build a world where the proliferation of nation states need not get in the way of enhanced monetary stability. Could something similar happen for the dollar or for currencies in Asia, leading to the creation of regional, rather than national, central banks?

I have written this final section with a heavy heart. The pressures on the West stemming from globalization may, ultimately, be politically too difficult to absorb. I already sense a shift away from multilateral to bilateral economic arrangements, whatever the G20 pretends to offer. These bilateral deals are not just those which will define the ongoing relationship between the US and China but also those which will carve up the rest of the world. Think, for example, of China's growing bilateral arrangements with selected African states. More worryingly, protectionist pressures are growing. Should they become strong enough, the West could quite easily turn its back on globalization, a knee-jerk reaction to its waning influence in world economic affairs. That would be a tragedy, not least because globalization has been instrumental in lifting so many people out of poverty. Unfortunately, history shows that our ability to avoid the tragic outcome has often been lacking.

History, politics and geography matter. Too often, economists end up lost in a mathematical world of esoteric equations which cannot provide answers to the really big questions affecting society. At the British Academy in the summer of 2009, the great and the good of the UK economics profession met to discuss the drafting of a letter to Her Majesty the Queen intended to explain why economists had failed to spot the credit crunch. The letter subsequently delivered to Buckingham Palace ended as follows:

> In summary, Your Majesty, the failure to foresee the timing, extent and severity of the crisis and to head it off, while it had many causes, was principally a failure of the collective imagination of many bright people, both in this country and internationally, to understand the risks to the system as a whole.

A simpler conclusion might have been to say that many bright people had failed to learn the lessons of history, politics and geography. Part One uses these lessons to explain why the West has, until now, enjoyed its time in the economic sun and why, in the years ahead, the sun will be shining on the other side of the world.

PART ONE

SCARCITY AND HISTORY

CHAPTER ONE

WIMBLEDON, THE OLYMPICS AND SCARCITY

For Margaret Goodson, my inspirational teacher at school, economics was about the allocation of scarce resources. The costs of using resources in one particular way were the opportunities foregone. These were 'opportunity costs'. Having more of one thing meant having to forego something else. Economics was, therefore, about the choices to be made in a world of scarcity.

Scarcity and choice dominate our lives in all sorts of different ways. I chose to go to university to study economics, thereby forfeiting any hopes of becoming a professional musician. By choosing one subject, I let go of another: both time and money were scarce. Western governments choose to cultivate bio-fuels to allow us access to cheaper energy. By doing so, the opportunity to grow sufficient crops to feed the starving and the destitute may be foregone.

At its worst, scarcity promotes armed conflict. In Africa and elsewhere, low incomes per head and a sense of hopelessness about the economic future lead all too frequently to war and war, in turn, lowers incomes per head. People choose (or are forced) to fight, rather than feed, each other.

In the West, where we've experienced steadily rising living standards for many years, we have often forgotten about the ultimate economic constraint of scarcity. Technologies will overcome temporary shortages. People and governments ignore budgetary constraints, hoping instead for continued access to credit. Governments boast about the pace of economic growth. We have come to expect – even to deserve – higher living standards, based on our faith in the success of technology and free markets. Those countries that do not deliver are labelled failures.

With the rise of the emerging nations, this kind of complacent thinking will have to change. Western living standards will not progress in the future as they have done in the past. Western economies are being pushed to one side by much more dynamic nations elsewhere in the world. Yet our leaders constantly promise more economic growth, seemingly unaware of the growing constraints being imposed on the West as a result of the economic success of nations elsewhere in the world.

There are many good examples of the hubris associated with Western economic progress. In his January 2007 State of the Union Address, President George W. Bush boasted of his past achievements:

> A future of hope and opportunity begins with a growing economy, and that is what we have. We are now in the 41st month of uninterrupted job growth, a recovery that has created 7.2 million new jobs so far. Unemployment is low, inflation is low, wages are rising. This economy is on the move. And our job is to keep it that way – not with more government but with more enterprise.[1]

Two years later, unemployment had soared, the budget deficit had exploded and the US had suffered its deepest recession since the 1930s.

Gordon Brown was similarly guilty. As Britain's Chancellor of the Exchequer, he said in his 2006 pre-Budget Report speech to the House of Commons:

> I can report not only the longest period of sustained growth in our history, but of all the major economies – America, France, Germany, Japan – Britain has enjoyed the longest post war period of continuous growth . . . In no other decade has Britain's personal wealth – up 60 per cent – grown so fast. And this Pre-Budget Report drives forward the great economic mission of our time – to meet the global challenge, to unleash the potential of all British people, so that the British economy outperforms our competitors – and deliver security, prosperity, and fairness for all.[2]

Suitably tub-thumping stuff, perhaps, but on the back of a housing collapse and banking implosion the UK was soon to join the US in what became a deep and protracted recession for the Western world as a whole.

Why were political leaders so confident? Why did policymakers believe they had found the holy grail of economic success? In part, I think, they had forgotten about the ultimate constraints of scarcity. They certainly chose to ignore the growing claims on the world's scarce resources being made by the increasingly dynamic emerging nations. They had, thus, forgotten about Mrs Goodson's fundamental economic choices.

PLAY UP! PLAY UP! AND PLAY THE GAME!

The rise – or more accurately, the economic re-emergence – of countries like China and India is profoundly changing the behaviour of the world economy and, within it, the West's relative economic power. To understand the growing influence of the emerging world, let me offer two trivial examples. The first concerns competition over scarce resources. The second is about opportunity.

Wimbledon

The tennis Championships at Wimbledon offer scarce resources. In the Ladies' Singles Championship, for example, there is only one trophy; so there can be only one winner. Before the First World War, when Wimbledon was very much an English affair (Wimbledon is, after all, the home of the All England Lawn Tennis and Croquet Club), the ladies' champion was almost always English. Indeed, the only interloper was May Sutton, an American, who won the trophy in 1905 and 1907.

During the interwar period, English dominance faded dramatically. The French and the Americans, in the shape of Suzanne Lenglen and Helen Wills Moody, dominated. Since the end of the Second World War, American supremacy has been maintained, but champions have also come from Germany, Brazil, the Czech Republic, Switzerland, Spain and Australia (two came from England, although one of them, Virginia Wade, spent the formative years of her life in South Africa).

Have English tennis players got worse over the years? Was something put in the nation's tea to undermine racquet skills? Not at all. England's players have, instead, become victims of globalization. Globalization – in its broadest terms, political and economic openness – has allowed players from an increasing number of countries to take part in the Wimbledon championships. The ladies' singles quarter-finals in 2008, for example, included two Americans, two Russians, a Czech, a Pole and, for the first time ever, two women from Asia, one from Thailand and one from China. For an Englishwoman, becoming Wimbledon champion today is considerably more difficult than it was a hundred years ago. Compare the current situation, for example, with the first ladies' event held in 1884, when Maud Watson emerged triumphant from a field of just thirteen competitors.

The Olympics

Apart from the occasional interruption for a world war, the summer Olympic Games have taken place every fourth year since the inaugural modern Games were held in Athens in 1896. Before the Second World War, the Olympics were a European and American affair, sometimes characterized more by their chaotic organization and quirky winners than by their sporting prowess. The St Louis Games held in 1904 are a case in point. According to the International Olympic Committee, 'The [St Louis] Olympic competitions, spread out over four and a half months, were lost in the chaos of a World's Fair. Of the 94 events generally considered to have been part of the Olympic program, only 42 included athletes who were not from the United States.' The highlight for that year was an American gymnast, George Eyser, 'who won six medals even though his left leg was made of wood'.[3]

Before the First World War, few nations joined in, partly because there were more empires, and hence fewer nations, than there are today. The Athens Olympics in 1896 included athletes representing just fourteen countries. Even during the interwar years, country representation wasn't very high, peaking at forty-nine for Hitler's Berlin Olympics in 1936 when Jesse Owens, an African-American, made a fool of the Nazi leader.[4]

After the Second World War, the Olympics changed rapidly. The number of participating countries increased dramatically. At the Beijing Olympics in 2008, for example, athletes from 204 countries took part. For the purposes of this book, though, the more interesting development has been the shift in Olympic geography. No longer do Europe and the US enjoy a monopoly over the location of the Games.

The initial experiment – very much a case of playing safe – took place in Melbourne in 1956, with the first-ever southern hemisphere

7

games. Since then, the Olympic movement has become far more adventurous. Of the sixteen summer games held since the Second World War, six have been held in Europe, two in the US and one in Canada. Five have been held in the Asia-Pacific area, one in Moscow and one in Mexico City. The likelihood of US or European cities becoming host nations has slowly declined. Admittedly, London is hosting the 2012 Olympics, but, despite the best efforts of President and Michelle Obama, the 2016 Olympics were awarded not to Chicago but, instead, to Rio de Janeiro, making Brazil the first South American country to host the games.[5] Meanwhile, even with the demise of America's Cold War rivals, the US medal count is not what it once was. The US Olympic team achieved an impressive gold medal haul of forty-four in the 1996 Atlanta Games, but this number dropped to thirty-six in the three subsequent competitions. China, meanwhile, has seen its gold medal tally rise from sixteen in 1996 to a massive fifty-one in Beijing in 2008.[6]

Both my examples demonstrate that for many years Westerners enjoyed the best sporting opportunities and the biggest sporting rewards. As, however, the world has opened up, becoming increasingly connected in the process, more and more nations and their people have striven for a piece of the sporting action. Western sportsmen and women and the Olympic Committees that support them have lost out, at least from the perspective of the number of medals and trophies won.

Wimbledon and the Olympics are simple metaphors for economic developments on the grandest of scales. As the emerging nations have become increasingly successful, extending their grip on the world's resources, so the Western world is discovering that its own claims on these resources are slowly diminishing.

In the second half of the twentieth century, the Western nations absolutely dominated the global economy. They had the tools to do so – the best technologies, the most effective forms of government and the most educated workforces. As we shall see in Chapter 2, history was squarely on the West's side. Meanwhile, the vast majority of the world's population was unable to make credible economic claims, which reflected both technological and (often self-imposed) political barriers alongside an absence of effective market mechanisms. That is all beginning to change. As existing technologies are replicated across more and more parts of the world, so the number of people hoping to enjoy 'Western' lifestyles is rising dramatically.

As a result, the demand for ultimately scarce resources – most obviously food and fuel – is growing rapidly. At the same time, the competitive environment is changing. Fragmented local labour markets are increasingly being joined together, reducing the relative bargaining power of many Western workers. The ability to negotiate pay increases and decent pensions is fading, constrained by the competitive onslaught from newly enfranchised workers elsewhere in the world.

Our belief in ever-rising living standards hinges on the idea that the West will continue to reap significant economic benefits from technological progress. As we shall see, however, this idea is unsound. Japan is one of the most technologically advanced countries in the world yet its economy has stagnated over the last twenty years. Technologies certainly help to raise living standards, but the story doesn't end there. Technologies also change the competitive nature of markets, to the advantage of some but to the disadvantage of others. And they allow more people to gain access to scarce resources. Rising incomes in the emerging world are increasingly affecting prices of goods, services, labour and capital in the Western world, forcing people to adjust to new, and often challenging, economic realities.

The rise of the emerging nations is, thus, of fundamental importance. The emerging nations' success undermines our understanding of what makes economies tick. The study of economics has, regrettably, become an increasingly technical discipline, ill-equipped to deal with the extraordinary upheavals now taking place in the world economy. In particular, economists have too often forgotten that economics is rooted in politics. The great economists of the past – Adam Smith, David Ricardo, John Stuart Mill and Karl Marx, to name but a few – understood that scarcity was linked to choice and choice, in turn, was linked to politics. The economics that mattered to these great thinkers and which still matters to the man and woman on the street is not just about the most efficient allocation of resources but also about the distribution of those resources: who ends up better off, who ends up worse off, who wins and who loses. We are, at long last, witnessing the return of what used to be called 'political economy'.

Political economy has too often been ignored, its imprecision and normative nature incompatible with the extraordinarily complex mathematical models that form the bread and butter of the typical economist's tools. Yet, as the emerging nations stake their claim on the world's scarce resources, the West's influence on global economic affairs is on the wane. How will scarce resources be distributed? Will the market be left in charge or will nation states increasingly call the shots? And is Western economic power beginning to fade? The interaction between the Western world and the emerging nations brings the politics back into economics (and, for that matter, takes the mathematics out).

FAITH IN THE MARKET

Market forces alone cannot deal with political economy. Nevertheless, for many years, policymakers were happy to leave difficulties over scarcity to the market and, in particular, to the price mechanism.

It is easy to see why. Since the end of the First World War, the political and economic debate both among and within the major powers has focused on the relative merits of market and state as providers of our economic well-being. Early in the twentieth century, the debate became increasingly polarized through the impact of the Russian Revolution in 1917, the strengthening of the trade-union movement in the UK in the 1920s and the US Great Depression of the 1930s.

The debate, in turn, reflected the search for an economic system that raised living standards for populations at large. With the end of Maoist policies in China in the late 1970s and the collapse of Soviet communism at the end of the 1980s, it seemed as though the market had emerged triumphant (that, at least, became the myth: public sectors in the Western world nevertheless consumed a much greater proportion of resources than they did at the end of the nineteenth century). Economic growth in North America, Europe, Japan, Australia and New Zealand (mostly the Western world) was faster, more sustainable and of better quality than under Chairman Mao's China and the Soviet regimes of Russia and Eastern Europe (which, too often, relied on slave labour). Eastern European countries became 'client states' of the Soviet Union, commanded to produce goods with no regard for the idiosyncratic economic advantages each country enjoyed. This was economic policy by edict. It was not a reflection of society's true preferences.[7]

At the level of the very small, markets often work very well. While we don't pop down to the local supermarket and studiously calculate the opportunity costs of each of our purchases, opportunity cost is still involved. Our budgets reflect scarce resources. And the way we allocate those resources depends on price. The price mechanism, in turn, is a remarkably efficient way of allowing us to make informed choices about scarcity. If something is expensive, its opportunity cost may be high. If something is cheap, its opportunity cost might be correspondingly low. Adam Smith (1723–1790), one of the economic greats and now deservedly immortalized on the Bank of England £20 note, called the price mechanism the 'invisible hand'.[8]

Many people have been seduced by Smith's ideas, sufficiently so as to claim that free markets are the sole reason behind the West's ongoing prosperity. Yet markets do not always work very well. They are not very good at identifying the environmental consequences of our actions. They do not cope well when there is a lack of well-established property rights. Why invest, for example, if your profits are siphoned off by an avaricious government or by a Mafia-style protection racket? With insufficient information, markets cannot always deliver desirable outcomes.[9] People too often try to rig markets for their personal gain. Monopolies, for example, may not act in the public interest, but they can certainly make their share-holders very happy. Markets do not always deal satisfactorily with choices over time. Capital markets, for example, are supposed to say something about the preference for consuming now as opposed to consuming in the future. Sub-prime crises, banking failures and equity market booms and busts suggest, though, that capital markets are not always entirely reliable. With time comes both risk (which can be quantified to a degree) and uncertainty (which cannot).

Good government is a precondition for effective markets, because without government there is no legal system and, hence, an absence of property rights. Governments may need to step in to 'correct' the perceived unfair distributional consequences of the billions of transactions that now occur in the global marketplace. In the presence of market failures, governments may also feel obliged to act through state provision of resources (roads, police and defence, for example), through regulation and through taxation. If the market cannot provide, the state will.[10]

We thus live in a world of mixed economies where the pluralism of markets is countered by state provision of countless goods and services and, separately, a legal and regulatory rulebook for markets and their participants. Whether market or state, however, the same difficulties apply: how are choices to be made in a world of scarcity?

And how are those choices to be expressed in a world where markets are increasingly connected but where individual nations wish to preserve their sovereignty?

BACK TO THE CLASSICAL ECONOMISTS

With scarce resources, there's no particular reason why higher living standards should always be achievable, no matter how market-friendly an economy might be. How, then, have some societies managed to perform what would seem to be a remarkable trick? If resources are scarce, how have living standards consistently risen? How has the curse of Thomas Malthus (1766–1834), author of *An Essay on the Principles of Population* (first published in 1798), been sidestepped? Is Western progress really just the result of market forces?

Malthus's arguments were, as far as I can tell, based on his view that labourers had voracious sexual appetites. In his words, 'in all societies, even those that are most vicious, the tendency to a virtuous attachment is so strong that there is a constant effort towards an increase of population. This constant effort . . . tends to subject the lower classes of the society to distress and to prevent any great permanent amelioration of their condition.'[11] In other words, the lower classes tended to produce offspring in such numbers that they'd remain, collectively, impoverished. Even if there was an improvement in technology that allowed people to have better lifestyles, those lifestyles would improve only temporarily. People with higher incomes would be tempted to have lots of children: the resulting population increase would place additional pressure on resources, increasing prices, lowering wages and pushing the population back to a life of subsistence.

Not surprisingly, others took exception to this provocative stance, and Malthus himself later admitted that perhaps he'd been a little harsh (even though, to be fair, his arguments were a reasonably accurate description of economic progress for the vast bulk of human history). In subsequent editions of his *Essay*, he accepted that people might abstain from sex, marry late or turn down the opportunity to have sex outside marriage (given the imminent arrival of the prudish Victorians, these observations were more accurate than he could possibly have imagined: Victoria became queen three years after Malthus's death). Oddly, he referred only to the lower classes. Perhaps he thought the landed gentry either didn't find each other attractive or, instead, were mostly homosexual.[12]

In the developed world, the Malthusian constraint has been overcome by human ingenuity, more specifically efficient economic organization, technical progress and contraception. Over time, we have learnt how to create more and more outputs from given inputs, and we have also managed to control the unintended consequences of our lasciviousness. That, at least, is the popular myth.

Long before Malthus's provocative *Essay*, Adam Smith had already emphasized the division of labour with his famous example of a pin factory and the skills specializations of its various workers. Through specialization, many more pins could be produced. Combine specialization with technical progress and society can deliver huge improvements in living standards. It's called productivity growth. Think, for example, of the first trains, planes and computers. Each was a remarkable achievement, but each was the beginning, not the end, of an endeavour. Stephenson's *Rocket* doesn't compare with Japan's Shinkansen (or 'Bullet' train). The Wright Brothers' inaugural flights cannot compete with the Airbus A380. The earliest mainframe computers had less processing power than the cheapest of today's laptops. In each case, innovations have led to enormous improvements in productivity. Capitalism, meanwhile, rewards some of the risk-taking innovators with profits (it also, of course, creates losses for others).

This constant process of innovation is capitalism's greatest strength. Karl Marx (1818–1883) understood this very well. Even though he implored the 'workers of the world [to] unite: you have nothing to lose but your chains',[13] he nevertheless recognized that capitalism was a critical stage in man's economic development: the revolution could only be a success if capitalists had created the wealth that could eventually be distributed among the proletariat.

Capitalism thrives best when ideas are allowed to flourish and where profitable opportunities can be developed. Remove those key incentives and economies atrophy. The success of the developed world partly rests, then, on freedom of expression and the rule of law (particularly with regard to the establishment of legally enforceable property rights, a point well understood by Adam Smith: the incentive to develop a new product is much reduced if there's no patent system, for example).[14]

Meanwhile, contraception has limited population growth in the developed world and, hence, has allowed ever-increasing income to be shared out among the lucky few. Ireland's Celtic Tiger boom in the 1980s and 1990s was achieved in part because women were able to go out to work rather than staying at home to endure far too many births: contraception can also play a big role in creating economic opportunity.

As Sir Isaac Newton might have said, we benefit economically from standing on the shoulders of centuries of creative, inventive and innovative giants. Each giant made his or her own contribution to the advancement of productivity. Productivity – measured either as output per hour or output per head – is the elixir of economic growth, the magical process that seemingly bypasses the problem of scarce resources. Productivity is, thus, the alchemy that turns base resources into economic gold.

There have been many interruptions along the way, including, most obviously, wars, the Great Depression of the 1930s and the stagflation of the 1970s.[15] Moreover, not all countries and continents have benefited from productivity's magical effects. While the developed world has become progressively richer over time, and the emerging world is now beginning to catch up, other countries and continents have suffered.

Some countries – notably in sub-Saharan Africa, parts of Central Asia and Central America – have been caught in seemingly irresolvable poverty traps. In many of those countries, the Malthusian constraint does, to a degree, hold. Parents choose to have many children not necessarily because, in Malthusian terms, they're addicted to sex, but, instead, because having more children supposedly guarantees greater economic security in old age (particularly so if property rights are poorly established and, thus, financial savings can easily be lost). Of course, if everyone thinks like this, the population multiplies too quickly and people, all too often, starve.

To remove the Malthusian constraint, then, any self-respecting political leader wants to have a piece of the productivity action. Higher productivity should deliver higher incomes. Yet, as I argue throughout this book, gains in productivity have not delivered universal benefits. With the rise of the emerging nations, the economic calculus is changing in ways that seem to be undermining Western hopes of ever-rising living standards, even allowing for continued technological progress across the world as a whole.

OPPORTUNITY FOR ALL

The changing fortunes exemplified by Wimbledon and the Olympics stem from two key aspects of globalization.

Political barriers have come down. Following the collapse of Soviet communism, estranged countries and their previously repressed people have become more closely connected with the Western world than before. On the streets of London and New York, Russian accents these days represent a combination of super-rich oligarchs and the new pioneering spirit from the East and not necessarily, as once might have been the case, the presence of the KGB.[16]

Technologies have enabled more and more people to join the international economic order. Where governments allow, migrants increasingly head to countries that offer better economic prospects. Capital heads towards countries where labour is cheaper. People are better connected and better informed. For example, a one-minute mobile phone call from India to the UK cost around IR100 per minute in 1995. Thirteen years later, the same phone call cost just IR9 per minute.[17]

Put simply, an increasing number of people have access to economic opportunity. These opportunities create incentives. Indians, Chinese, Russians and others can go to college knowing full well that their opportunities upon graduation will be much better than before. Multinationals increasingly hire all over the world. They're no longer restricted to Harvard, Yale, Oxford or Cambridge. And, even if multinationals only focused on the West's best educational establishments, they'd happily find that the best universities, in turn, cast their nets further and further afield to grab the world's brightest young people.[18] Meanwhile, entrepreneurs can come from all over the world. There's no reason why, for example, software development should reside only in Silicon Valley. Nowadays, India has its own technology industry.

The economic effects of this 'opening up' are extraordinary. Since the 1980s, for example, Chinese incomes have risen at a faster rate than those in Europe for the first time in six centuries, thanks to Deng Xiaoping's willingness to encourage China to engage with the rest of the world. China's share of global output has consequently soared (from a low of 5 per cent in 1950 to 15 per cent by the beginning of the twenty-first century).[19] So has its share of world trade. Chairman Mao famously boasted in the 1950s about China's Great Leap Forward. As it turned out, he was forty or fifty years too early.

Similar stories can be found all over what is now called the emerging world. India's growth rate has accelerated in recent decades, helped along by the so-called green revolution of the 1960s and 1970s, during which crop yields rose dramatically. The collapse of the Soviet Union led India's leaders to realign their interests with the West. Trade barriers have been slowly reduced and trade has flourished as a result. Meanwhile, for former members of the Soviet Empire, openness is, in some cases, resulting in a mini-version of China's experience. 1917 marked the start of the 'short-century' economic and political mistake in Russia, and, through its repressive influence, Russia's western and southern neighbours. Taken together, the emerging nations are now at least as big economically as the US and they're growing around three times faster.

Admittedly, despite their gains, many in the emerging nations are still very poor. For example, the median income per capita for China's rural workers in 2008 stood at RMB4, 700 or, in 2008 dollars, $691. Yet, for urban workers, life is getting better; income per capita for Chinese urbanites in 2008 was RMB15,000 or $2,205. Within this urban group, there are now millions of people earning annual incomes in the $5,000–10,000 range. At these levels, citizens begin to place increasing demands on the world's scarce resources. They want cars, holidays, central heating, air-conditioning and all the paraphernalia of modern life.[20] They aspire to Western diets. Meat, poultry and dairy are favoured, while the simple bowl of rice is treated with disdain. Feeding people via animals, though, is highly inefficient: to feed the animals that then are used to feed humans requires many more crops compared with feeding humans from the fields directly.

China's increased command over the world's resources can be seen in all sorts of different ways. Since the beginning of the twenty-first century, it has been the single biggest contributor to increased global energy demand. China is now the most important marginal consumer of aluminium and copper. The proliferation of Starbucks in Beijing and Shanghai demonstrates the Chinese middle classes' desire to have Western diets (ostensibly, Starbucks sells coffee, but, given that its most popular products are lattes, cappuccinos and frappucinos, its sales are effectively dominated by milk). Meanwhile, China represents Ferrari's fastest-growing market in the world.

China is not the first Asian country to gain a foothold on the ladder of economic progress. From the 1950s through to the 1980s, Japan's economy grew at a faster rate than that of either the US or the major European countries. South Korea followed Japan's example later. Sixty years ago, after the Korean War, South Korea was impoverished, with the majority of people living off subsistence agriculture. Now Seoul is the home of well-known multinationals such as Samsung and LG.

Yet while the Japanese and Korean experiences are of considerable interest, in global terms China and India are in a different league. Japan has a population of 120 million. South Korea's population is around 80 million. These numbers are dwarfed by China and India. At the last count, China had a population of 1.3 billion while India's population amounted to 1.1 billion. India's population will soon exceed China's, reflecting a relatively high Indian birth rate, falling infant mortality and, for China, the restrictions imposed by the one-child policy. Whatever the relativities, however, the aggregate populations of China and India are enormous in global terms. Taken together, China and India account for well over one-third of the world's population, currently estimated to be 6.6 billion. Even if only a fraction of Chinese and Indians have the opportunity to make effective claims on the world's resources, the balance of economic power will probably shift dramatically. No productivity miracle is likely to be big enough to cope with this demographic pressure.

China is the first economy of size still to have remarkably low per-capita incomes by global standards. In the past, there has been a strong correlation between overall output and output per head. For example, the US is the world's biggest economy and, of the major industrial nations, has one of the highest levels of income per capita. Conversely, the majority of poor countries are poor both in per-capita terms and also in total. China is unique. Following thirty years of rapid economic growth it is still poor in relation to the industrialized world, but already it has become a huge global player in resource markets. Imagine, then, that China keeps growing at its current rate. In thirty years' time China would be roughly the same size in economic terms as the US. Its per-capita incomes would still be much lower, but its citizens would, collectively, be placing huge demands on the world's resources. Simple calculations suggest that, by the middle of the twenty-first century, China would be trying to consume the equivalent of all today's global oil output.

That, of course, will not happen. Oil prices will rise, energy efficiency will increase and, if we're lucky, new, cleaner sources of energy will be harnessed. Nevertheless. China's success places a burden on the world as a whole. Across a huge range of resources, competition is hotting up (as, indeed, is the climate). As China makes new friends in Africa and Central Asia and the US deals with old enemies in the Middle East, the economic and political map is being redrawn to reflect the increasing claims on ultimately scarce resources by the Chinese and others. Countries have gone to war over far more trivial matters.

TECHNOLOGY REPLICATION AND RESOURCE SCARCITY

No amount of free trade, comparative advantage or capital-market openness will change this new economic reality. Globalization creates a new kind of economic growth. I call it growth through technology replication rather than technology improvement. Let me explain why.

In the 1950s, the jet airline industry was in its infancy. The first commercial jet airliner was the British Comet. Shortly afterwards,

Boeing developed the 707, which became the workhorse for many commercial fleets in the years to come. These airliners were inefficient. Piston planes offered better fuel economy. Moreover, Comets suffered from metal fatigue and had an alarming habit of falling out of the sky. Nevertheless, jet planes were clearly the way ahead: in time, they delivered greater fuel efficiency, could fly longer distances and, for their passengers, offered reduced noise and more comfort.

The arrival of the Airbus A380, the world's biggest commercial passenger aircraft yet, enables us to assess progress so far. According to industry sources, the giant Airbus is three to four times more efficient than the Comet 4. The resources used per passenger mile are less than 30 per cent of those used in the Comet. This vast improvement in productivity is, of course, good news both for the passengers and the environment. The calculation, however, reflects only technology improvement. In a world of scarce resources, what matters is not so much the improvement in technology but on how many occasions that technology is replicated.

Before the arrival of Deng Xiaoping and the collapse of the Berlin Wall, technology replication was limited. Too many countries were shut off from new technologies and, even where they had access, they channelled those technologies into military, rather than civilian, ventures. No longer is this the case. More and more countries are using technology replication to improve the lives of their citizens. It may be that the Airbus A380 is much more fuel-efficient than the Comet, but, with a sevenfold rise in passenger numbers over the last forty years, greater efficiency is still consistent with higher resource utilization. In other words, the numbers of people making claims on resources has risen faster than the technological efficiency with which those resources are utilized. Put another way, even though the flight cost per passenger has gone down, the number of passengers now flying has risen dramatically. This shift in demand necessarily puts pressure on scarce resources, most obviously the metals and plastics used in the manufacture of aircraft components and the fuel needed to keep aeroplanes in the air.

Technology replication is a direct result of globalization. More people can aspire to the lifestyles enjoyed by rich Westerners. More people have the ability to meet their aspirations. As they strive to do so, competition over access to raw materials and technologies will only increase. In this environment, can we really be confident that globalization has the potential to make everybody winners?

My thesis is simple. For the Western world, the emerging economies increasingly threaten the cosy expectations of ever-rising living standards which characterized the second half of the twentieth century. Through the destruction of political and technological barriers and through technology replication, more and more countries will be trying to lay claim to only limited global resources. Economic claims from a wide variety of hitherto poor nations are becoming ever more credible. Understanding how the West is vulnerable as a result of these mounting claims is the theme of this book. Our hallowed assumptions about the world economy are fast breaking down. The world economy is undergoing a major transformation. The Western powers are, in so many different ways, losing control.

There are, of course, many ways in which the Western powers are vulnerable. This book, though, is not about military strength, nor is it about new political alliances, even though I touch upon both issues. It is, instead, about the economic mechanisms that will allow the emerging markets to claim more, and the developed world to consume less, of the world's resources.

Before turning to the future, however, I want to turn to the past. Chapter 2 looks at the reasons behind the West's economic progress over the last few hundred years. Market forces, technological gains and productivity surges have all been important. They are not, however, the full story. Western economic success has also depended

on conquests, land grabs, slavery, state capitalism and, more generally, a willingness to rig markets for the benefit of a privileged
minority. The West's ability to rig markets to keep its citizens happy
is now under serious pressure, a direct result of the success of the
emerging nations.

CHAPTER TWO

THE SECRETS OF WESTERN SUCCESS

The Western world's economic development over the last five hundred years was not the result of productivity gains or market forces alone. Western nations became wealthier because they were increasingly able to rig the global economy to suit their own aims, using a combination of economic, political and military power. Specifically, they were able to engage in what economists call 'rent-seeking behaviour'. In very simple terms, those who successfully seek rents are paid above the free market price. Most of us are rent seekers. We like to be paid more even if there has been no rise in demand for our services or increase in our efforts. For the successful rent seeker, the Malthusian constraint can be removed even while others are still suffering.

David Ricardo (1772–1823) related economic rent to only one factor of production, namely land.[1] It can, however, be used for any factor of production where there is, for a while, limited supply. Economic rent can be defined as the payment made to a factor of production – land, labour or capital – over and above the minimum required to keep the factor of production in its current use (the minimum payment is known as the transfer earnings of the factor of production in question). Those who earn rents thus receive a higher income than they require to remain engaged in a particular line of economic activity. For some, bankers' bonuses fall into this category. Others might worry more about the earnings of top soccer, baseball and film stars.

Obvious ways to increase rental payments include the development of economies of scale, the creation of barriers to entry which keep competitors out, becoming a Hollywood superstar, friendly government regulation (otherwise known as protectionism), military action, bribery, racism in its many forms and slavery. Apart from Hollywood, these examples suggest that nation states have strong incentives to collude with commercial interests. Rent-seeking is not confined to the private sector alone. In modern-day parlance, we might call linkages between governments and commercial interests 'state capitalism'. Western governments have used the methods of state capitalism for hundreds of years in their bid to shape the world around them.

Indeed, rent-seeking behaviour was, over the centuries, closely linked to colonization. The discovery and exploitation of lands and peoples offered an abundance of raw materials and cheap labour designed to furnish Western economic tastes. So long as the local population could be bribed, destroyed or enslaved, the Malthusian constraint, at least for the West, could be removed (Incas, Aztecs, Native Americans, Aborigines and Black Africans doubtless didn't feel the same). Productivity may have been increasing, but so too were supplies of the raw materials and cheap labour necessary to feed Europe's expansion. I'll call them 'enabling' resources.

Before the Industrial Revolution, which raised productivity and, hence, output per worker, slaves were the enabling resources. As the revolution took hold, two additional resources became crucial. The first was land. The New World offered land in abundance, particularly given the willingness of the settlers to take it away from the indigenous population. The second was coal.

These 'enabling' resources allowed countries to exploit new technologies to the full. Slavery became less important, not just because of a sudden moment of ethical illumination but also because, economically, the coal-powered steam engine was much more efficient than a group of slaves, no matter how numerous they were or how hard they were made to work. Meanwhile, no longer did people have to make difficult choices over cultivating land for either food or fuel. Land could now be used exclusively for food because fuel was to be found underneath: nations could have both guns and butter. The available land, and the fuel that could be found below its surface, increased dramatically as the eighteenth and nineteenth centuries progressed.

Not surprisingly, as the West became economically more powerful, the interests of government and commerce became increasingly inter-related. The idea that market forces alone led to the West's success is nonsense. Take, for example, the development of the British East India Company (founded in 1600). As its ventures in India became more complex, so it built up a large private army to protect its interests (matching the earlier behaviour of the Dutch East India Company). It wasn't long before a commercial operation turned into political ambition, thereby providing an early example of today's state capitalism, a theme I explore in greater detail in Chapter 7. The mercenaries of the private army became regular soldiers, and India was absorbed into the British Empire.

The Opium Wars of the nineteenth century provide a similar example. Again, the East India Company was involved, increasingly exporting opium to a lucrative Chinese market. Again, the British government supported Britain's commercial interests. The rising demand in Britain for Chinese luxuries such as porcelain and silk had to be paid for somehow. As a consequence, the UK became the world's biggest drug dealer. It could do so because, despite two huge uprisings, the Chinese didn't possess the military means to end Britain's interests in a trade that was, to say the least, morally dubious.

Meanwhile, others just didn't have the means or desire to stake a claim on the world's resources. Europe's economic progress from the fifteenth century onwards (and its eventual spread into North America, Australia and New Zealand) was not matched elsewhere. The Renaissance, the Reformation and the later Age of Enlightenment were all crucial staging posts in European development, signalling the growing dominance of science, the reduced power of the church and the emergence of a new political philosophy consistent with the rights of man (and his property). All this, in turn, allowed the creation of increasingly complex markets for goods, services and, crucially, capital.

Market complexity still didn't indicate market freedom. It wasn't until 1789, well after the establishment of stock markets,[2] that William Wilberforce spoke in favour of the abolition of slavery.[3] US citizens fought each other in the Civil War of 1861–5 partly over the issue of slavery. Meanwhile, many nineteenth-century US industries were built up not in the face of fierce competition from Europe but, instead, behind protectionist barriers. The infant industry arguments so beloved of Japan, South Korea and China in the second half of the twentieth century were utilized heavily by the Americans 150 years ago and by British wool-makers even earlier.[4]

THE FAILURE TO ADVANCE

Other countries and empires fell behind, even when they were not being repressed by avaricious Europeans. Islam made extraordinary advances, both military and scientific, from its earliest days through to the 1400s, but thereafter became increasingly introspective and, in relation to Christian Europe, increasingly repressive. Having finally been forced out of Spain in 1492, with defeat at Grenada, Muslim leaders chose to focus on problems closer to home in response to growing strains between the Sunnis of the Ottoman Empire and the Shiites in Persia.[5] Economically and politically, Islam suffered a double blow. In the same year that the Moors were expelled from Spain Columbus discovered the Americas. Eight years later, Vasco da Gama rounded the South African Cape and sailed to India. These discoveries mattered for three reasons: (i) Europeans were fast developing ocean-going sailing skills which left Islamic nations at a nautical disadvantage; (ii) now that Europeans could sail to India and elsewhere in the Indian Ocean, they were no longer dependent on the Middle East for supplies of exotic spices and silks, thereby reducing the incomes – and, thus, the rents – of Arab middlemen (Venice, which had been the European hub for the land-based spice trade, also went into relative decline at this time); (iii) as opportunities in the Americas expanded, so Europeans were able to cultivate crops that hitherto had been supplied via Islamic lands. Chief among these were coffee and sugar.

The Islamic leaders of the Ottoman Empire did not emulate the separation of sacred from secular taking place in Christian Europe (the Prophet Mohammed was, after all, not just a spiritual leader but also a political and military hero, thereby inextricably linking the spiritual, political, legal and material worlds). Scientific progress, itself dependent on open debate, became more of a challenge, limiting the opportunities for technical progress.

Meanwhile, after a brief flirtation with various European nations in the Indian Ocean, the leaders of the Ming Dynasty in China became increasingly worried about the influx of new, and possibly corrupting, influences on the Chinese Empire. In the early 1430s, Chinese leaders chose to destroy their entire ocean-going fleet. As a symbolic act, it was, economically, one of the most costly moments in human history. At the time, Chinese ships were bigger and better than their European counterparts. Chinese sailors navigated using the magnetic compass as a matter of routine. And, in Admiral Zheng He, a seven-foot tall Muslim Mongolian eunuch, China had the greatest sailor of the day, whose exploits included visits to thirty-seven countries over twenty-eight years with a fleet of around 300 ships and 28,000 sailors (it's now thought that Zheng found the Americas before Columbus). Through closing itself off to the rest of the world, China was starved of the ideas and innovations that contributed so much to the productivity gains seen in Europe over the last five hundred years. Openness matters.

Angus Maddison, the renowned economic historian, has constructed some estimates of per-capita incomes in China and Europe going back over two millennia.[6] Of course, these are no more than the vaguest of guesses, but they're based on some simple – and not very controversial – observations. Until 1400, both Europe and China were subject to Malthusian constraints. Europe lost out in relation to China in both the fourth century (when the Roman Empire collapsed in the West) and the seventh century (when the Arabs captured Spain and large parts of western Asia, which destroyed European trade in the Mediterranean). China made progress during the Sung dynasty (960–1279), largely through advances in rice production, but population growth placed a lid on per-capita incomes: for most people, the Malthusian curse was an everyday reality. From the 1500s onwards, however, Europe began to move ahead. Removed from the shackles of agricultural subsistence, Europe started to benefit from technical advances: better ships, printing presses and, in time, steam power and railways.[7] China, closed off from the rest of the world, did nothing. In 1000, Chinese per-capita incomes were slightly higher than those in Europe. By 1820 they were only half European levels (although the huge size of China's population meant that its economy was still roughly the same size as all the Western economies added together).

According to Maddison's data, the gap grew progressively wider until the 1950s. The Great Leap Forward of that decade and the Cultural Revolution that followed in the late 1960s did little to help the situation: Chinese per-capita incomes stabilized at around 8 per cent of European levels. The best that can be said about Mao Zedong's reign is that China's relative economic decline came to a halt: but, with Chinese per-capita incomes now averaging just 8 per cent of those in Western Europe, Chairman Mao managed only to confirm China's huge loss of global economic status.

In simple terms, then, the history of economic development over at least the last four or five hundred years has been a story of Western progress while other nations stagnated. By the beginning of the twentieth century, the world economy was completely dominated by the Western powers, who directly produced more than 50 per cent of the world's GDP, a result of their rapid economic growth over many previous decades. By the mid-twentieth century, other nations just didn't seem to matter: their shares of world income were tiny and their incomes per capita were minute. Across East Asia, for example, incomes per capita were less than one-tenth of those of the United States.

THE NEW FORCES OF GLOBALIZATION

While the progress of Western economies was, thus, hugely impressive compared with the competition, their progress did not depend purely on technology gains and the benefits of free markets, important though these sometimes were. There were three other vital ingredients. First, economies of scale made it more difficult for other countries to enter certain industries. Second, virgin lands with abundant raw materials and labour were discovered and exploited. Third, populations in other parts of the world were unable to stake meaningful economic claims. They were disconnected from the world's productivity engines through the suppression of ideas, innovations and linkages with other nations, or by the violence meted out to them by the Western powers. Throughout its period of rapid economic development, then, the West was able to benefit from rent-seeking behaviour in all its forms.

Since the 1950s, however, there has been a remarkable change. Asia as a whole has delivered more than half a century of annual economic growth running at 3.5 per cent per capita, representing the fastest economic advance of any region in the entire economic history of the planet. China has overtaken Germany to become the third-biggest economy in the world and, on some measures, is ahead of Japan, thus making China second only to the US in economic terms. In just a handful of decades, China will probably also move ahead of the US to become the world's dominant economic powerhouse. Other emerging nations are also growing rapidly. Their success is generating a new 'gravitational pull' in the world economy. No longer is the global economic agenda being set by the Western powers. The West's influence is waning. New relationships are being forged which, over time, threaten to leave the West economically disadvantaged.

Globalization dramatically changes the ability of incumbent governments, companies and citizens in the West to continue benefiting from their earlier rent-seeking – or cheating – ways. Because capital can move around relatively easily, economies of scale can be created in an increasing number of countries (the US car industry is on its knees partly because of this enhanced capital mobility). There is only a finite amount of virgin territory to exploit and, in the absence of colonization (usually frowned upon these days), competing political interests may make the extraction of ever-increasing amounts of raw materials more and more difficult (as BP discovered in its Russian ventures). Most importantly, the populations of previously unsuccessful economies are now begin-ning to make their voices heard. China's remarkable economic growth over the last thirty years hasn't been enough to remove the majority of its population from poverty, but it now boasts a newly affluent middle class of roughly 300 million people.

For some, this isn't a problem. Globalization is a natural feature of the economic landscape, leading to a happier, more contented, global community driven on by the ideas of the Enlightenment and the spread of liberal democracy. In this view of the world, it is relatively easy to incorporate the hopes, aspirations and economic muscle of the emerging nations into an already established world economic order. This is the kind of message that found favour in books such as Francis Fukuyama's *The End of History* and which still finds sympathy today in international gatherings such as the World Economic Forum in Davos, Switzerland (where the great and the good of the global community can solve mass poverty for the benefit of the international media before heading off to the nearest champagne reception or ski slope).

Admittedly it's a seductive view. If globalization is inevitable, the only things that can hold it back are evil men, stupid ideas and wars. For extreme optimists, the events of the last hundred years can thus be regarded as no more than an awkward interruption, a pause for breath before the forces of globalization are allowed to scale even greater heights. On this interpretation, we have finally returned to an economic roadmap that had apparently reached a dead end as the nineteenth century drew to a close. With the free market restored, with world trade rising rapidly, with cross-border capital flows surging and with command economies increasingly no more than historical relics, the battle over political and economic ideas that led to the violence of the twentieth century is now over. We are back to 'business as usual', only with more nations able to take advantage of the ideas that first began to develop in Europe during the Enlightenment. Seen this way, we can all be rich.

It's a pleasing idea, but it's also largely wrong. We may be living in a world of relative peace and prosperity, with capital flowing more easily across borders, but there's no guarantee that this land of economic milk and honey will remain bountiful for ever. There is, in fact, no 'business as usual'. The world economy is constantly evolving and, as it does so, it offers new challenges. We cannot just travel back in a time machine to conditions that last prevailed at the end of the nineteenth century. As we shall see, the world today looks very different from how it appeared then. In any case, those who look back at the late nineteenth century with rose-tinted spectacles forget the obvious weakness in their approach: the relative peace of the nineteenth century was shattered by the destructive violence of the twentieth century. Globalization depends on co-operation but can all too easily be knocked off course by conflict.

DON'T MENTION THE WAR

Before the outbreak of the First World War, the idea that globalization was inevitable was widely shared in part because the costs of any reversal were, rightly, seen to be huge. Globalization was not, however, an immutable process. Its pre-First World War protagonists were nicely lampooned by John Maynard Keynes in his *Economic Consequences of the Peace*[8] in a much quoted, yet highly relevant, passage caricaturing a typical English gentleman in the summer of 1914. The complacency it reveals is commonplace today:

> The inhabitant of London could order by telephone, sipping his morning tea in bed, the various products of the whole earth, in such quantity as he might see fit, and reasonably expect their early delivery upon his doorstep; he could at the same moment and by the same means adventure his wealth in the natural resources and new enterprises of any quarter of the world, and share, without

exertion or even trouble, in their prospective fruits and advantages ... The projects and politics of militarism and imperialism, of racial and cultural rivalries, of monopolies, restrictions, and exclusion ... were little more than the amusements of his daily newspaper, and appeared to exercise almost no influence at all on the ordinary course of social and economic life, the internationalisation of which was nearly complete in practice.

From an Englishman's perspective, at least, the early years of the twentieth century were halcyon times. The looming disaster of the Great War and the subsequent collapse of the international economic order were impossible to imagine. A major conflagration was clearly in nobody's interest: war simply couldn't happen. Meanwhile, markets were able to function unimpeded for the most part by the actions of nations.

Keynes's description reflected a model of globalization linked to empire, ideas, technology and cross-border mobility of both labour and capital. By the end of the nineteenth century, Britain had an empire covering a third of the Earth's land mass. Other European nations, notably France and Russia, also built up sizeable empires. Europe's overall control of the Earth's surface rose from 37 per cent in 1800 to 67 per cent in 1878 and 84 per cent by 1914.[9] Critically, by the mid-nineteenth century Britain had become the philosophical and practical cheerleader for free trade. The Royal Navy ruled the high seas, acting as a global policeman either to enforce liberal trade or to impose Britain's sovereign power over others.[10] The Royal Navy generally succeeded in keeping international trade afloat, bringing benefits to trading nations all over the world (it acted as a gunboat version of today's World Trade Organization).

Meanwhile, the Industrial Revolution was in full flow, with canals, steamships and railways all contributing to a remarkable reduction in transportation costs, while the laying of telegraph cables – the first transatlantic success was in 1866 – marked the beginnings of an information technology revolution which that was to become a defining feature of the late twentieth century. Labour easily moved across countries, continents and oceans, often in search of empty yet potentially productive lands. Capital also moved around with remarkable ease. According to Maurice Obstfeld and Alan Taylor, the stock of foreign investment (investment made by people outside their home country) rose from 7 per cent of world GDP in 1870 to nearly 20 per cent by 1914, a figure not surpassed until the early 1980s.[11] Moreover, before the First World War, a big element of cross-border investment went from the developed nations to what we now label emerging markets. And people lived in a world of 'small government'. In nominal terms, government spending in 1913 amounted to just over 13 per cent of GDP in the UK, 8.9 per cent in France, 13.3 per cent in Germany and 8.0 per cent in the US. Market forces truly dominated.

ECONOMIC INTEGRATION, POLITICAL PROLIFERATION

Globalization in the nineteenth century ultimately depended on the redrawing of the political map of Europe (and, by extension, other parts of the world) by a group of great men representing the Great Powers. International relations in the nineteenth century were shaped by the Congress of Vienna in 1815 (following the Napoleonic Wars), at which Europe was divided into spheres of influence, primarily reflecting the interests of the victorious Great Powers – the UK, Austria, Russia and Prussia (although, even after Napoleon's departure following mounting defeats, France somehow still managed to get a seat at the table through the efforts of Charles-Maurice de Talleyrand, Louis XVIII's envoy, who used his wily diplomatic skills to create friction between the victors). The voices of the people went unheeded and unheard. This was a world of empires and imperfect suffrage.

Under the influence of self-determination, sponsored by an increasingly powerful US hostile to colonial influence, the empires of the nineteenth century collapsed in the wars and economic crises that followed. The biggest casualty, most obviously, was the British Empire. The Ottoman Empire went the same way and, with the fall of the Berlin Wall in 1989, so did the Soviet Union's twentieth-century empire. The result was a huge proliferation of nation states. According to Freedom House, there were only fifty-five sovereign countries in 1900, alongside thirteen empires. That compares with the 192 states which, in 2009, were members of the United Nations. Of today's nations, 113 used to be part of colonial and imperial systems, while a further thirty-three were parts of other states.

Economic globalization has, therefore, been associated with political disintegration. This is a very odd result. At the very least, it suggests the political challenges associated with modern-day globalization are very different from the challenges that emerged, so tragically, in the second decade of the twentieth century. How, for example, can there be global agreement on capital markets, climate change or currency markets if multitudinous nation states all wish to pursue their own individual agendas? If, as was argued in Chapter 1, good government is essential for sustained economic progress, how easy is it to deliver good government at the international level in the absence of nineteenth-century empires?

The good news is that there has been considerable progress. Trade flows have gradually been rebuilt, partly through regional trading blocs but, most importantly, through the creation of global rules through the General Agreement on Tariffs and Trade (GATT) and its successor, the World Trade Organization (WTO), which China signed up to in 2001, heralding a new era for international trade. Soviet communism has gone and Chinese communism is not what it used to be. The British Empire has been replaced by American hegemony. As a substitute for the Gold Standard, more and more countries have embraced the case for sound money through, most obviously, the use of inflation targets and links to the US dollar.

Meanwhile, in more recent times, cross-border capital flows have risen dramatically, reflecting in part the gradual abolition of capital controls and, for a while, a growing acceptance that cross-border capital flows subjected nations to useful market disciplines. Even as the Berlin Wall came down in 1989, many Western European countries still routinely used such controls. Only with the creation of the Single Market in 1992, just seven years before the creation of the euro, was a formal commitment made to free cross-border movements of capital within the European Union.

But does this really represent a return to the roadmap abandoned at the beginning of the twentieth century? I don't think so. The political and economic backdrop to late-nineteenth-century globalization was fundamentally different from today's version. There was a global law-enforcement officer, in the form of the Royal Navy, which kept the sea lanes open. The US, the most powerful nation on earth today, does not share the same commitment. It has no physical empire to protect and it chooses not to offer unequivocal support to the organizations that might enforce international law.

As we shall see in Chapter 8, there were huge movements of people across borders on a scale that can hardly be imagined today, at least in proportion to the size of indigenous populations. While border controls were, primarily, a twentieth-century innovation, they continue to distort the allocation of productive resources in the twenty-first century. Even where immigration controls have been lifted – in parts of the European Union, for example – this has generally been a patchwork affair.

The most powerful nation on Earth, the UK, ran a balance of payments current-account surplus in the late nineteenth century, using its excess savings to invest in potentially lucrative opportunities in less advantaged parts of the world.[12] Since 1977, the US has, for the most part, run an ever-widening balance of payments current-account deficit (punctuated by occasional recession-induced surpluses). By the beginning of the twenty-first century, the US had become enormously dependent on the deep pockets of emerging creditor nations.

Before the First World War, public sectors were small. Over the last hundred years, the role of the state in economic affairs has expanded enormously. Government spending in the Organization for Economic Co-operation and Development (OECD) area, for example, varies from around 30 per cent in South Korea and 35 per cent in the US through to around 50 per cent in the UK, France and Germany and approaching 60 per cent in Sweden.[13] The market's influence on the allocation of resources is only a shadow of its nineteenth-century self, notwithstanding the efforts of Margaret Thatcher and Ronald Reagan.

The global rules that used to be set by the imperial powers are now agreed upon in shifting multilateral groupings, from the G20 through to NATO, from the North American Free Trade Association through to the European Union and from the United Nations through to, as we shall see, the Shanghai Co-operation Organization. Organizations exist to promote global commerce – alongside the regional arrangements in Europe and North America, the World Trade Organization plays a vital role. And there has been some, very limited, progress on climate change, even though the 2009 Copenhagen summit ended in acrimony.

There is, however, no such forum within which the perils and pitfalls of global capital markets can be acted upon, even though the massive growth of capital markets is surely *the* defining feature of modern-day globalization. Until recently, the closest we had was the International Monetary Fund (IMF). In the world of capital markets, though, the IMF has little information, no teeth and, across the emerging world, little trust. Nor can it offer the gunboat diplomacy that, in the nineteenth century, proved a useful way of enforcing – or imposing – property rights. As a result, we have a system of capital markets that has proved to be beyond regulation and supervision. Moreover, it is a system in which powerful nation states, not private investors, are beginning to play the dominant role. The United States provides the world's reserve currency even though the Federal Reserve, the US central bank, has only to worry about monetary conditions in the US. Governments, central banks and sovereign wealth funds in the emerging world increasingly play a pivotal role as agents to transfer their nations' savings to the developed world. And those nations which, in the nineteenth century, would have had the dominant say in global economic affairs are no more than has-beens. For them, the economic and political swagger of yesteryear has gone. The globalization roadmap is being redrawn.

NEW ARRANGEMENTS FOR A NEW DISORDER

The United States and Western Europe are being forced to come to terms with this new world order. They are, slowly but surely, having to accept that the rules of the global game are changing. The most obvious sign of this change, to date, is the arrival of the G20 as a potentially influential global organization,[14] in effect replacing the G8.

The US and other Western nations now have to accept their growing dependence on developments in parts of the world which, a few decades earlier, they would have treated as largely irrelevant. China, kicked about by the imperial powers in the nineteenth century, partially occupied by the Japanese in the 1930s, and economically handicapped through the policies of Mao Zedong in the 1950s and 1960s, suddenly finds itself in a pivotal position in the world economy. If, in the first decade of the twenty-first century, the US was the world's biggest borrower, China had become the world's biggest lender. China was not alone. Other creditor nations included Saudi Arabia and Russia.

The G20 is, so far, only a club for economies, not nation states. It is not designed to represent military powers or particular political systems (those issues are far too awkward). It is a modus vivendi, designed to deal with economic matters while conveniently ignoring other, perhaps more important, political affairs. Its existence is built on a pretence, namely that politics and economics can somehow be separated. That, I believe, is a false distinction. The distinction was made because the credit crunch that began in 2007 cried out for a global solution; for a while, then, there was a commonality of interest.

History suggests, however, that commonalities of interest do not last very long. Until and unless the G20 is able to confront the difficulties outlined in this book, it is likely to head the same way as the League of Nations and the Bretton Woods exchange-rate system – in other words, into the dustbin of history. The G20 doesn't really have the teeth to offer the international rule of law which was, in effect, forced upon the world by the imperial powers in the nineteenth century.

What might a new international order begin to look like? Already, there are clues dotted around the world. I suspect governments will increasingly use their influence to conduct foreign policy through their influence on international markets, encouraging the creation of bilateral relationships that appear to be driven by commercial interests but which, in reality, are an important part of modern-day realpolitik. Think, for example, of Gazprom's dominance of the European energy market or Halliburton's involvement over the years in Iraq. The connections between these firms and their political masters are enormously strong. More broadly, as countries push forward their own agendas, we are seeing the renaissance of 'state capitalism'.

As already noted, state capitalism has been a fact of economic life for centuries. The East India Company, with its mercenaries and its cross-border drug dealing, was perhaps its greatest exponent. Nations have always happily traded land with each other in quasi-commercial strategic deals. Buying and selling is considerably less painful than shooting and bombing. To pretend that the private sector alone should be responsible for trading is pure fantasy.

A fine example is the Louisiana Purchase of 1803, when the US paid France $15 million for what now amounts to about 23 per cent of US territory, including all of present-day Arkansas, Iowa, Kansas, Missouri, Nebraska and Oklahoma, together with assorted bits and pieces of other US states, most obviously Louisiana west of the Mississippi, including New Orleans (interestingly, the US could solve its current debt problems by selling California to the Chinese although it somehow seems an unlikely gambit).

Thomas Jefferson, the US president at that time, was particularly worried about American access to New Orleans, by then a major port, and feared that trade could be undermined by French and Spanish hostility. Napoleon Bonaparte, meanwhile, had seen French power ebb away in Haiti and in the Caribbean more broadly. Without the economic benefits stemming from access to the lucrative sugar plantations, Napoleon was happy to strike a deal. Huge swathes of North American territory fell into US hands, prompting Napoleon to comment, 'This accession of territory affirms for ever the power of the United States, and I have given England a maritime rival who sooner or later will humble her pride.'[15]

He was right. His conclusion prompts the obvious question. Confronted with increasing economic and political connections across the emerging world, will the US, like the UK before it, find that, at some point, its pride will be humbled? After all, the US was the nineteenth century's emerging market. At the beginning of the twenty-first century, it sits upon the summit of economic and political power, waiting, like the UK a hundred years ago, for someone to knock it off. There is no shortage of pretenders to the throne.

These, of course, are major long-term issues. I will return to them in Parts Three and Four. In Part Two, I turn to some more immediate difficulties. The rise of the emerging nations appears to be connected with greater economic instability – equity bubbles, financial crises, housing booms, credit crunches and global imbalances (to name but a few). Is there a link? Can Western policymakers really deliver on their promises or are they, instead, losing control of our economic destiny?

BROKEN ECONOMIC BAROMETERS

PART TWO

BROKEN
GOVERNMENT,
BROKEN TRUST

CHAPTER THREE

THE PLEASURES AND PERILS OF TRADE

BLACK HOLES

Black holes cannot be observed directly. Their effect can be seen only through their gravitational pull. Celestial objects that used to behave in a predictable manner begin to act differently as they approach a black hole. They may start to move faster than normal. They may heat up and emit radiation as they're sucked in to the void. The presence of a black hole can be detected only through these indirect routes.

The emerging nations are a bit like a black hole. There is little available data, the data that is published is often deemed unreliable and historical comparisons are typically meaningless. For example, communist Czechoslovakia, hidden behind the Iron Curtain, was a very different economy from the capitalist Czech Republic, which now nestles in the bosom of the European Union.

Proving that emerging nations are economically influential is, therefore, tricky, at least for statisticians. The available information is not generally up to the task in hand. An alternative approach is to

47

think about the influence of the emerging nations indirectly. What effects are emerging economies having on the Western world? And have policymakers in the Western world properly come to terms with these effects?

These are key questions. For Western policymakers, economic success is in part a question about expectations management. If, for example, a policymaker claims that rising US exports to China are a 'good thing', US workers can reasonably expect to experience rising incomes as trade with China opens up. Similarly, if a policymaker claims the delivery of persistently low inflation is the best single way of producing lasting economic health, investors should not have to worry about impending economic and financial crises.

Yet the promises of policymakers have not been met. World trade has increased dramatically as emerging nations have made their presence felt, but the trade flows we're seeing today are not purely the result of comparative advantage, the mainstay of the free-trade argument, and have certainly not delivered rising incomes for all concerned. Meanwhile, after years in which inflation has been broadly under control, the early years of the twenty-first century witnessed the most extraordinary economic and financial boom and bust. If price stability was such a good thing, why did the world go on to experience an economic crisis second only to the disasters of the 1930s?

It seems to me that the gravitational pull of the emerging nations has upset the barometers we typically use to calibrate economic success. In Part Two, I examine this gravitational pull in three different areas – trade, capital markets and price stability. Has increased trade brought benefits for all? Have the economic special-izations associated with higher trade volumes – for the US and the UK, primarily in financial services – genuinely contributed to lasting economic stability? Why, despite the rapid growth of emerging nations, have returns for investors been so poor? And, most controversially, has the achievement of low inflation in the Western world become a source of economic instability?

VORSPRUNG DURCH TECHNIK

One of the more obvious theoretical benefits of globalization is its impact on trade. Why should the West worry if, for example, rising demand in China, India and elsewhere boosts export opportunities for Western companies and, in the process, creates Western jobs? Certainly, standard trade theories suggest that increased specialization brings benefits to all involved. The reality, however, is more complex. The world trade system is undergoing a series of seismic shocks, creating both winners and losers in the process. To understand why, we need to go back to the economic world as it was before the destruction of the Berlin Wall, a world where many would-be workers and consumers simply did not have access to Western markets and capital.

Had you been living in affluent West Germany in the early 1980s you might have treated yourself to an Audi Quattro, one of the most desirable automobiles ever made. It certainly wasn't the most expensive car available at the time, but it was the first to feature both four-wheel drive and a turbo-charged engine. Its huge success in rallying provided an extra mystique. For its day, the Quattro offered an exhilarating performance, with a 0–60mph time of only around seven seconds. Over 10,000 of these cars were sold in Western Europe in the early 1980s, with a few hundred more sold in North America.[1]

If you had been living in East Germany in the early 1980s, you might have known about the Audi, but you wouldn't have been able to get your hands on one unless a kindly West German had given you a very generous gift.[2] East Germany's economy was under the shackles of Soviet-style communism. The regime survived only by protecting itself from the competitive pressures coming from the

West. The dreams of central planners had turned into nightmares of bureaucracy and corruption, leaving East German consumers with products that wouldn't survive in a world dominated by free market choice. While the West Germans could whiz around in their Audis, the East Germans had to make do with Trabants. Although the cars are treated with nostalgic affection today, Trabant production lasted only a couple of years after the fall of the Berlin Wall in 1989. Given the choice, East Germans preferred to scrap their heavily polluting and remarkably slow Trabants (0–60mph in 21 seconds) and replace them with second-hand cars from Western Europe. The Trabant was dumped onto the scrapheap of Soviet communism. Those employed making Trabants and other relics of the Soviet era ended up without jobs, and were supported instead by handouts from the wealthy citizens of former West Germany.[3]

Not all Soviet-era car companies went the same way. Škoda was a Czech car company originally founded in 1895 as a manufacturer of bicycles. After the Second World War, the company was nationalized. It went on to produce a number of innovative designs in the 1960s and 1970s but could make only limited headway in Western markets, where advances in motor technology and marketing were far greater. Indeed, by the 1980s, the Škoda brand had become something of a joke. In the UK, Škoda gags became very popular.[4] (Q: 'How do you double the value of a Škoda?' A: 'Fill its tank with gas'.)

With the fall of the Berlin Wall it became clear that Škoda, like the manufacturers of the Trabant, would not be able to survive as an independent company. In 1991, it became part of the Volkswagen Group, alongside Audi and Seat. Since then, its fortunes have been transformed and the jokes have been long forgotten. In 2008, Škoda managed 674,530 sales, the largest number in its long and sometimes turbulent history. Its biggest markets, interestingly, are other emerging economies. Sales to Russia, China and India have proved to be particularly important. Škoda still benefits from low Eastern European wages, which allow cars to be produced relatively cheaply, but it now also benefits from the technologies, management know-how and cheap international finance available to the Volkswagen Group.

Škoda's experience neatly encapsulates the difficulties in making sense of international trade and investment since the fall of the Berlin Wall. Škoda exports from its Mladá Boleslav assembly plant in the Czech Republic to customers all over the world. It offers competition to other car manufacturers which, in earlier decades, did not have to cope with the cheaper labour available on the eastern side of the Berlin Wall. It provides employment for Czech workers and tax revenues for the Czech government. It also provides employment in its dealerships across the world.

Škoda's profits now go to the shareholders of Volkswagen AG who, in turn, are based in Frankfurt, London, New York and countless other locations. While Škoda's geographical location says something about trading relationships – Czech car exports may be higher as a result – the idea that the Czech Republic and its people are somehow the sole beneficiaries of Škoda's revitalization is untrue. There are winners spread all over the world. There are also losers. Trabant production didn't survive but nor did Britain's Rover Group. America's Big Three didn't do too well either. With the competitive pressures unleashed by globalization, unprofitable, poorly managed companies have no place to hide.

COMPARATIVE ADVANTAGE AND ECONOMIC DISADVANTAGE

Political arrangements can get in the way of economic opportunity and preserve economic rents for the lucky few. They create barriers to free trade, migration and capital flows. Since the 1980s, those barriers have slowly come down. The developed world is now trading with countries that, only a few years ago, were treated as strange lands. In analysing these new patterns of trade, economists

51

routinely resort to the principles of comparative advantage famously described by David Ricardo in *On the Principles of Political Economy and Taxation*, published in 1817. Today's trade patterns, however, are much more a story about outsourcing, off-shoring, upscaling and downsizing. The developed world has increasingly been exporting its *factories* to the emerging economies. I'm not sure we've understood the full implications.

Ricardo was, rightly, keen to extol the advantages of trade. He had a brilliant argument to do so. Both England and Portugal could produce wine and cloth, but Portugal was better at producing both goods. Portugal therefore had an *absolute* advantage in the production of both wine and cloth. Trade between the two countries therefore did not seem to be promising; certainly, there appeared to be little benefit for Portugal.

Ricardo was not put off. If the cost of producing cloth in Portugal was relatively high, in terms of the reduced production of bottles of Portuguese wine, and wasn't so high in England, it would make sense for Portugal to devote more of its resources to the production of wine, which could then be traded for cloth produced in England. The net result would be higher output and higher consumption in both Portugal and England.

Ricardo's argument is in effect an international extension of the economic principles established by Adam Smith and others fifty years earlier. Each of us should specialize in the things we are *relatively* good at. A dentist might be better as a dental nurse than the dental nurse she employs, but if she spent all her time being a dental nurse, she wouldn't be able to practise dentistry to the best of her ability and her patients would be left with toothache. Similarly, if Portuguese wine is particularly good and English cloth just about passes muster, it benefits everyone if the Portuguese spend their time tending their vines. I've drunk English wine and, with perhaps one or two exceptions, I'd rather leave viticulture to the Portuguese.

If all trade were the result of Ricardo's comparative advantage, then we'd all be potentially better off. Yet comparative advantage is not the only reason for trade. Ricardo's arguments work only under specific assumptions which do not always hold true. Of these, perhaps the most important are, first, that capital and labour are immobile across nations and, second, that capital and labour are very mobile within nations.

Neither of these assumptions typically holds. If, for example, the opening up of trade between England and Portugal leaves lots of wine producers in England threatened with unemployment, comparative advantage works best only when those workers can easily get new jobs making cloth. Let's imagine that wages in cloth making are much lower than wages in wine manufacturing. If so, those who are forced to leave the wine-making industry might end up taking a pay cut. Alternatively, they might fail to gain employment because of a lack of suitable qualifications or willingness to work at the new, lower wage. England and Portugal might both be better off in aggregate as a result of the opening up of trade, but some individuals in England may still be worse off. There is, therefore, a possible unwelcome redistributional consequence of trade.

As for the immobility of labour and capital between nations, that is only true under certain strict conditions. Ricardo's arguments work only if national borders cannot shift. Yet borders are constantly being redrawn. Take California and Oregon. We consider California and Oregon to be part of a single, very large economy. California, however, wasn't always part of the US, only ending up in US hands following the signing of the Treaty of Guadalupe Hidalgo in 1848 after two years of fighting in the Mexican–American war.[5] Do these changing circumstances imply that the principles of comparative advantage worked only while California was 'south of the border' and not when it subsequently fell into US hands? Possibly, but given the number of Mexicans living in California and the number of US companies operating in Mexico, the more likely answer is that Ricardo's assumptions of labour and capital immobility across borders were never going to stand up to close scrutiny. The movement of American capital south of the border and the movement of Mexican labour north of the border may have benefited the owners of capital (because they now make more profit) and Mexican workers, but not necessarily US workers.

But it's not just borders that are being redrawn. International relations are also constantly evolving. If we go back to the late 1960s, when China was completely shut off from the rest of the world, where the Cultural Revolution was at its height and when President Nixon's visit to Beijing was still fantasy rather than fact, we go back to a time when US companies built factories mostly in the US. US workers didn't have to worry about competition from Chinese workers because the Chinese had no access to the world's best capital (and, even if they did, it would presumably have been destroyed in the madness of the Cultural Revolution).

Now move forward to the 1980s. In a new spirit of openness, the Chinese authorities welcomed an influx of capital from the West. Suddenly, companies that previously had to tie their capital to expensive Western labour could, instead, relocate their capital to China to take advantage of cheap Chinese labour. The exodus of capital enabled companies to produce products more cheaply (which is why the price of manufactured goods, in particular, has come down so rapidly in recent years), clearly benefiting consumers all over the world. But falling goods prices meant that companies and workers still operating in the US found themselves suffering a persistent deterioration in their terms of trade. No matter how hard they worked, their profits and wages came under persistent downward pressure (the slow demise of General Motors and Chrysler owes much over the long term to this process).

The Ricardian model of comparative advantage thus works best if each country is endowed with a certain mix of factors of production that cannot easily be transferred (Portugal has a comparative advantage in the production of wine because its climate and soil offer better opportunities for wine producers than wet and windy England). If, however, these endowments can shift, it's no longer clear that comparative advantage works so well: shifting factors of production destroy the economic rents of those who were lucky enough not to have been properly exposed to competition before. In this sense, it's not obvious that everyone benefits from free trade even if global output is raised.[6]

Ricardian assumptions worked better in the 1950s and 1960s, a world in which capital flows across borders were relatively limited and where trade flows took place between a group of economically 'like-minded' OECD countries. The world has substantially changed since then. Indeed, conditions have changed so much that it is no longer clear what the process of 'exporting' actually involves. According to the *Oxford English Dictionary*, to export is 'to send (goods or services) to another country for sale'. An easy definition, admittedly, but it doesn't entirely capture what is taking place economically. Many exports these days take place within firms as part of global production platforms: any internal 'sale' is economically meaningless.

JAPAN'S *KUDOKA* – AN ANTIDOTE TO THE GLORIES OF FREE TRADE

A good way to understand the problems associated with changing global trading patterns comes from Japan's economic experience since the 1990s. Japan's economic miracle – a combination of exceptionally strong growth and generally low inflation – came to an abrupt end at the end of the 1980s. Policymakers in the US and

Europe tend to argue that Japan's failures stemmed from a disincli-
nation to use macroeconomic policy to reflate Japan's economy in
the wake of the collapse in share and land prices in the early years of
the 1990s, which, in turn, contributed to a world of deflation.[7]
Japanese policymakers hold a rather different view. With the ticking
clock of population ageing, Japan's economic expansion was going
to slow in any case. In addition, policymakers rightly recognize the
changes forced upon the Japanese economy and, in particular, on its
industrial sector by China's re-awakening. These massive structural
shifts are known as *kudoka* or 'hollowing out'.

At first sight, it's not obvious what was going on. The share of
Japanese exports going to China steadily increased from the beginning of the 1990s. In 1990 itself, a mere 2.1 per cent of Japan's exports
went to China. Five years later, the number had more than doubled
to around 5 per cent. By 2001, the share had risen to 7.7 per cent and,
by 2008, it was up to 16 per cent. On the face of it, then, China's emergence has been great news for Japan: Japanese exports to the Middle
Kingdom have soared in recent decades.

So why are Japanese policymakers so uneasy about this process?
Other than the mutual scars of history, the key concern is the *composition* of Japanese exports to China. Since the early 1990s, Japan's
exports to China have been dominated by exports of capital goods –
most obviously, machinery of one sort or another – and industrial
materials. Given low incomes per capita in China, this is perhaps not
surprising: China needs all the capital goods it can get to drive the
process of industrial catch-up that will take its people into the
twenty-first century; Beijing's subway system, for example, is tiny
compared with the London Underground, even though Beijing's
population is somewhat larger. In the process, China has become the
emerging world's single biggest recipient of foreign direct investment.

This development, though, has proved to be a major threat to
Japan's industrial structure. Japanese multinationals used to depend

for their supplies of industrial components on the domestic so-called *keiretsu* firms, which were typically competing with each other for the attentions of the Japanese multinational 'sole-buyer'. As Japanese multinationals headed elsewhere for their supplies in the 1990s in a bid to lower costs, so China gained and the domestic Japanese *keiretsu* lost out. Expensive Japanese workers were, in effect, replaced by cheaper Chinese workers who could perform similar tasks at a fraction of the price. In this sense, the export of capital goods from Japan to China was synonymous with the export of jobs. While this was good news for Japanese multinationals, able to reduce their dependency on Japanese suppliers alone and, therefore, to increase their profits, the impact on the Japanese industrial base was less encouraging. 'Hollowing out' contributed significantly to Japan's stagnation in the 1990s and beyond. For the average Japanese citizen, it's not at all obvious that the opportunities presented by the emerging superpower across the way were entirely golden, no matter what the export data suggested. Japan's growth rate dropped from around 4 per cent a year in the 1980s to only 1 per cent a year thereafter. Even if Japan's multinationals – and their foreign shareholders – may have benefited from a new 'global' strategy, this has not necessarily brought many benefits for the Japanese people. While many Japanese companies are well-established household names, the Japanese stock market, replete with companies vulnerable to the process of hollowing out, has delivered an abysmal performance since the beginning of the 1990s. Meanwhile, wages have stagnated and, by Japanese standards, unemployment has remained painfully high.

Put another way, Japanese multinationals are no longer Japanese in the conventional sense. They may be headquartered in Japan but, in many ways, they are no more beholden to their domestic economy than any foreign company that might choose to operate in Japan. For multinationals, national borders are increasingly irrelevant.

Japan's 'hollowing out' process has also increasingly been seen elsewhere. The World Investment Report (WIR), published on an annual basis by the United Nations Conference on Trade and Development (UNCTAD), contains a wealth of useful information on multinational investments in foreign lands. At the last count, 71,385 foreign companies had bases in the Czech Republic, while Romania had 89,911, Hungary 26,019 and Turkey 18,308. The biggest of all, though, was China: 286,232 foreign companies were based there in 2007.

These trends are set to continue. Surveys conducted by UNCTAD persistently show that favoured destinations for future foreign direct investment include China, India, the Russian Federation, Brazil and Vietnam, alongside the US. Few European countries make it to the top ten: Germany and the UK are clinging on for dear life.

There is nothing new, of course, in the idea of companies operating at the regional or global level. Companies often open plants in other parts of the world either to reduce the risks associated with protectionism (Japanese car companies to the US in the 1980s) or to produce goods to reflect local needs (US car companies to Europe in the 1950s and 1960s: the Pontiac Catalina would have struggled to find its way through the narrow streets of London, Rome or Paris). Ranked by size of foreign assets, the top ten non-financial multinationals are what might reasonably be described as 'the usual suspects'.[8] What is new, however, is the increased motivation to invest in other parts of the world as a result of access to workers who are willing to work for much lower wages than those on offer in the developed world.

It's worth spending a moment or two reflecting on how extreme the differences are. In 1960 an average Chinese citizen's per-capita income was 3 per cent of an American's. By 1970, following the Cultural Revolution, the ratio had dropped to just 1.5 per cent before rising to around 5 per cent in the first decade of the new century.

China's living standards have thus risen quickly since the 1970s but, on average, Chinese incomes are still very low. Brazil and Russia are doing little better, with incomes per capita around 12 to 15 per cent of those in the US in recent times; in *relative* terms, this still leaves them in the position last held by Japan in 1960. India, meanwhile, remains extremely poor, with per-capita incomes less than 2 per cent of the US average.[9]

In previous centuries, workers in these countries had no access to global capital. Now they do. David Ricardo's theory of comparative advantage no longer applies. His arguments were based on the assumption that factors of production could not travel across borders. The rapid growth of the emerging economies, however, depends critically on the ability of capital, in particular, to hop across borders with impunity. And so it has proved to be. The motivation for companies, domestic or multinational, to invest in these countries is not so much because their investments provide access to billions of new consumers who might buy their products (although there are plenty of eager emerging consumers keen to be seen with Gucci loafers, Louis Vuitton handbags or Cartier trinkets) but, rather, because factories can recruit cheap labour. Economists often talk about the advantages of trade, but this is more a story about a major global redistribution of income, from those who have always enjoyed access to the best capital to those who, for the first time, have managed to place their feet on the rungs of the development ladder.

GEOGRAPHY MATTERS

Japan's 'hollowing-out' experience may be happening elsewhere. US trade experience in recent years, for example, is certainly consistent with the Japanese story. In 1988, the year before the Berlin Wall came down, China accounted for 1.6 per cent of US export of goods. Ten years later, China accounted for 2.1 per cent of US exports. By 2008, that share had risen to 5.5 per cent, overtaking Japan (5.1 per cent), Germany (4.2 per cent) and the UK (4.1 per cent) in the process.

China is not the only emerging economy to become an important destination for US exports. Also playing a crucial role in 2008 were Mexico (11.7 per cent), Brazil (2.5 per cent), an assortment of other Latin American economies and the United Arab Emirates (1.2 per cent).

At the margin, exports to emerging economies are beginning to dominate world trade. For any given increase in US exports, for example, an expanding proportion is likely to be heading to the emerging world. Some simple arithmetical manipulation can be used to calculate so-called 'percentage-point contributions' to overall export growth.[10] These calculations can be used to explain what proportion of any given increase in exports is heading to any one country or region. Not surprisingly, the main drivers of US export growth are Canada and Mexico (this was the case even before the signing of the North American Free Trade Agreement). Elsewhere, however, there have been some major changes. China didn't make any sort of impression in 1988 but has rapidly moved up the rankings since then. So has Brazil. Japan, meanwhile, has headed in entirely the opposite direction: it may still account for over 5 per cent of US exports but its contribution to US export growth has been in rapid decline. France and the UK have also fallen by the wayside. The United States' most important trading partners, those helping to shape the country's economic future, now come from the poor South and West and not, as was true for many decades, from wealthy Europe.

The US is not the only country to have experienced huge changes in exports patterns in recent years. As an export destination, the US itself is on the wane: although it still accounts for a large share of German, French, British and Japanese exports, it is less important than it once was. The growth markets are to be found elsewhere: for

Europe, China, Russia, Poland, the Middle East and other countries in Asia all score increasingly highly.

Of course, this is not just one-way traffic. US concerns about Chinese economic muscle do not stem from China's growing role as a market for US exports. Instead, they are a reflection of China's growing penetration in US markets. For every dollar of US exports to China, around $4 comes back the other way, giving an overall deficit on the US current account position with China of $308bn in 2008. China has a huge bilateral trade surplus with the US notwithstanding the substantial increase in US exports to China in recent years. China's trade surplus, in turn, has become a major source of friction between these two great powers.[11]

The position is somewhat ironic. In the 1980s, when China's subsequent economic success was no more than a distant dream, the US became concerned about other trading relationships. Before the Berlin Wall came down, the country generating the biggest concerns was Japan. America's bilateral deficit with Japan had been steadily expanding through the 1980s, helped along in the first half of that decade by a massive appreciation of the US dollar, which had dampened the competitive position of US exporters. Japan came under tremendous pressure to open up its domestic markets which, for services in particular, had been closed to foreign competitors. As far as the US authorities were concerned, Japan was pursuing a mercantilist policy that threatened the fabric of economic life in the US. Germany was tarred with the same brush. In a conversation in the late 1980s, an American economist made the absurd claim to me that 'what the Japanese and Germans are trying to do to us economically today is what they failed to do to us militarily during World War Two'. Those who believe that the US always happily embraces free trade need to wake up. Isolationism and exceptionalism are characteristics that have stuck like leeches to the US nation throughout its history. In Chapter 10, I discuss this issue in more detail; for the time being, it's worth noting that free movement of goods and capital across borders is far from guaranteed.

In the 1980s, the US had a huge bilateral trade deficit with Japan. It still does.[12] Yet concerns about Japan's industrial muscle have faded even though Toyota, for example, is a far more successful car manufacturer than its American counterparts. Why has Japan faded from view? The answer doubtless lies with Japan's multi-year economic stagnation. The biggest perceived threat to American economic prosperity in the 1980s is now regarded as only a second-tier economic power. US diplomatic interest has shifted to the other side of the East China Sea. China may not be as wealthy per capita as Japan, but it's the world's biggest consumer of a variety of industrial raw materials, it's growing very quickly and, unlike Japan, it has nuclear weapons. China bestraddles the global stage in ways unimaginable only a few decades ago. Japan, meanwhile, is merely a shadow of its former economic self. America's fear is ultimately that the US could be heading the same way as Japan.

THE US BANK: HAVE WE TRADED MANUFACTURING SKILLS FOR FINANCIAL INSTABILITY?

One possible defence of the comparative-advantage argument is to suggest that the US, unlike Japan, can more easily cope with the rise of China because America's economy is unusually flexible. It's worth considering, for example, the implications of heightened foreign direct investment for the relative shares of different types of economic activity in the developed and the emerging worlds.

One particularly significant change in recent decades has been a wholesale shift in manufacturing capacity from the developed to the emerging world. It's no surprise that, these days, Germany and Japan regard emerging economies as some of their biggest customers: as the world's most important producers of capital goods, sustained increases in plant and machinery investment within the emerging world are good news for the likes of Siemens and Komatsu. Overall, the share of global industrial 'added value' coming from the developed nations has dropped from 68.3 per cent in 1971 to 51.9 per cent in 2008, while the share accruing to Brazil, Russia, India and China (BRIC), has risen from 2.6 to 16.5 per cent over the same period (similar figures apply to capital spending). For GDP as a whole, the G7 share has fallen more moderately from 70.5 per cent in 1971 to 61.1 per cent in 2008, with the share for China et al. rising from 3.3 to 11.6 per cent over the period:[13] in other words, the developed nations have moved away from manufacturing while the BRICs have become increasingly dependent on it.

The Ricardian interpretation of these developments is simple. All that's happened is that each area of the world has focused on its comparative advantage. As barriers came down, there was swift recognition of the huge cost advantage offered by potential manufacturing workers in the emerging world. Many of these people were, in effect, underemployed in the agricultural sector. Their drift into urban factories both raised productivity in the agricultural sector (fewer workers but a similar output) while raising incomes as a whole because, on average, productivity is higher in manufacturing than in agriculture.[14]

But if the emerging economies are now focused on manufacturing production, a Ricardian interpretation requires the developed world to specialize in something else. The answer, it seems, has been a massive growth in financial services (alongside design, the media and other service industries). In effect, emerging economies make things but capital markets in the developed world determine what things should be made through their banks, stock markets and bond markets.

Think of China, for example, as a naive saver who regularly deposits his income into the local bank which, for the purposes of this argument, I'll call American Thrift Inc. As a naive saver, China does not want a particularly high return on his savings: instead, he just wants to know that he can get access to those savings at a moment's notice. American Thrift Inc. offers a very modest return to its depositors but then takes the money to invest in higher-returning opportunities elsewhere.

This, of course, is not quite the whole picture. While China treats America as its bank, China invests largely in Treasuries rather than in any particular financial establishment. As we shall see in Chapter 4, the higher demand for Treasuries raises the price of Treasuries and, thus, lowers the yield. This lower level of interest rates makes other investments seem more attractive, including investments by US multinationals into China. The increased flow of foreign direct investment into China is profitable for US multinationals, creates additional Chinese jobs and, at the same time, allows the American financial-services industry to expand. What better illustration could there be of the benefits of comparative advantage?

Unfortunately, this is not all good news. The argument works only if there are no distortions created as a result of treating the US as China's bank. Yet there are distortions aplenty. Although the Chinese deposit their savings with the US, they have no say over how those savings are then invested. While US companies might choose to invest in China, they could just as easily invest in a domestic housing boom (as, in fact, they did in the early years of the twenty-first century). For those lucky enough to be working in financial markets during the boom years, the winning mentality prevailed. But as the dependency on financial systems as sources of income and wealth has increased in the developed world, so the risk of financial crises may have risen. As manufacturing has headed elsewhere, the developed world has increasingly found its comparative advantage to be in the world of financial roulette. As we discovered in 2008 and 2009, this was, perhaps, a gamble that did not pay off.

Indeed, the outsourcing and off-shoring synonymous with the rise of the emerging world have revealed underlying weaknesses in the developed economies. Rent-seeking behaviour has increased in the financial industry where monetary rewards have, in some cases, soared into the stratosphere. Yet the returns delivered by the financial industry have been generally poor, at least since the 1990s. As we'll see in Chapter 6, the vast majority of people in the West have not substantially gained from increased globalization. Moreover, to the extent that weaknesses within the financial system, revealed in 2008 and 2009, will have to be paid for by current and future taxpayers, the ultimate benefits of globalization for the West have either already been taken off the table by those in the financial world who were lucky or, instead, have been significantly overstated. The rapid growth of the financial services industry appears both to have masked a competitive loss in other areas of economic endeavour and to have created a huge future tax burden. The implications of this will be explored more fully in the following chapters. At this stage, however, it's worth emphasizing that the changing patterns of trade seen since the 1980s do not reflect the simple homilies of comparative advantage.

We are only now beginning to see the full consequences of the changing trading patterns associated with the rise of the emerging economies. Parts of the developed world have swapped the cyclicality of manufacturing activity for the instability of high finance. Other parts of the developed world have stagnated. Companies have, rightly, taken advantage of the new investment opportunities that have opened up around the world. Governments, however, have been slow to understand the full implications of outsourcing, off-shoring and all the rest. They've ended up with economies that have developed an alarming taste for cowboy capitalism.

The commitment to free trade, where it exists, is, in general, admirable. The failure to think about the consequences of restructuring for broader economic stability is not so admirable. As emerging economies have increasingly specialized in the activities that used to take place in the West, the developed world has struggled to work out what to do next. In Japan, the cost has been seen in economic stagnation. In the US and the UK, the costs can be seen in the form of inflated financial sectors operating in a global casino which, unlike Las Vegas, has no hard-and-fast rules. As Chapter 4 reveals, capital markets have as a result become increasingly unstable.

CHAPTER FOUR

INTERNATIONAL ROULETTE: ANARCHY IN CAPITAL MARKETS

While emerging economies have had a huge influence on capital market performance, it has not been the influence expected by the majority of investors. Many thought a gold mine of investment opportunities awaited them. On the whole, these hopes have been dashed. There has been no gold mine. Instead, we have been living through a modern-day version of the Californian gold rush. Too often, only fool's gold has been on offer. Capital markets have not delivered decent returns while financial systems overall have become increasingly unhinged. The gravitational pull of the emerging nations has left interest rates and the prices of a wide range of financial and real assets increasingly warped. The consequence has been a vast increase in financial-market volatility and a reduction in rates of return.

AT THE END OF THE RAINBOW

As the emerging economies awoke from their decades and, in some cases, centuries of economic hibernation, corporate investors and fund managers around the world licked their lips. Companies saw tremendous opportunities ahead of them. No longer were their customers and workers confined to the developed world. Corporate executives were, instead, faced with a brave new world offering higher sales volumes at lower cost and, hence, higher profit.

Fund managers began to offer new products tailored to the exciting new opportunities available in the emerging world. In the summer of 2009, for example, Fidelity International – one of the world's biggest and most successful fund managers – offered to investors a total of well over thirty separate funds tailored specifically to emerging markets.

As for individual savers, they could benefit in one of two ways. Either they could buy one of the thousands of funds that directly invested in emerging world companies; or, instead, they could buy shares in companies based in the developed world, which, in turn, would invest the additional funds in exciting new opportunities in the emerging world.

Yet for investors, it's been a roller-coaster ride with more downs than ups, particularly since the beginning of the new millennium. While some years have offered spectacular returns in specific markets, overall returns have been poor. In the ten years ending in 2008 (a year in which equities collapsed) or 2009 (when equities rebounded), investors would have been better off investing in safe, boring, US Treasuries – simple claims on future US taxpayers – than in US equities or, indeed, in the equities of many emerging markets (see Figures 4.1 and 4.2). Given that many profit-hungry US companies chose to invest all over the world – including its emerging parts – this is a remarkable and historically unprecedented result. Partly, it reflects the increasing instability of the financial system as a whole. Following the collapse of the Berlin Wall, crisis layered upon crisis: an early 1990s credit crunch, the 1992 European exchange-rate crisis, the Mexican 'tequila' crisis, the Asian crisis, the Russian and Argentine

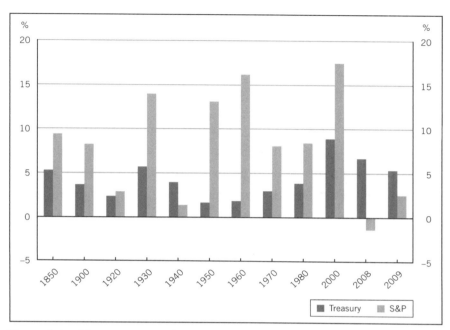

Figure 4.1: 10-year returns for US government bonds and US equities
Source: HSBC

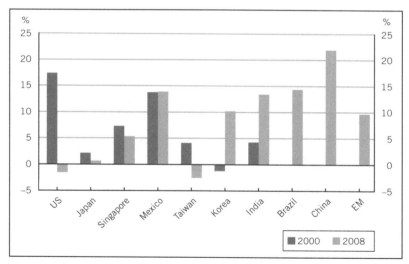

Figure 4.2: 10-year annualized returns across developed and emerging nations
Source: HSBC. Returns data for the ten years to 2000 are not available for Brazil and China and, hence, for the emerging nations as a whole. EM refers to emerging markets and is an aggregate measure of their performance.

defaults, the dot.com bubble and subsequent bust, the sub-prime crisis and, of course, the global meltdown that followed.

THE ROLE OF CAPITAL MARKETS

Capital markets bring together savers and borrowers. They allow us to plan for our futures. They enable us to smooth our consumption patterns over our lifetimes (and, if bequests are included, beyond our lifetimes). They help determine the amount, and type, of investment in an economy. They link the real economy with the financial economy.

Capital market participants – bankers, fund managers, private-equity investors and other 'go-betweens' – package their products in all sorts of ways, ranging from simple bank deposits and loans through to the ever-more complex instruments that make up the lexicon of international finance: syndicated loans, equities, corporate bonds, commercial paper, asset-backed securities, collateralized debt obligations and structured products. Ultimately, each of these products offers a claim on future economic wealth (or, put another way, a reward for abstinence today). Banks provide loans in exchange for an interest payment. Shareholders hold equities because they expect a dividend or a capital gain. Issuers of asset-backed securities provide a return in exchange for the apparent protection associated with the underlying asset.

That most people have no idea of what these products are is one of the wonderful tricks of modern international finance. Ultimately, savers end up buying products they often don't understand. Not surprisingly, the business of global capital markets has, over the years, attracted more than its fair share of snake-oil salesmen. There is no shortage of rent-seeking behaviour in the capital markets.

THE HUNT FOR YIELD

Yet despite these difficulties, we desperately want our capital markets to perform well. With baby boomers approaching retirement, the developed world is facing new challenges. The proportion of people in work is diminishing. With fewer workers, how will it be possible to deliver the income needed to feed not just the workers themselves but also the increasing numbers of people in retirement?

In recent years, the answer has come in the form of a 'hunt for yield', a search for a range of magic assets that would either deliver higher interest rates or dividends than in the past or, alternatively, produce higher capital returns than before without any additional risk. There is, apparently, a pot of gold at the end of the investment rainbow. Even for those countries facing tremendous economic challenges this belief is difficult to shake off. The pressure to earn a high rate of return is intense, even if the domestic economy is stagnant. During the 1990s, I was constantly amazed by Japanese fund managers who believed they could squeeze double-digit returns from an economy that had lost the ability to expand.

On paper, the arrival on the global economic stage of the emerging economies thus seemed to offer manna from heaven. Suddenly, arthritic growth in the developed world was no longer a constraint on capital returns. Instead, the West could invest in the emerging world. Companies could produce goods more cheaply and widen their customer base, thereby boosting their profits and keeping their shareholders and bank managers happy. All in all, the emerging economies gave a shot in the arm to global growth, implying higher future levels of output and, hence, higher capital returns.

You could almost hear the collective sigh of relief. With China opening its borders, with the Soviet Union's collapse triggering outbreaks of capitalist endeavour across Eastern Europe and with India deciding its long-term interests were best served by embracing the market economy as opposed to its earlier flirtations with socialism, it suddenly appeared that ageing Westerners would no longer see their living standards coming under downward pressure. Wrinkly Americans and greying Europeans would be able to head off to Naples Beach or Cannes for their summer holidays, happy in the knowledge that wealth accumulation was safe and sound, given the new opportunities presenting themselves in the emerging economies.

NO PROMISED LAND

That, at least, was the theory. The practice has been entirely different. The financial industry takes pride in the idea that its many skilled practitioners are able to deliver returns superior to those available to ordinary folk who probably don't know the difference between an equity, a corporate bond and a structured product. Yet the various financial mishaps of recent years paint an entirely different picture. It is extraordinary that savers would have been better off leaving their investments in safe US Treasuries than investing in some of the products that, supposedly, deliver superior returns over a longer time period.

For every emerging-market investment that appears to have performed well, others have performed poorly. As for the US, the recent ups and downs in its financial markets offer a match for Japan and its lost decades.

This is a puzzling outcome. After all, the emerging economies have delivered rapid growth since the 1980s, expanding at a rate two or three times faster than the typical pace seen in the industrialized world. If growth has been so good for the vast majority of the time, surely it should have been easy to unearth profitable investment opportunities? Either investors could have put their money directly into emerging markets or, instead, they could have invested in companies that, in turn, had strategic profitable aims in the emerging world.

The hunt for yield, however, went off in an altogether different direction. It was as if someone had rearranged all the road signs, sending travellers to entirely inappropriate destinations. The proof comes from the emergence of the so-called 'global imbalances'. If emerging economies offered such wonderful investment prospects, a reasonable conclusion might be that savings would accumulate in the developed world and then flow into investment prospects in the emerging world. That, after all, was the nineteenth-century model of globalization, with savings from the UK heading to emerging nations to take advantage of exciting investment opportunities. In this 'win-win' situation, capital inflows would, in theory, fuel higher growth in emerging markets, generating rising living standards for more and more people. Meanwhile, the new investment opportunities would enable Western companies to make higher profits, thereby satisfying the hunt for yield for Western holders of capital.

The outcome has been exactly the opposite. On balance, savings and, hence, capital have flowed not from the developed world to the emerging world but, instead, from the emerging world to the developed world. The US, for example, has run a bigger and bigger current-account deficit over the last three decades (admittedly with the occasional interruption for a recession). To do so – and it's no more than a simple rule of accounting – the US has had to attract increasing amounts of capital from abroad.

In the 1980s, the primary sources of this capital were Japan and Germany. At that time, global imbalances were the G7's problem. The inability of the G7 to reach any kind of credible agreement, notwithstanding the Plaza and Louvre accords in 1985 and 1987 respectively, led to upheavals in currency markets and, eventually, the 1987 stock-market crash.[1]

Japan and Germany remain important providers of capital, but from the mid-1990s onwards the really big suppliers have been China, the Middle East, Russia and an assortment of other emerging economies.

Ben Bernanke, the Chairman of the Board of Governors of the Federal Reserve, famously referred to these imbalances as 'The Global Savings Glut'.[2] The argument boils down to a matter of supply and demand in the capital markets. If the rapidly expanding US current-account deficit reflected a rise in US demand for global capital, that increased demand should have raised the 'price' of capital. In other words, US interest rates should have gone up to attract the additional funds US borrowers wanted to suck in from abroad.

This didn't happen. For the most part, US interest rates have not only been low but persistently lower than the vast majority of economists expected.[3] Put another way, the US borrowed in size precisely because interest rates were so low. Interest rates were low, in turn, because countries elsewhere in the world were generating huge amounts of surplus savings. It wasn't so much, then, that a rising demand for loans in the US was driving interest rates up, but, rather, that a rising *supply* of loans outside the US was driving interest rates down. Americans may have a reputation as spendthrifts, but, on this interpretation, their high levels of indebtedness were merely a response to high levels of saving elsewhere in the world which lowered the cost of borrowing.

THE EMERGING-NATION WAR CHEST

One of the big messages from the Asian economic crisis in 1997 and 1998 was that emerging economies could sometimes struggle under the burden of huge capital inflows. At that time, many emerging economies ran current-account deficits. In other words, domestic investment was higher than domestic saving, requiring inflows of capital from abroad to balance the books. These capital inflows were too often invested in unsound property deals or corrupt business ventures, leading to accusations of 'crony capitalism'. As foreign investors took fright, capital left Asia and headed elsewhere. Without the inflows, Asia could no longer maintain its earlier standard of living: demand fell, imports dropped, exchange rates plummeted and economies collapsed.

The Asian crisis demonstrated two things. First, in their hunt for yield, Western investors were happy to chase returns regardless of the risks involved. Second, Asian countries were not able to offer the depth or sophistication of capital markets that could easily handle the inflows associated with the hunt for yield.[4]

For some Asian policymakers, the Asian crisis offered a remarkably simple lesson (through both the law of unintended consequences and the hunt for yield, this lesson undoubtedly contributed to the 2007/8 sub-prime crisis and the credit crunch that followed). Many Asian leaders – and, indeed, policymakers in other emerging economies – decided to build war chests of foreign-exchange reserves to protect themselves against the risk of future balance-of-payments and currency crises. Their motives were entirely understandable. In some cases, their economies had shrunk in the late 1990s at a double-digit rate. They needed the economic equivalent of a force field to prevent any reoccurrence. The force field came in the form of persistent – and, in some cases, persistently rising – current-account surpluses. Domestic savings started to outstrip domestic investment. The surplus savings had to go somewhere. Ultimately, through rising foreign-exchange reserves, they were invested by emerging-market central banks in safe and liquid US Treasuries, demonstrating a level of risk aversion not normally shown by private-sector investors. Yields dropped, US households borrowed more and consumer spending boomed.

THE HOLE IN THE STORY

This is a neat argument, but it doesn't quite let policymakers off the hook. Knowing that American consumers were borrowing more because interest rates were lower does not mean they *should* have been borrowing more. After all, no one argues that the increase in drug usage that follows a fall in the street price of crack cocaine is a good thing, even though it's a perfectly reasonable example of the market at work.

The influence on the world's capital markets of savings behaviour in emerging economies is, in fact, considerably more complicated than the simple global savings glut thesis suggests. And, because this influence has not been properly recognized, the Western world has been subject to increasing financial shocks.

While many countries shifted from current-account deficit to surplus, one emerging Asian economy started with a large current-account surplus and saw the surplus get bigger and bigger over time. China wasn't significantly affected by the Asian crisis. Why, then, did it allow its current-account surplus to rise so much? Why did it resist exchange-rate appreciation, at the risk of facing the wrath of an angry US Congress? Why was it seemingly unable to stimulate domestic demand sufficiently to bring its current-account surplus down to a level that would have made the US happier?

The answer that finds favour in a US Congress with its finger on the protectionist trigger is that China has deliberately manipulated its exchange rate in the pursuit of a mercantilist trade policy. According to this argument, the rise in China's foreign-exchange reserves in recent years demonstrates that China has deliberately undervalued its exchange rate in the pursuit of a rising share of global trade.[5]

It is certainly true that China's share of world trade has risen. It's equally true that, had the Chinese allowed the renminbi to rise further in value, Chinese foreign-exchange reserves would probably be a lot lower. But are these really signs of a mercantilist policy or, instead, are they indications of something more fundamental?

One of the most striking features of China's economy is the combination of a very high level of capital spending within total gross domestic product together with a substantial current-account surplus. Many countries with high investment shares in total domestic expenditure do not have sufficient domestic funds to support the investment and, as a result, they depend on inflows of foreign savings. In other words, they run current-account deficits. China has such high domestic savings that it can afford to fund huge amounts of domestic capital spending and still have more than loose change to send abroad in the form of what, post-millennium, proved to be the single biggest current-account surplus in the world.

Arguing that the high level of domestic savings stems from a deliberately undervalued exchange rate is, at best, misleading and, at worst, no more than protectionist posturing. China's labour costs are dramatically lower than those in the developed world. No amount of nominal exchange-rate appreciation is going to change this simple fact of economic life. Indeed, were the renminbi to rise dramatically, the chances are either that Chinese wages would fall (because of the greater difficulty in exporting products) or that US wages would rise (in response to higher import prices). Chinese wages are low because of China's lack of development over hundreds of years. Chinese workers do not expect to be paid, and nor can they command, the wages received by Americans: exchange-rate manipulation will not be enough to change this underlying economic fact.

Moreover, even if Chinese wages did rise to American levels over time, there is no particular reason to believe that China's current-account surplus would materially decline. To understand why, you need only look at economic developments in Japan, China's near neighbour and long-term rival.

JAPAN'S CURRENCY APPRECIATION: LESSONS FOR CHINA

Japan is a rich country. Despite the economic problems of the last two decades, the Japanese enjoy per-capita incomes that compare very favourably with rich countries elsewhere in the world. Over the last forty years, the Japanese yen has steadily appreciated against the world's other major currencies. In the early 1970s, a dollar would buy more than ¥300. By the 1980s, a dollar would buy, on average, around ¥200. In the new millennium, a dollar was sufficient to buy a paltry ¥114. If nominal exchange-rate appreciation is supposed to remove global imbalances, Japan's experience should surely support this claim.

But it doesn't. In the 1970s, Japan's current-account surplus averaged 0.7 per cent of gross domestic product (GDP). In the 1980s, the surplus had risen to 2 per cent of GDP. In the first eight years of the twenty-first century, the surplus averaged approaching 3.5 per cent of GDP. Despite, therefore, persistent gains in the yen's value on the foreign-exchange markets, Japan's rising current-account surplus has added to global imbalances over the last forty years.

Those who believe in the efficacy of exchange-rate moves would doubtless argue that Japan should have allowed its exchange rate to rise even further. This argument doesn't wash. Had the revaluation protagonists entered the medical profession, they'd still be advocating amputation to deal with early signs of gangrene when a dose of antibiotics would be more effective and less painful, and carry fewer side effects. The evidence is overwhelming: over the long term, movements in nominal exchange rates do little to alter global imbalances.

People in China and other emerging countries save a lot (or borrow very little which, in net terms, amounts to much the same thing) primarily because they lack the institutions that have dramatically lowered savings rates in the industrialized world. What we call the 'savings industry' is, in theory, a brilliant way of spreading risk and allowing people to smooth their consumption patterns over their lifetimes. Even with radical advances in genetic knowledge in recent years, none of us can predict how long we'll live. Those who die before reaching retirement (or soon after) effectively subsidize the pension incomes of those who live for many more years. Insurance works on much the same basis (indeed, pensions are a form of insurance: everyone contributes, but those who end up six feet under a day after retirement gain little financial benefit). For those who cannot afford to pay into private-sector pension and insurance schemes, most Western economies offer 'social insurance' in the form of state pensions, unemployment benefit, tertiary education and the like. The spread of social security was a direct response to the impact of the Great Depression in the 1930s: as nation states took on the burden of providing insurance to those who were at risk of economic disadvantage, so the need for individuals to save for 'precautionary' reasons fell. Meanwhile, with the rise of consumer credit, Western individuals have increasingly been able to borrow from 'future' income to fund current consumption. In response to all these changes, savings ratios (the ratio of household income not consumed to total income) declined through much of the post-war period.

This process has yet to happen in China and many other emerging economies. Why should it? The declines in household saving ratios in the Western world over the last forty years may have been a response to the spreading benefits of pensions, insurance and state education, but the ability of nations to deliver these benefits has, in turn, depended on hundreds of years of per-capita income growth and financial evolution, from the diamond traders of Antwerp and the share dealers of London coffee houses in the eighteenth century through to the modern-day alchemists of global finance. It's not realistic to expect emerging economies to compress three or four centuries of economic and financial development into a handful of years. Americans may be able to walk into the nearest car showroom and drive off with the latest model just by taking out a loan, but for the vast majority of workers in the emerging world that option does not exist, whatever the level of the exchange rate.

This, in turn, implies that policymakers on either side of the Atlantic have been looking at the problem of global imbalances from entirely the wrong perspective. Demanding that China, for example, should dramatically reduce its current-account surplus is all very well, but there is no obvious mechanism to achieve this outcome. Cyclically, China's surplus will decline every time the US has a recession, for the simple reason that around 20 per cent of China's exports of goods go to the US. But to reduce global imbalances through a US recession is an unattractive outcome that creates misery for all concerned.

The correct and constructive way of thinking about global imbalances is to consider how they influence cross-border capital flows and how those flows, in turn, distort capital allocation across countries and within nations. Policymakers should not merely indulge in a spot of wishful thinking that, one morning, global imbalances will just disappear. They are, instead, a fact of economic and political life. They also carry all sorts of implications for economic stability – or the lack of it – in the developed world.

Excess savings in the emerging economies create two problems. First, if emerging economies save large amounts of money, the rest of the world must borrow large amounts of money. Second, the excess savings in the emerging world have tended to be invested in a narrow range of seemingly 'safe' assets such as US Treasuries, primarily because the vast majority of excess savings are held in the form of foreign-exchange reserves. Reserve managers do not share the investment objectives of a typical New York or London fund manager. They focus on liquidity rather than return. The reserves are held as a cushion against 'sudden stops', whereby inflows of capital from abroad dry up. They are, therefore, designed to be not just a nest egg for future generations but also a tool to deliver macro-economic stability in the short run. Moreover, as we shall see in Chapter 7, the diversification options for many emerging nations are rather narrow, in part because the West is unwilling to sell controlling interests in its companies and resources to state investors elsewhere in the world.

THE MIS-PRICING OF WESTERN CAPITAL MARKETS

This combination is potentially lethal for Western capital markets. If the emerging world is busily buying US Treasuries, the price on Treasuries will be higher, and the yield lower, than might be the case in a 'free market' situation, where the only focus of fund managers is to maximize returns for a given amount of risk. This creates problems for Western investors who, as argued above, are actively engaged in the 'hunt for yield'. If Treasury yields are unusually low, investors will be forced to buy something else.

What is that 'something else'? In the late 1990s, following the onset of the Asian crisis, the asset of choice was equities, helped along by the new technologies associated with the dot.com boom. Seemingly, any fool capable of putting together an investment prospectus was able to raise funds, not because the business case was necessarily sound but because the funds were so freely available. The Federal Reserve added fuel to the fire by keeping policy rates relatively low, because of the unjustified fears of global recession stemming from the Asian crisis and, later on, the concerns associated with computer failures linked to the new millennium (although why monetary policy had to play a role in the Y2K threat is, to say the least, puzzling).

The decision to keep interest rates low after the Asian crisis is understandable but, in hindsight, was based on a misinterpretation of the effects of the crisis. Economic models are mostly driven by real, rather than financial, flows: changes in the value of exports and imports, not changes in the value of holdings of financial assets. Admittedly, policy rates and exchange rates play a role, but the Asian crisis filtered through the policymakers' models only via trade. If demand was collapsing in Asia, it followed that US and European exports to Asia would collapse, leaving the Western world facing recession.

There was no recession. The collapse in Asia was precipitated by capital flight. Funds that had happily nestled in Asia went back to the US and Europe. As Asian current-account deficits diminished, so the US current-account deficit grew bigger, funded by the capital which was now fleeing Asia. The inflows helped push down short- and long-term interest rates, lifted the US equity market and contributed to an ongoing boom in domestic demand. This was, perhaps, the first indication that the US economy could be at the mercy of international capital flows over which policymakers had no direct control.

The bubble in equities could not be sustained. While it lasted many people were happy to extol the wonders of the 'new economy'. There certainly was an improvement in productivity growth led by cutting-edge technologies, but, as time passed, the impact of these technologies on rising living standards began to fade. Economic growth in the developed world slowed following the 2000 stock-market crash and would have been slower still in the absence of a global housing boom and a massive, and unsustainable, expansion of credit.

The belief in the wonders of new technologies was fuelled by a stock market that, for a while, seemed to defy the laws of gravity. This became a circular process: the stock market went up because of new technologies, but investment in new technologies was forthcoming because the stock market was going up.

Bubbles burst. The stock-market boom in the late 1990s, fuelled by capital inflows from Asia and other emerging economies, was no exception. The Federal Reserve belatedly applied the monetary brakes, signalling its disagreement with those more optimistic investors who believed US economic growth might be sustained at a 4 per cent annual rate for evermore. By past standards, interest rates didn't rise very far. They didn't have to. The message got through. All those expectations of exuberant profits growth in the years to come began to fade and, as they did so, stock markets collapsed. No matter how much capital was pouring into the US economy from Asia and other parts of the emerging world, ultimately reality triumphed over inflated stock-market aspirations. Moreover, as the stock market plummeted, so the usual scams emerged, in the form of Enron, WorldCom and the rest. Trust collapsed and equity markets were unable to recover their earlier poise.

Yet investors and policymakers failed to learn the lesson. The hunt for yield did not disappear. And with emerging economies building up ever-larger savings surpluses, distortions in global capital markets got worse, not better. The belief in the pot of gold refused to go away. Since equities couldn't deliver the necessary returns, and government bond yields were ludicrously low, investors went in search of other assets that might do the trick. As with any other market, an increase in demand for high-returning non-equity assets was met with an increase in supply. Asset-backed securities, mortgage-backed securities, collateralized debt obligations and so on became the investments *du jour*. Banks packaged up vast quanti-ties of loans into these securities and either tucked them away under the mattress as off-balance-sheet items in the form of conduits and special investment vehicles (SIVs) or, instead, sold them off to other investors – insurance companies, pension funds, hedge funds and, in some cases, local councils – who, collectively, became known as the 'shadow banking system'. These institutions lent money to the banks who, in turn, lent the money on to their customers. These customers included, most obviously, sub-prime borrowers in the US.

Lenders did not restrict themselves to lending merely to US borrowers with questionable credit histories. They also, increasingly, lent to customers within the emerging world. After all, emerging economies were growing quickly and, therefore, seemed to have many of the attributes required to justify a 'hunt for yield'. For the daring investor, the opportunity to make high returns was there to be grabbed, notwithstanding the paltry long-run returns that had been made since the 1980s.

Some emerging economies – most obviously, those in Central and Eastern Europe – saw capital inflows rising much more quickly than capital outflows, leaving them with balance of payments current-account deficits. Others coped with rising capital inflows by creating even bigger capital outflows, often in the form of rapidly rising foreign-exchange reserves. China is a fine example of this reaction. Between 1997 and 2008, for example, foreign direct-investment inflows into China rose by $723bn: simultaneously, foreign-exchange reserves (in effect, investments made abroad by China's central bank for the benefit of the people) rose by $1,841bn.[6]

FOREIGN-EXCHANGE RESERVES AND A CAPITAL 'MARKET' RUN FOR THE BENEFIT OF GOVERNMENTS

China and other emerging nations became major participants in a global liquidity game played more by governments than by private institutions. Some limited clues to the changing status of international capital markets, and the growing role of state investors and borrowers, comes from the IMF's data on the currency composition of official foreign-exchange reserves (COFER), outlined in Figure 4.3.

Reserve holdings	1995 (US$bn)	2008 (US$bn)
World	1389	6645
World (per cent of GDP)	*5.0*	*11.0*
Advanced economies	918	2451
Advanced economies (per cent of GDP)	*3.7*	*6.0*
claims in dollars	408	1462
claims in Deutsche Marks	121	0
claims in ECU/euros	88	488
claims in yen	54	92
unallocated	165	293
Developing economies	472	4194
Developing economies (per cent of GDP)	*9.1*	*25.0*
claims in dollars	203	1237
claims in Deutsche Marks	42	0
claims in ECU/euros	0	627
claims in yen	16	38
unallocated	190	2141

Figure 4.3: The changing pattern of foreign-exchange reserve holdings
Source: IMF Currency Composition of Foreign Exchange Reserves

In 1995, before the onset of the Asian crisis, global foreign-exchange holdings amounted to $1.4trn (around 5 per cent of global GDP). Within the total, $0.9trn was held in the developed world (around 3.7 per cent of developed world GDP) with the remaining $0.5trn held in the emerging and developing economies (around 9.1 per cent of their GDP).

By 2008, the picture had radically changed. Global foreign-exchange reserves had jumped to an extraordinary $6.7trn (around 11 per cent of global GDP). Of this, $2.5trn was held in the developed world (around 6 per cent of developed world GDP) with $4.2trn held in the emerging and developing economies (around 25 per cent of their GDP). Many of these reserves were 'unallocated' and hidden away within the emerging world. Secrecy doesn't help but, given that around 60 per cent of allocated emerging reserves were held in dollars, there's every chance that much of their mysterious $2.1trn was also dollar-denominated. Assuming that the dollar share was, again, 60 per cent, overall holdings of dollars within emerging country foreign-exchange reserves would have amounted to $2.6trn, the equivalent of 15 per cent of emerging world GDP.

While large, these numbers almost certainly understate the seismic shift in capital markets that has taken place over the last twenty years. Foreign-exchange reserves have risen rapidly, but so too have other forms of state ownership, as we shall see in Chapter 7 with the rise of sovereign wealth funds (SWFs). Because the distinction between reserves and SWFs is so vague, the true size of government holdings of foreign assets is difficult to pin down. For example, according to Bloomberg, Saudi Arabia's reserve holdings amounted to just $27bn at the beginning of 2009, or just 0.4 per cent of the global total. For a major oil producer which has run current-account surpluses for decades, these numbers appear implausibly low, suggesting that Saudi Arabia's overseas assets are locked away in other forms. In many emerging nations, the distinction between state-owned and privately owned assets is far from clear.

While the official international savings of emerging economies have risen dramatically, so too have the international borrowings of the US government. In 1950, US federal debt outstanding amounted to around $257bn. At approaching 100 per cent of US national income, this was a huge legacy of the military expenditures associated with the Second World War. Almost all this debt was funded by Americans who were happy to lend to their government. Less than 2 per cent of the total was funded by foreigners, partly because of a wave of capital and foreign-exchange controls throughout the world.

By 2008, US government debt had risen to $9.6trn. As a share of national income, this stood at 68 per cent, lower than the immediate post-war extremes but, nevertheless, a sizeable increase compared with the 1981 trough of 33 per cent. Foreign participation had grown hugely. The amount of US government debt held by foreign lenders had risen to $3.2trn, or around one-third of the amount outstanding. Foreigners had also piled into bonds issued by, for example, Fannie Mae and Freddie Mac, the home-loan specialists. These and other government-sponsored enterprises were assumed to have an implicit US government guarantee, making the paper they issued about as safe as US Treasuries (in the light of the 2008 financial meltdown and the taxpayer-funded bailout that followed, this proved to be an accurate assumption). By 2008, foreigners owned $1.4trn of this paper, up from hardly anything in 1950. They also held $2.8trn of 'corporate' bonds, most of which turned out to be mortgage-backed securities, ultimately dependent on the health of the US housing market and the US banking system. Many of these pieces of paper also had an implicit US taxpayer guarantee, at least to the extent that the banking bailouts at the height of the credit crunch required a huge injection of taxpayers' money to buy up the 'toxic' assets hidden away in banks' balance sheets in the form of conduits and SIVs.

These numbers are huge. Over 50 per cent of US assets by value held by foreigners are these IOUs, while fewer than 13 per cent of foreign-owned US assets are equities and only around 20 per cent are in the form of foreign direct investment. Seen this way, the current and future US taxpayer is enormously in debt to the rest of the world and, in particular, to foreign governments. Around 50 per cent of new US debt issued each and every year is now purchased by foreign investors. Many of these investors are state entities. We thus have a global capital market dominated by borrowing and lending governments, not by the millions of investors required by a free market.

LIQUIDITY AND GREED

The action of both borrowing and lending governments has ensured the creation of a 'virtuous' circle of excess liquidity. Too many emerging economies wanted to run large current-account surpluses and resist exchange-rate appreciation. To do so, they lent to Western governments through rising foreign-exchange reserves that were often invested in liquid government paper, lowering the yields on this paper. Too many investors in developed markets were happy to chase higher yields on riskier assets, disregarding the associated dangers. As they did so, they allowed banks to raise funds well beyond their deposits through the creation of securitized products. Many of these funds were lent to US households with questionable credit histories in the form of sub-prime mortgages. Some of the funds raised, though, were lent back to the emerging economies.

This wasn't quite a Ponzi scheme (although Ponzi schemes, most obviously Bernard L. Madoff Investment Securities LLC, nevertheless developed), but it had much the same effect. The combination of rapidly growing emerging economies, 1990s Asian failures and a hunt for yield left investors with the belief that capital gains had to be plucked from the tree without any real regard for risk. Even sensible investors were forced to take part. I recall talking to one particularly cautious bond investor in 2007 who was lamenting his company's determination to deliver to its investors a particularly high rate of return. The investor found himself having to buy Ukrainian government debt at a yield of 6.5 per cent which, at the time, was considerably more attractive than the paltry 4.5 per cent available on US Treasuries. It was the only way he could ensure that his portfolio would keep up with the competition and that he, in turn, would keep his job. Two years later, the value of his investment had collapsed: the yield on Ukrainian debt rose from a trough of 5.8 per cent to a peak of 40.4 per cent, implying a huge loss. This was a catastrophe for the investor, his company and the company's clients.[7]

The pot of gold mentality did not, therefore, have a distorting effect on capital markets in the developed world alone. It also led to excessive flows of savings into emerging investments where returns for investors were, frankly, suspect. Rent-seeking behaviour is not confined to greedy Western capitalists. It is found all over the emerging world where the distinction between private companies and government control is, at best, tenuous. Pretending that corporate governance will somehow be good enough to protect the interest of developed-world investors is, in some cases, laughable.

In *The Writing on the Wall*, Will Hutton criticizes China's Communist Party for failing to disentangle itself from corporate China, arguing that China is suffering as a result from endemic corruption or, in Ricardo's terminology, abusive rent-seeking behaviour. Whether or not the corruption is endemic, the key point is, surely, that investors in the developed world have no guarantee that they'll receive the returns they expect from investing in Chinese capital markets. China was hardly treated well by the imperial powers in the nineteenth century. It isn't likely to be well disposed to investors who have every intention of extracting short-run gains at the possible expense of China's long-term development. Indeed, although China's economy has performed powerfully since the 1980s, the returns to investors have been mixed. Those who hunted for yield didn't ask enough of the right questions. They were too greedy.

THE GOLD RUSH REVISITED

Ultimately, we have lived through decades of false hopes. The savings industry has failed to deliver the returns investors expected, partly because of the distortions arising from excessive government lending and borrowing. For those of us who have worked in financial markets, this is a deeply depressing conclusion. We have, it seems, been living through a modern-day version of the Californian gold rush in the mid-nineteenth century.

The gold rush was, arguably, the ultimate triumph of hope over what would eventually prove to be bitter experience. Sam Brannan, one of the gold-rush pioneers, made a killing in the mid-nineteenth century not because he discovered very much gold but, instead, because he bought up every pick and shovel in the area; he then sold the tools to dreamy prospectors, making a mint in the process. The prospectors literally believed in a pot (or nugget) of gold, and were happy to hand over their savings to Brannan who, presumably, was happier still. Levi Strauss, a Bavarian who arrived in the US just before the gold rush, founded his eponymous company in 1853, making a fortune from the sale of heavy-duty clothing for those who would end up doing the hard yet unrewarding work of gold prospecting. In 1873, he made his clothing even stronger with the use of copper rivets, and so jeans were born.

The gold rush, then, marked a huge redistribution of wealth from those who invested everything in their dreams to those who furnished the pursuit of those dreams. The modern-day equivalents are surely the investment banks, the pension funds, the insurance companies, the providers of screen services and so on, who, like those who went before them, have benefited from others' dreams. In the nineteenth century, people believed gold would make them wealthy. In the late twentieth century, people believed their pension contributions would make them secure in their retirement. Anything supporting this idea was seized upon, including the pioneering investor spirit unleashed by the arrival of the emerging economies. Yet, as with the gold rush, the real winners may not have been those who dreamt.

While emerging economies have had an important influence on developments in world capital markets since the 1980s, their impact has been poorly understood. The most glaring error has been the belief that capital-market prices have been free of distortion. This required the heroic assumption that the rise of the emerging economies would be entirely consistent with free-market behaviour.

As we shall see in Chapter 7, this is simply not true. More importantly, policymakers in the developed world have been far too happy
to go along with the 'pot of gold' mentality. Far better, it seems, to
have pretended our savings were safe than to have faced up to the
reality of poor returns, excessive risk, false promise and, through
much higher cross-border capital flows, a loss of control.

Why were policymakers happy to go along with the pretence? In
part, they had become victims of their own propaganda. With the
defeat of inflation, they believed they had discovered the secrets of
economic management. In fact, their focus on inflation led them
away from some of the really big threats facing Western economies.
Even worse, in a world where prices of goods, services, labour and
assets were increasingly being distorted by the gravitational pull of
the emerging nations, the single-minded pursuit of price stability
only increased the risks of economic instability. The next chapter
explains why.

CHAPTER FIVE

PRICE STABILITY BRINGS ECONOMIC INSTABILITY

For many years, policymakers have pursued low and stable inflation with virtuous zeal. Understandably, they have no desire to return to the dark days of the 1970s and early 1980s, a time when inflation in all its many forms was rampant and economic performance in the Western world was, at best, disappointing. Low and stable inflation is now typically seen as a necessary condition for economic stability.

Yet, with the rise of the emerging nations, it is no longer so clear that the single-minded pursuit of price stability is delivering the goods. If anything, in a world where price disturbances in the West are increasingly the result of economic developments in the emerging world, the pursuit of price stability has contributed to mounting economic instability. Policymakers – governments, central bankers – like to take credit for the achievement of low inflation. Their institutions are specifically designed to prioritize price stability above all else, often based on the premise that price stability can easily be encapsulated in a single inflation target. This premise is wrong. Policymakers have chosen to ignore the ways in which emerging nations bend, twist and warp prices. The blinkered pursuit of low inflation in the West has been a mistake, leading to asset-price bubbles, economic booms and busts and excessive accumulation of debt. It is time for a rethink. That rethink must involve a better understanding of the role of emerging nations in determining inflation, both in the emerging world and in the West.[1]

BACK TO THE 1970S

For those brought up in the 1970s, the achievement of price stability became the big macroeconomic prize. During that decade, one economic disaster followed another, largely because there was no monetary discipline and, hence, no anchor for inflationary expectations. The commodity price surge at the beginning of the 1970s came about partly because the US over-stimulated demand in a bid to fund the Vietnam War. The collapse of the Bretton Woods exchange-rate system, and the volatility that followed, reflected the willingness to tolerate inflation as the 'acceptable' cost of delivering a low rate of unemployment. The quadrupling of oil prices at the end of 1973, as a consequence of the Arab oil embargo (itself a reaction to the Yom Kippur War), was only possible because the inflation genie was already out of the bottle. As inflation – and expectations of inflation – picked up, so industrial relations deteriorated, creating a legacy of strikes, huge wage and price increases and the beginnings of so-called 'stagflation', whereby inflation went up but economic growth and employment came down. Meanwhile, those on fixed monetary incomes – most obviously, pensioners – were often robbed of their savings through ever-bigger price increases.

While the desire to control inflation is now a central tenet of monetary policy, the shift during the 1970s towards a focus on inflation rather than unemployment as the main macroeconomic policy objective represented a remarkable change of view compared with the 1960s, when most policymakers believed in the pursuit of full employment and didn't worry too much about inflation. The best economic ideas tend, eventually, to go out of fashion, upstaged by unexpected or irregular economic developments.

The shift in stance is summed up nicely in two well-known quotes. The first, 'we are all Keynesians now', is commonly attributed to US President Richard Nixon in 1971, although the original source was a tongue-in-cheek Milton Friedman in a 1965 edition of *Time* magazine, lamenting the dominance at the time of the intellectual ideas stemming from John Maynard Keynes's *General Theory of Employment, Interest and Money*.[2] The conventional wisdom held that Keynesian demand-management policies – changes in tax and public-spending levels to foster a desired level of economic activity – would bring about full employment. These policies were to be actively used at all times to avoid a repeat of the economic calamities of the 1930s Depression.

A handful of years later, with the onset of the excessive inflation of the 1970s, this view of the world was gradually rejected. Jim Callaghan, the UK prime minister at the time, administered the *coup de grâce* for Keynesian demand-management policies, at least from a British point of view, at the Labour Party conference in 1976:

> We used to think that you could spend your way out of a recession and increase employment by cutting taxes and boosting govern-ment spending. I tell you in all candour that that option no longer exists, and in so far as it ever did exist, it only worked on each occasion since the war by injecting a bigger dose of inflation into the economy, followed by a higher level of unemployment as the next step.[3]

Put another way, if everyone knew a government was prepared to guarantee full employment through demand-management policies, it no longer mattered how far individual prices and wages rose. With everyone thinking along similar lines, inflation was bound to take off. Meanwhile, if some prices and wages rose faster than others, there would be an arbitrary and unfair redistribution of income and wealth. Those on fixed incomes – savers, pensioners – would lose out. Others – debtors, unionized workers able to demand annual wage increases – would gain. Meanwhile, increasingly volatile movements in prices and wages would make life impossible for businesses. They would not easily be able to single out profitable investment opportunities, leaving capital spending unnecessarily depressed, as proved to be the case in many countries during the 1970s. Socially, economically and politically, excessive inflation was a corrosive disaster.

Callaghan's comments marked the beginnings of an experiment with monetarism, the belief that controlling the money supply would be the best way of stabilizing inflation and, hence, restoring economic stability. This approach was wholeheartedly embraced by Paul Volcker's new-look US Federal Reserve and Margaret Thatcher's new-look British Conservative government at the end of the 1970s via the use of monetary targets. The overriding ambition at the macroeconomic level became the control of inflation, a controversial idea at the time but one that is now entirely mainstream. Liberated markets, with reduced union power and only modest government intervention, would in turn sort out problems of unemployment.

Monetary targets didn't quite go according to plan. Money supply was difficult to control and its relationship with the economy as a whole was nothing like as steady or predictable as monetarists had claimed. Nevertheless, policymakers were keen to stick to simple macroeconomic rules in the pursuit of underlying economic stability. Monetary targets were replaced by other targets, the most enduring of which have proved to be inflation targets (in the developed world) and exchange-rate targets (in the emerging world). Meanwhile, to rid policymakers of undue political influence, many central banks were granted independence, to a greater or lesser degree, from their ultimate political masters.

Central bankers have become the high priests of price stability and pursue their beliefs with a theocratic orthodoxy. They believe not only that price stability is good but that its achievement is the single best 'top-down' way of delivering overall economic well-being. They also believe they have the tools to keep inflation under control at all times. Most obviously, they control short-term interest rates in the hope of meeting their broader economic aims.

Changes in short-term interest rates feed through to the economy and to inflation through a series of different channels. They work on people's expectations. Rate increases, for example, are commonly regarded as a sign of more austere times ahead and can, therefore, act to constrain wage demands. Interest rates can affect asset prices. Other things equal, lower interest rates make other assets easier and more attractive to purchase. Lower mortgage rates, for example, tend to increase demand for housing, thereby pushing up house prices. More generally, lower interest rates reduce the returns on bank deposits in relation to other, more risky, investments such as equities and commercial property, thereby stimulating asset-price increases. Changes in interest rates will directly impact on the willingness of companies to borrow for investment projects.

In an international context, higher interest rates will make a given currency more attractive to foreign investors, thereby driving the currency's value up on the foreign exchanges. Imports end up cheaper while exporters are forced to control their costs with more rigour. All in all, changes in interest rates alter demand and cost pressures within an economy, have an impact on people's expectations about the future path of the economy and, if credible, influence inflation and inflationary expectations.

Yet if the channels between changes in policy rates and their ultimate effect on inflation are distorted, closed off, diverted or overwhelmed by events taking place elsewhere in the world, it's not at all obvious that the revolutionary claims of political leaders at the end of the 1970s or the beginning of the 1980s – namely that the control of inflation brings with it lasting economic stability – can still be met. Either inflation itself cannot be controlled or, more likely, its control leads to unexpected problems elsewhere in an economy.

Indeed, the relentless pursuit of near-term price stability is increasingly likely to be a source of economic and financial *instability*. Linked with the growing size and influence of the emerging world, the battle against inflation is changing. Unfortunately, central banks are still pursuing the tactics of yesterday's war. For them, price stability is a necessary condition of overall economic stability. This may still be true at the global level but, at the national or regional level, I am not convinced this claim still holds.

DEFINING INFLATION . . . AND CONTROLLING IT

Typically, inflation is defined either as a sustained rise in the general price level or a sustained decline in the value of money. Deflation, conversely, is a sustained fall in the general price level or sustained rise in the value of money. The general price level, in turn, refers to prices of everything – goods, services, labour and capital. A central bank that safeguards the value of money is, therefore, delivering price stability.

Which prices should be included? The consumer price indices which normally are the focus of an inflation-targeting regime are based on a 'typical person's' basket of goods and services. This immediately raises some awkward issues. The spending pattern of the wealthy Upper East Side resident will not match that of someone who hails from the mean streets of Detroit. What, then, does inflation refer to?[4]

Even if all US citizens were the same, what should be in the basket? Are volatile components, such as food and energy, to be included even when they might give misleading indications of inflation 'in the long run'? How should changes in the quality of goods be accounted for? Should only goods and services be included or should the prices of assets also be included?

Conventional measures of inflation – and conventional inflation targets – focus on consumer prices. The pursuit of price stability, however, ultimately has to take into account not just prices but also costs. A world in which both prices and wages are rising – the inflation of the 1970s – is a very different world from one in which prices are rising but wages are not. Both worlds see a pick-up in measured inflation in the short term, but while the first leaves spending power unchanged, the second makes workers poorer. The second example can be better described, therefore, as a redistribution of income away from workers. Many of the uncertainties over inflation we see today are routinely of this second variety. Commodity prices go up and, in the developed world, the price level rises in relation to wages. Manufactured goods prices – laptops, iPods, flat-screen TVs – come down and the price level falls in relation to wages.

The problems of defining inflation don't end there. What about the relative price of goods and services in one country against another? If both countries have the identical domestic inflation rate, it's still possible that the relative price of goods and services in one country will rise or fall against another country as a result of movements in the exchange rate. Moreover, sudden changes in demand in one country can easily have spill-over effects in other countries. Because many of these spill-over effects may surprise both in timing and magnitude, there's a good chance that policymakers will make mistakes.

A good example comes from the 1970s, when Germany and Switzerland burnished their anti-inflation credentials. Most countries benefited from relatively low inflation in the 1950s and early

1960s. By the late 1960s, however, many policymakers were beginning to lose the price-stability plot. Fearing a major rise in unemployment – and, in the US, spending vast amounts of money on the Vietnam War – they left monetary conditions too loose, and it wasn't long before inflation globally started to accelerate.

In the midst of this storm, Germany and Switzerland managed to deliver relatively modest inflation rates. While UK inflation went up into the stratosphere and US inflation headed into double digits, the Bundesbank (Germany's central bank) and the Swiss National Bank steadfastly defended their reputations as guardians of their respective currencies.

While their joint performance was impressive by the standards of the day, their performances judged against today's ambitions for price stability can only be described as failures. German and Swiss inflation averaged around 5 per cent per year through the 1970s. Today's inflation targets allow for annual increases in a country's or region's price level of only around 2 per cent. Through the 1970s as a whole, German and Swiss prices rose over 60 per cent – a very odd kind of price stability.

The German and Swiss experiences show that if other countries allow inflation to run out of control or more generally do not have a commitment to sound money, even the very best performers find the achievement of price stability too difficult. Even if the ambition to achieve stable prices was there – a view some would debate – the ability was not. Monetary sovereignty doesn't simply grow on trees.

Theoretically, Germany and Switzerland might still have been able to achieve price stability had they allowed their currencies to appreciate sufficiently. What, however, counts as sufficient? To this day, central banks struggle with the competing claims of 'internal' price stability, as measured by consumer price inflation, and 'external' price stability, as measured by the exchange rate. When, for example, the UK was forced out of the European exchange-rate mechanism in

1992, leading to a collapse in sterling's value on the foreign exchanges, many commentators believed inflation would surge, emphasizing the impact on future inflation of sterling's precipitous decline. They were wrong, largely because the weakness of the domestic economy completely overwhelmed any exchange-rate influence on inflation.

The tension between internal and external influences on prices can lead to serious errors of judgement. Imagine a world of just two countries, Lilliput and Blefuscu.[5] At first, both countries successfully achieve price stability. Then the powers that be in Lilliput decide to go on an extended inflationary spending spree, leading to a doubling of the money supply (schillings, say) and of the price level and, hence, a halving of the value of the schillings in people's pockets. The Lilliputian schilling should halve in value against the Blefuscucian lira. The wise people of Blefuscu, however, see the lira rising in value against the schilling. Unaware of the foolish inflationary policies being pursued by the Lilliputians, they fear a serious loss of export competitiveness. The central bank cuts interest rates in the hope of preventing an 'excessive' appreciation of the exchange rate. In doing so, domestic inflationary pressures begin to rise. Blefuscu has inadvertently imported inflation from its neighbour.

The exchange rate is only useful as an indicator of inflationary pressures if the policymaker knows as much about inflation in other countries as he or she knows about inflation in the home economy. Rarely does this prove to be the case. Assessing monetary progress through the exchange rate is rather like assessing your driving speed by counting the number of cars you're overtaking. It's an odd approach. Your relative speed might result either from others driving with excessive caution or, instead, from your own unbelievable recklessness.

The obvious lesson from all this is that central banks are still largely dependent on each other's behaviour, if only because they all belong to a common global economic and monetary system. Yet they do not all abide by the same rules, they do not all share the same objectives and, when it comes to political independence, some are more fortunate than others.

WE ARE NOT ALONE

Price stability was enshrined in most central bank constitutions in the 1990s, a time when emerging economies were only just beginning to make their presence felt.[6] At that time, economists had tremendous difficulties incorporating emerging economic developments into their world views – partly because of a dearth of reliable data – and often they didn't even bother to try.

In the years following German reunification, for example, it was commonplace for economists merely to forecast progress in the former West Germany. It was easier to maintain the pretence of statistical certainty than to admit to the inevitable economic ignorance associated with the joining up of the two Germanys, even though this was one of the most exciting political and economic events in decades. I remember a colleague running through his views of the (West) German economy in 1992 to an investor in the Gulf. After the presentation had finished, the investor sat back, lit a cigarette, and asked my colleague whether he'd heard the news. 'What news?' my colleague asked. 'Have you not heard? Two years ago, there was something called reunification.' My colleague spluttered his excuses and left.

For central bankers in the developed world, the rise of the emerging economies did not seem crucially important, at least not at first. The assumption was, and still is, that individual central banks enjoy sovereignty over both monetary policy and its impact on the inflation rate (in much the same way that economists happily pretended that West Germany enjoyed sovereignty from East Germany in the early 1990s). Even among those central banks without a formal inflation target – the best known of which is the US Federal Reserve – policymakers generally believe that price stability must be achieved before anything else. The Federal Reserve's own publications include the following wording:

> The goals of monetary policy are spelled out in the Federal Reserve Act, which specifies that '[the Fed] should seek to promote effectively the goals of maximum employment, stable prices, and moderate long-term interest rates'. Stable prices in the long run are a precondition for maximum sustainable output growth and employment as well as moderate long-term interest rates. When prices are stable and believed likely to remain so, the prices of goods, services, materials and labor are undistorted by inflation and serve as clearer signals and guides to the efficient allocation of resources and thus contribute to higher standards of living.[7]

Or, for a more British flavour, the aims and objectives of UK monetary policy are set out, rather quaintly, in a letter from the Chancellor of the Exchequer to the Governor of the Bank of England. The April 2009 version instructed the Bank to:

> maintain price stability . . . the operational target for monetary policy remains an underlying inflation rate . . . of 2 per cent. The inflation target is 2 per cent at all times: that is the rate which the Monetary Policy Committee is required to achieve and for which it is accountable . . . the framework is based on the recognition that the actual inflation rate will on occasions depart from its target as a result of shocks and disturbances. Attempts to keep inflation at the inflation target in these circumstances may cause undesirable volatility in output. But if inflation moves away from the target by more than 1 percentage point . . . I shall expect you to send an open letter to me . . . setting out . . . the reasons why inflation has moved away from target . . . the policy action which you

are taking to deal with it . . . [and] the period within which you expect inflation to return to the target.[8]

In other words, price stability is, like the UK prime minister, first among equals. Even for those central banks with more than one economic objective, price stability is typically the most important. The central bank's job is thus to safeguard the value of the currency. Price stability matters because Adam Smith's invisible hand works best free of distortions. But in both the American and British mandates, there is no explicit recognition that inflation is determined not just by domestic policies but also by developments elsewhere in the world, other than by reference to 'shocks and disturbances'. The rise of the emerging economies appears to be of no significant consequence. Yet exchange rates, interest rates, commodity prices, manufactured-goods prices and all sorts of other prices are now increasingly under the emerging economies' spell.

For a while, it was possible for central banks to kid themselves that their sovereignty was still intact. From the late 1980s through to the early years of the new millennium, the developed world supposedly benefited from the 'Great Moderation', a process whereby inflation and interest rates gradually fell, where business cycles became less volatile and where global economic growth strengthened in relation to the 1970s and early 1980s.[9] Yet this moderation was followed by possibly the worst, and certainly the most synchronized, global economic downswing since the 1930s. If inflation was so low, why did things go so badly wrong?

FROM STABILITY TO INSTABILITY: WHY PRICE STABILITY DOESN'T ALWAYS LIVE UP TO ITS PROMISE

Part of the explanation relates to an increased globalization of the inflation process. For central banks, charged with the need to deliver price stability at the national or continental level, this change has created three significant challenges. First, inflationary surprises in either direction may have nothing to do with the amount of money swirling around an economy, or the prevailing interest rate. The Great Moderation, for example, may have been more a result of good luck rather than inspired monetary judgement, reflecting the impact of outsourcing and off-shoring on the prices of manufactured goods. Responding through monetary policy to these kinds of inflationary surprises may, thus, *add* to economic and financial instability. If prices fall in relation to wages, as happened during the Moderation, why encourage even more spending by keeping interest rates low as well?

Second, changes in monetary policy in, say, the US, have an impact not just in the US but also, in particular, in emerging countries whose central banks piggyback off the Federal Reserve by linking their currencies to the US dollar. Subsequent economic developments in the piggyback countries, in turn, may affect the US economy in unforeseen ways – through, for example, oil-price spikes. If the Fed thinks about only the near-term domestic consequences of its monetary actions, it may ignore inflationary effects coming through the emerging nation back door.

Third, changes in domestic interest rates may shift global capital flows to a degree sufficient to alter the link between policy decisions and subsequent economic outcomes. For example, the Bank of England's policy of raising interest rates more or less continuously from 2003 through to 2007 triggered huge capital inflows from abroad. These were then invested by UK financial institutions in low-quality junk bonds, helping fuel a real-estate boom. While the inflows also pushed up the sterling exchange rate, thereby keeping a lid on inflation, the economy as a whole became increasingly unbalanced, paving the way for the credit crunch that followed later in the decade.

EMERGING ECONOMIES AND GLOBAL INFLATION: SIZE INCREASINGLY MATTERS

Policymakers in emerging economies, understandably, have chosen to make economic growth a priority. Per-capita incomes in emerging economies are, after all, very low. But, as emerging economies get bigger, their impact on the economies of the developed world, for good or bad, begins to increase. This gravitational pull means that, even if price stability is actually achieved in developed nations, it may not be the guarantee of lasting economic or financial stability that policymakers hope for. Price stability can, instead, offer false reassurance in a world of rapid economic change. Its achievement can lead to instability elsewhere within the economic system.

There are many different ways of assessing the size of economies. On the most conservative estimates, which merely measure the size of each economy in dollars, low- and medium-income economies (which include all the emerging markets) are, collectively, about the same size as the US economy. If we pretend that the identical product should have the same cost across different countries and geographies (using either formal purchasing power parity calculations or *The Economist*'s Big Mac index), the emerging economies are, collectively, about twice the size of the US.[10]

The emerging economies have come a long way since the 1970s, a result of rapid economic growth year-in, year-out. Yet they still have a long way to go. Per-capita incomes are in some cases only a tiny fraction of those in the US or in the developed world more generally. With further increases in income levels within the emerging world, the control of inflation in the developed world is likely to become increasingly complicated because the developed world will no longer have a monopoly influence over the global price level, whether for commodities, manufactured goods, workers on assembly lines, university graduates or London real estate.

Consider China. As we have seen, in modern economic history China is the first economy to be both poor in per-capita terms but large in terms of its global influence. China's expansion has, to date, been very commodity-intensive. China is now the second-biggest energy consumer in the world, behind the US but ahead of the European Union. In 1980 it was an economic minnow, with its national income only 7 per cent of America's in dollar terms and only 9 per cent using purchasing power parity.

Already, China's expansion has had a huge impact on demand for basic materials. In the early years of the new millennium, China absolutely dominated the consumption of metals, accounting for almost all the increase in global demand for tin and nickel and more than all the increase in global demand for lead and zinc. For aluminium and copper, China accounted for around half of the increase in global consumption. China was also responsible for 30 per cent of the increase in global demand for oil.

The story doesn't end there. China's per-capita incomes may have risen rapidly in recent years but, at current levels, there's a long way to go before the Chinese begin to enjoy living standards anywhere near those taken for granted in the developed world. As China's incomes rise, so its consumption of the world's scarce resources will continue to increase. As noted in Chapter 1, simple back-of-the-envelope calculations suggest that, at current growth rates, China would be attempting to consume the equivalent of all of the world's current oil production by the middle of the twenty-first century. As the IMF explained in the September 2006 *World Economic Outlook*, 'historical patterns suggest that consumption of metals typically grows together with income until about $15,000–$20,000 per capita (in purchasing power parity adjusted dollars) as countries go through a period of industrialization and infrastructure building . . . So far, China has generally tracked the patterns of Japan and Korea during their initial development phase.'[11] Meanwhile, like other countries before it, China's economic success is prompting a shift to protein-based diets, which will have a major long-term effect on the demand for grain.

Perhaps China's economic progress will moderate (or, as some pessimists would argue, come to a grinding halt). Maybe someone will discover an alternative energy source which will, once again, liberate us from the Malthusian constraint. In the absence of these outcomes, however, it seems likely that commodity prices will rise (indeed, higher energy prices may be necessary to encourage energy-saving innovations). If they do, what happens to inflation?

INFLATION AS AN INSTRUMENT OF INCOME AND WEALTH REDISTRIBUTION

The easy answer, one which you'll hear from many central bankers, is 'nothing'. If inflation is merely a monetary phenomenon, there is no reason to believe that a rise in the price of one particular good or service will lead to an increase in the general price level. In a fantasy world in which all prices are flexible, increases in some prices will be offset by declines in others, leaving overall inflation unchanged.

Returning to the real world, not all prices are fully flexible. In particular, it's typically easier for wages (which are, after all, the price of labour) to rise rather than fall, even allowing for greater 'flexibility' in recent years. If, however, commodity prices are persistently rising, there is a problem.

To see why, we should think about inflation not so much from a price perspective but, instead, from the point of view of costs. After all, the price of anything is, ultimately, a reflection of its production costs, whether they be labour costs, raw-materials costs or profits (which are the costs of capital). If raw-materials prices start to rise rapidly, it follows that other costs will have to come down.

Try telling a population used to ever-rising living standards that, from now on, they can expect to experience wage and profit squeezes – maybe even cuts in pay or in dividends – to make room for the demands coming from China, India and other fast-growing emerging economies. It's not very plausible. If inflation targeting requires people to be made worse off 'up front', it's going to find fewer and fewer supporters. 'Making room' for the economic demands of the Chinese and the populations of other emerging nations was never going to be easy, but inflation targeting highlights the immediate problems associated with the developed world's loss of control over commodity prices. Whether or not Western nations adhere to inflation targets in these circumstances may be a second-order question, given that rising commodity prices will make commodity-importing nations worse off, either through a squeeze on real spending power or through a return to 1970-style inflation accommodation. Nevertheless, seen through the framework of inflation targeting, the issue is made particularly stark.

Commodity prices are increasingly affected by movements in demand in other, poorer, parts of the world, for better or worse. In the first few years of the twenty-first century, emerging economies' success contributed to rising commodity prices: in the last decade of the twentieth century, their failure contributed to collapsing commodity prices, primarily as the result of the Asian crisis beginning in 1997 and its broader ramifications for emerging economies more generally.

These waves of influence are hardly trivial. In the late 1990s, both central bankers (notably Alan Greenspan, the then Chairman of the Federal Reserve) and economic commentators argued in favour of the so-called new economy, a view that undoubtedly contributed to large – and ultimately unsustainable – increases in equity prices, as observed in Chapter 4. The new economy was being driven, apparently, by sweeping productivity gains that would lead to both elevated economic growth and ever higher stock prices.

In the late 1990s, there certainly was some evidence consistent with the 'new economy'. In the US, growth was unexpectedly strong and inflation was unusually low. But does this constitute proof? Not necessarily.

First, although US economic growth was, indeed, exceptionally strong in the late 1990s, this strength came after a period of disappointing weakness in the first half of the 1990s. If one takes the peak of the 1990s economic cycle and compares it with the previous peak, the US economy enjoyed growth through the 1990s as a whole of 3 per cent, no faster than the average through the 1980s economic cycle. And, as the US entered the new millennium, the growth rate slowed down abruptly. The US expanded at a rate of only 2.5 per cent per year. Not a big difference from one year to the next, perhaps, but, over a number of years, the compound effect becomes very large. A decade of growth at 3 per cent leaves income levels almost 5 per cent higher than a decade of growth at 2.5 per cent.

On a per-capita basis, the numbers are even less impressive: after twenty years of per-capita income growth averaging 2 per cent per annum, the economic cycle in the early years of the twenty-first century generated per-capita gains of only 1.4 per cent per year.

Second, while technology innovations can improve productivity growth and, hence, allow an economy to grow more quickly without bumping into an inflationary constraint, commodity-price declines create a very similar effect, at least for commodity-consuming nations. It's easy to be seduced by the idea that economic success comes from technological improvements or wise policy decisions. As perceptions about the new economy began to pick up in the late 1990s, Alan Greenspan, who had famously warned of 'irrational exuberance' in 1996,[12] seemed happy to jump on the new economy bandwagon later in the decade. His case was helped by the improving split between growth and inflation. But was he right?

When the Asian crisis struck in 1997, triggered by a collapse in the value of the Thai baht, many argued that the end of the economic world was nigh. The Asian tigers had, apparently, been the main engines of global growth for a number of years. Their collapse, it seemed, would prompt a worldwide economic crisis. For a short while, economists busily slashed their forecasts for growth in the US and other developed markets, reasoning that a drop in Asian demand would, inevitably, feed through into lower world trade growth and, hence, a global recession.

The economists were largely wrong. World trade certainly did collapse, but the US economy boomed. A couple of years later, the European economy followed suit. How was it that, faced with a collapse in demand in Asia and other emerging markets, the Western developed markets could perform so well? There are two reasons. First, as explained in Chapter 4, capital that had been attracted to Asia in pursuit of high local returns went home. This provided a spur to equity markets in the US and Europe. Second, because Asia had become an important source of demand for commodities, its collapse led to much lower commodity prices. This proved to be very good news for commodity-importing nations (the US and Europe) and very bad news for commodity-producing nations (Russia and Brazil).

The Asian crisis thereby triggered a massive redistribution of income away from commodity-producing nations towards commodity-importing nations. For a short period the commodity-importing nations were made better off. Rather than accepting their temporary good fortune, however, they thought they'd discovered the elixir of ever-rising riches. No longer, it seemed, was there a constraint on growth because no longer did there seem to be a major problem with inflation.

In response, they were able to keep interest rates lower than might otherwise have been the case. This was a major mistake. Inflation was low, but that was more a matter of luck than good monetary judgement. In a world of already robust asset-price gains, keeping interest rates low just encouraged investors to borrow even more money, driving equity prices in particular up to ever-higher levels. Inflation might have been well behaved, but its good behaviour said little about whether central bankers were getting their monetary policies right. The downward shift in inflation rates was a sign of changing real economic phenomena, which led to the creation of new winners and losers in the global economy. It didn't necessarily need a monetary response.

While it seems reasonable for central banks to safeguard the value of the currency – which is effectively what price stability implies – it is becoming increasingly difficult to decide whether that goal is being achieved from one month to the next. If there's a late 1990s-type emerging-market collapse, inflation in the US and Europe is likely to come in lower than expected. Does this require lower interest rates? Probably not. After all, a fall in commodity prices would leave prices of goods in the developed world lower in relation to both wages and profits. Real spending power is, therefore, boosted. Why add to this beneficial effect by offering to cut interest rates?

Similarly, persistently higher emerging-market demand might raise commodity prices. Other things equal, prices of goods will rise in relation to wages and profits. People in the developed world are genuinely worse off through, for example, higher petrol prices. Does their misery need to be compounded by a tightening of the monetary screws? In the first decade of the twenty-first century, ahead of the 2007/8 credit crunch, this was precisely the dilemma central banks were faced with. Remarkably enough, faced with an identical shock, they responded in very different ways.

The US couldn't fully come to terms with the idea that commodity price movements were no longer determined by developments in the world's biggest economy. Oil, metals and other commodity prices soared, even though the US economy moved along at only a very modest pace by its own high standards. The Federal Reserve took the optimistic view that increases in commodity prices in any one year would be followed by declines in subsequent years. In other words, it ignored movements in commodity prices altogether, focusing purely on so-called core inflation, excluding food and energy. By doing so, it left interest rates low enough to help stimulate a housing boom and the sub-prime crisis that followed.

The European Central Bank, at the opposite extreme, thought that commodity prices might persistently rise, reflecting high structural growth in the emerging economies and, perhaps, the emerging economies' overly loose monetary policies. Unlike the Federal Reserve, it chose to focus on headline inflation. By doing so, it provided a more 'hair-shirt' approach to monetary policy. It worried that 'this year's' higher headline inflation might feed through to inflation expectations, making 'next year's' core inflation more difficult to manage.

The Bank of England attempted to navigate a middle course, admitting that there had been a structural increase in commodity prices as a result of strong demand stemming from emerging markets, but arguing that this was a 'one-off' that would not add to inflationary pressures in the longer term.

Who was right? In 'real time', it was never that obvious. To see why, it's worth disentangling real and monetary drivers of inflation in industrial countries.

INFLATION AS A RESULT OF CURRENCY LINKAGES

So far I have argued that 'real' effects on inflation stemming from emerging economies can play havoc with monetary policy decisions. Rises or declines in commodity prices as a result of substantial changes in emerging economic prospects should not automatically be met by an interest rate response. As the price level moves in relation to the level of wages and profits, people's spending power adjusts to new economic realities.

What happens, however, if the inflation imported from the emerging world is not a reflection of real factors but, instead, a consequence of monetary misjudgements? What happens if the imported inflation is of the Blefuscucian variety?

Emerging economies have problems with inflation. First, they're not helped by their track records. Financial markets have long memories: it wasn't so long ago that many emerging markets suffered from hyper-inflations, currency crises or both. Look at Latin America in the 1970s and 1980s. Second, given low levels of per-capita incomes, policymakers in emerging economies are often reluctant to slam on the brakes to prevent inflation from shooting upwards. Third, policymakers often attempt to 'hide' inflation by offering subsidies on basic items such as food and energy, typically to protect those in rural poverty. Fourth, for many emerging economies, the appropriate framework for conducting monetary policy has yet to be discovered. In the absence of any credible domestic arrangement, most policymakers instead choose to jump into bed with a central bank that does appear to know what it's doing. Typically, it's the Federal Reserve. It's not always a match made in heaven.

In the developed world, inflation targeting isn't easy. It's much more difficult in the emerging world. Volatile food and energy prices, typically ignored by a Federal Reserve that prefers to focus on core inflation, are much more important in the emerging world. These countries are poor. Their people spend a large amount of their income on the basics.

Put another way, unforeseen movements in volatile food and energy prices can send inflation in emerging markets all over the place. One minute, inflation is roaring ahead, the next prices are collapsing. Inflation targeting in this environment is rather meaningless. It's like aiming at a dartboard made of mercury: the target is constantly moving and the policy darts simply won't stick.

It's for this reason that many emerging economies choose not to commit solely to an inflation target. But they still need to show they support the principles of 'sound money'. Lenin allegedly said that the best way to undermine the capitalist system was to debauch the currency.[13] Some emerging economies have done so in the past with considerable aplomb. Nowadays, however, many emerging economies support the aims of sound money by tying their currencies, loosely or tightly, to the US dollar.[14] After all, the Federal Reserve has delivered sound money over many years. Maybe, through their ties to the US dollar, other countries might be able to do the same.

One problem with this approach is the possible inconsistency between an exchange-rate target and domestic price stability. Emerging economies are, for the most part, enjoying an extended period of economic 'catch-up', whereby their per-capita incomes gravitate towards higher levels in the developed world. This, though, creates a possible problem known as the Balassa–Samuelson condition.[15]

Typically, productivity gains for fast-growing economies are to be found in the tradable goods sector, where cutting-edge technologies can be most easily deployed. Wages begin to rise in these productive areas, as the benefits of rapid growth begin to trickle down into the population at large. But if wages are rising in the increasingly productive areas of the economy, what happens to wages in areas where productivity hasn't moved an inch? What happens to the incomes of hairdressers, waiters, taxi drivers and the like? According to Balassa–Samuelson, their wages also rise. They need to, in part, because otherwise everyone would rush off to the super modern factories, leaving restaurants bereft of staff and the population as a whole with very long hair.

If wages rise in line with productivity gains, nothing very much happens to inflation. People are paid more, but they're also producing more, so the cost per item produced doesn't change very much. If, instead, wages rise faster than productivity gains (and, for taxi drivers in heavily congested cities, this is likely to be a fact of life), inflation will rise. Across the emerging world, the desire to link currencies to the US dollar inevitably implies upward pressure on inflation as the taxi drivers, waiters and hairdressers benefit from productivity gains in other parts of the economy.

There is nothing wrong with this process. It is an essential part of economic catch-up. As people become richer, their domestic wages rise. This, in turn, increases their purchasing power over goods and services priced in foreign currency. It's one reason why global commodity prices have tended to rise since the late 1990s. As people become richer, their command over global resources tends to rise.

In the emerging world, however, not all people get richer at the same pace. As I shall explain in more detail in Chapter 6, levels of income inequality are remarkably high. China, for example, has a level of income inequality similar to that of the US, an ironic result given the countries' differing political systems. In an attempt to deliver social cohesion in the light of rising commodity prices, many fast-growing emerging markets choose to subsidize the prices of staples such as food and energy. This effectively raises consumption over and above the market clearing level. Higher consumption in the emerging world must, though, imply lower consumption elsewhere: the developed world ends up paying an even higher price for access to the world's raw materials.

Inflation in the emerging markets may tend to drift higher as a result of economic catch-up accompanied by fixed nominal exchange rates, but there is also a danger of nasty inflation surprises that stem from emerging-market linkages to the US dollar. These surprises are not confined to the emerging world alone.

WHY THE FED SHOULD SPEND MORE TIME WORRYING ABOUT THE EMERGING WORLD

When the Federal Open Markets Committee (FOMC) sits down every six weeks in Washington DC to debate the appropriate level of US interest rates, there's very little discussion about anything other than the outlook for the US economy. A quick glance through the published minutes of the numerous meetings held since the 1990s reveals that there's no time for a detailed discussion of what's going on in emerging economies.[16] On occasion, they are considered important, but only because they sometimes provide a clear and present danger to the US economy. Their day-to-day problems are really of no concern to the august members of the FOMC.

Yet the Federal Reserve's decisions have a direct impact on many emerging economies precisely because these countries link their currencies to the dollar. If the Fed chooses to cut interest rates, emerging-market central banks may have to follow suit. Otherwise, their currencies will tend to rise against the dollar. The same arguments apply, in reverse, if the Fed chooses to raise interest rates. The Fed ends up setting monetary conditions in a dollar bloc that spreads far and wide around the world.

This might not matter if most emerging economies' business cycles were tied to the US business cycle because, in those circumstances, Fed policy that was good for the US goose would also be good for the emerging-market gander. But emerging-market business cycles are not perfectly linked with the US. In the late 1990s, at the time of the Asian crisis, the US economy was booming. In the early years of the twenty-first century, when the US economy was struggling to cope with the consequences of the collapse in its late 1990s technology bubble, emerging markets were booming.

Consider once again the linkages between US monetary policy and monetary conditions in emerging markets. If the US economy is relatively weak, the Federal Reserve will naturally have a bias towards 'easy' monetary policy. Indeed, in 2003, Fed funds, the key US policy rate, fell to just 1 per cent, a remarkably low number compared with earlier history. The dollar came under tremendous downward pressure as investors pulled their savings out of the US to hunt for returns elsewhere in the world. A lot of money poured into the emerging markets. In a world of flexible exchange rates, emerging-market currencies should have risen rapidly. Some of them, for example the Brazilian real, did (although the real's increase eventually proved too much for the Brazilian authorities, who eventually had to intervene in the foreign-exchange markets to prevent further appreciation in an attempt to keep exporters happy). Most of them did not.

In the absence of any other nominal anchor, and with a fear of lost export opportunities, the majority of emerging economies resisted exchange-rate appreciation. Like Muhammad Ali in the rumble in the jungle, they merely absorbed the pressure. But, rather than sitting on the ropes being pummelled by George Foreman, they instead allowed their foreign-exchange reserves to rise.

This approach had two broad consequences. First, resistance to exchange-rate appreciation meant that emerging economies were left with too much money swilling around, the result of low interest rates and high foreign-exchange reserves. Arguably, the rapid increases in emerging-market domestic demand which followed contributed to huge gains in commodity prices. Second, because foreign-exchange reserves were heavily invested in 'low-risk' dollar assets, notably Treasuries, the price of these assets went up and the yield came down, as explained in Chapter 4. Put another way, although the Federal Reserve maintained control over short-term interest rates, it increasingly lost control of the longer-term interest rates that matter for businesses and households. The same applied in the UK where, as noted earlier, rising official interest rates were associated with falling yields on junk bonds. The global housing boom of recent years was partly the result of this distortion in the level of interest rates.

Other countries also lost their grip on the monetary reins. Low interest rates in the US, combined with even lower interest rates in Japan and relatively high risk in some of the emerging markets, persuaded many investors to take advantage of so-called carry trades, borrowing in dollars or yen and reinvesting in higher-yielding currencies like sterling, the New Zealand dollar and the Icelandic krona. The resulting inflows allowed the banking systems of these countries to expand rapidly, seemingly beyond the control of central bankers and regulators. Indeed, the more central banks raised their interest rates to contain inflationary pressures, the bigger the carry trade. And, as commercial banks found themselves awash with liquidity from abroad, so they loosened their lending terms. The housing boom spread like wildfire through the Western banking system in part because individual central banks were powerless to stop the domestic consequences of carry trades and, more broadly, return-hungry international capital flows.

CONCLUSIONS

Four broad conclusions follow.

First, the arrival on the world stage of the new economic super-powers has made the interpretation of price movements much more difficult. Inflation can go up and down for non-monetary reasons and, on some occasions, a monetary response is neither necessary nor desirable. The gravitational pull exerted by the new powers, whether to raise or lower inflation, may be related to 'real' economic factors such as beneficial productivity shocks or unhelpful commodity-price shocks. Central bankers who tweak interest rates in the hope of limiting the inflationary consequences of these effects may, in fact, be doing the wrong thing.

Second, the successful pursuit of price stability provides no guarantee of lasting economic stability. History is replete with periods of low and stable inflation followed by economic meltdown (the 1930s Depression followed a period of remarkably well-behaved US inflation in the 1920s, for example). A failure to understand the relative consequences for the levels of wages and prices in the developed world of the increased influence of the emerging economies on labour and commodity markets threatens to encourage persistent errors in the calibration of monetary policy. There are occasions when the price level needs to adjust in relation to the level of wages and profits. Using interest rates to prevent this mechanism from working risks heightened economic instability.

Third, the Federal Reserve and other developed-world central banks need to spend more time thinking about the global consequences of their monetary policy decisions. Central bankers may wish for fully flexible exchange rates to provide a guarantee of complete monetary sovereignty, but, in the real world, exchange-rate regimes are a mixture of floating, fixed and every variation in between. When the Federal Reserve sets interest rates, it's doing so not just for the US but also for huge chunks of the emerging world, whether it likes it or not. By ignoring their needs, global monetary conditions can end up either too tight or too loose.

Fourth, monetary sovereignty is a myth. Whether through currency pegs, carry trades, unexpected price shocks or any one of a number of other examples, central banks are, individually, not as powerful as they'd like to believe. The gravitational pull being exercised by the emerging markets should change for ever the cosy Western attitudes towards monetary policy. No longer are developed-world central banks in control.

The key question for policymakers to ask is this: if price stability is all it's believed to be, why was its achievement during the Great Moderation followed by one of the biggest economic crises of the past hundred years? The standard response is to argue that price stability is a necessary but not sufficient guarantee of lasting economic success. Pursued too blindly, however, it seems to me that the achievement of price stability has, in fact, become a potential source of economic failure.

Central bankers do not take seriously enough the distortions to prices and wages stemming from the emerging world. These distortions are only going to get bigger over time. As they do so, the Fed, the European Central Bank and the Bank of England will make more and more monetary mistakes until and unless they begin to recognize the crucial importance of the emerging economies in setting the global inflation agenda. I fear we are entering a period of economic uncertainty similar to that of the 1970s; not so much because of the sudden reappearance of inflation but, instead, because attempts to control inflation are proving to be the equivalent of the Keynesian demand management policies of the 1960s: well intentioned but, in a changing world, ultimately misconceived. Some bouts of high or low inflation do require a monetary response but others do not: distinguishing between the two is what ultimately makes central banking an art rather than a science.

PART THREE

THE RETURN OF POLITICAL ECONOMY

CHAPTER SIX

HAVES AND HAVE-NOTS

NEW MODES OF REDISTRIBUTION

Part Two argued that traditional barometers of economic success are giving out faulty readings. The emerging nations have become an increasingly important destination for Western exporters, but it's hard to argue that higher exports, on their own, are a sign of Western success. Capital markets have become significantly bigger, but they have also become increasingly distorted through the dominance of decisions made by sovereign nations as opposed to the decisions of millions of underlying investors. Inflation targeting is now a cornerstone of Western policymaking, yet is often poorly positioned to deal with the real and monetary shocks stemming from economic developments in the emerging nations. Indeed, a narrowly based focus on price stability has not provided the guarantees of economic stability many policymakers hoped for.

There is a simple reason why the traditional barometers of economic success have failed. Many of our economic barometers now tell us less about macroeconomic health and more about the winners and losers stemming from globalization. The old economic certainties have gone, while the gravitational pull of the emerging nations has increased. Globalization doesn't just lead to a superior allocation of resources and, therefore, to higher levels of global economic activity, as is so often claimed. It also leads to a redistribution of that activity. For some, globalization leads to a bigger slice of an expanding economic pie. For others, globalization leads to a smaller slice, either relatively or, in some cases, absolutely. Moreover, globalization creates a central paradox. Across nations, income and wealth inequality is narrowing, as the emerging nations catch up with the West. Within nations, income and wealth inequality is on the rise. Because our political systems are, for the most part, designed to meet the needs of nation states, this is potentially a big problem. How do governments defend the concept of globalization when their own populations may include both winners and losers?

In 1960, rising economic wealth was seen to benefit everyone. As John F. Kennedy put it, 'A rising tide lifts all the boats.'[1] Almost fifty years later, in 2007, Gordon Brown announced, 'It is time to train British workers for the British jobs that will be available over the coming few years and to make sure that people who are inactive and unemployed are able to get the new jobs on offer in our country.'[2] This protectionist rhetoric betrays a clear anxiety about globalization. If people from low-income countries can travel across borders more easily than before, what happens to the competitive position and earnings power of relatively wealthy indigenous populations? And if those indigenous populations do not like the outcome, what economic and political implications might follow?

These are big issues. They put the politics back into economics. Governments have to make choices. Do they use their tax and spending powers to redistribute income from the winners to the losers? Do they try to use their financial clout to seek controlling interests in companies to ensure that the benefits of globalization stay at home rather than leak abroad? Do they erect barriers to the free flow of capital and labour across borders to insulate domestic companies and workers from the full force of global competition?

By ignoring the underlying reasons that are driving prices, capital markets and trade, we are in danger of ignoring one of the biggest political implications of globalization. The competitive forces disrupting our economic barometers are also responsible for heightened income inequality. How governments react to this challenge will help determine the future of globalization. For governments dissatisfied with and uneasy about 'market' outcomes, the incentive is surely to intervene, for better or worse.

Part Three offers three perspectives on this return of 'political economy'. This chapter explores the reasons behind rising income inequality both in the West and in the emerging nations. Many explanations for rising inequality are domestically focused, but I contend that one of the most important reasons behind rising inequality, too often ignored, is the integration of previously independent economies. We are seeing, slowly but surely, the formation of global markets in both labour and capital which are undermining the rent-seeking behaviour of Western workers.

Chapters 7 and 8 examine the ways in which nations are trying to override these market outcomes, either through the growing influence of governments on the ownership and control of capital or through the often ill-conceived attempts to limit the cross-border migration of labour. The incentives to ignore market mechanisms are enormous. If governments can control capital, they can extract economic rents for the benefit of their constituents at the expense of people elsewhere in the world (a fabulous example from the 1970s is OPEC). If governments can control cross-border migration, they might, for a while, protect workers' incomes in the West. Tough controls over migration ultimately, however, may be self-defeating.

As the West ages, its greying population will increasingly depend on the support of immigrant workers. To turn them away will eventually leave the West weaker, not stronger. The demographic clock is ticking and alarm bells should be ringing for Western nations.

CONVERSATIONS WITH CAB DRIVERS

A few years ago, I had encounters with two cab drivers, one of whom had embraced everything good about globalization while the other feared everything bad. The first was a Romanian Jew who had escaped the clutches of the Ceauşescu regime and had headed for New York. He was a groundbreaker for globalization, having departed from his home country well before the collapse of Soviet communism. His experience is becoming increasingly commonplace. He managed to find work in New York, he paid for his sons' education and they, in turn, found work in government and the legal profession. In the space of a generation, opportunities denied to the father were granted to the sons.

The second cab driver was Italian. I was in Milan for a conference and, on the way back to the airport, got stuck in traffic. The cab driver became increasingly frustrated. Eventually, the source of the jam became apparent. A lorry was having difficulty reversing into a building site, and, through constant manoeuvring, was blocking the road. A construction worker of North African origin had stepped in to solve the problem. On seeing the worker, the cab driver opened his window and launched a ferociously racist diatribe. My Italian colleague was able to translate, but no translation was required. The message was simple. The worker should 'go back from where he came from . . . he wasn't up to the task and, frankly, he was stealing jobs from good, hard-working, Italians'.*

---

* This is unashamedly a paraphrase: the actual language used is not fit to print.

One cab driver, therefore, took advantage of the opportunities in front of him while the other lived a life of hatred and, perhaps, fear. Such is human nature. In the developed world, fear and uncertainty are likely to increase further in the years ahead. No amount of education, careful financial planning or flexibility is likely to provide insulation against the redistributional forces unleashed as a consequence of the rise of emerging economies. While some might regard these forces as merely an attack on free-market principles (China is growing quickly because it deliberately maintains a competitive advantage through an undervalued exchange rate), the story is, in fact, much bigger. The arrival of the emerging world dramatically alters the degree to which individuals are able to extract economic rents. Some are winners. Others will lose out.

A THREE-COUNTRY MODEL

Market forces allocate resources blindly. If market conditions shift, there is no reason to believe that everyone benefits equally. Indeed, it's perfectly possible that some will lose out. Even if the economic cake grows bigger as a result of globalization, those who enjoyed big slices before may suddenly find themselves on an unwanted diet.

The 'enlightened' political response to these challenges has been twofold. Economies in the developed world should become more 'flexible' and, therefore, more easily able to adapt to changing economic circumstances, consistent with the flexibility required by David Ricardo's theory of comparative advantage. Meanwhile, investment in education should be increased, both in an attempt to produce more graduates and, also, to allow people to acquire new skills later in life.

There's nothing particularly wrong with these ideas, but it's likely they promise too much. Flexibility is all very well, but, as argued in Chapter 5, it can just as easily mean pay cuts as pay increases. Education is desirable in its own right, but with millions of graduates now pouring out of Chinese and Indian universities, it's not obvious that education alone will safeguard the living standards of those living in the developed world, even if the quality of US and European graduates may, for the time being, still be higher.

It's easy to develop a simple theoretical explanation for rising income inequality dependent upon both the increased interconnectedness between the developed and emerging worlds and, within the emerging world, changing consumer preferences, particularly with regard to food. This model casts doubt on 'domestic' explanations of rising income inequality. It's consistent with the idea that we're living in a world of winners and losers, a response to the growing influence of the emerging economies. Globalization is not lifting all the boats. Some boats are sinking.

Consider the implications of globalization in a world containing just three countries. The first, a rich country, I'll call the US. The second, a poor country, I'll call China. The third is an oil producer, which I'll call Saudi Arabia.

Pre-globalization, the US is an immensely successful economy whereas China is very poor and, economically, has failed. China's backwardness is not the failure of nations stuck in poverty through no fault of their own.[3] Instead, China's failure stems from (i) a deep suspicion of Western attitudes, leaving it with an insular economy closed off from external influence; (ii) a lack of appropriate information technologies to allow engagement to take place; and (iii) an over-reliance on the state, rather than the market, to allocate resources. Saudi Arabia might be rich or poor but, crucially, it has monopoly powers over global oil production. In the pre-globalization world, Saudi Arabia has a strong relationship with the US but much less interest in China, which is too poor to be a big player in the oil market. Labour and capital cannot flow between the US and China. All the technologically advanced capital resides in the US and, as a result, US incomes are much higher than those in China.

In the US, there are three primary sources of income: wages in manufacturing, wages in financial services and income from capital in the form of capital gains, dividends and interest. In China, there is no significant financial sector, and income from capital is minimal. Labour is either involved in agriculture or manufacturing. Saudi Arabia produces oil and nothing else.

Imagine that barriers to trade, to capital flows and to labour migration are removed. What then happens? Capital should head from the US to China, seeking cheaper labour. Labour should head from China to the US, seeking higher wages. American owners of capital should end up richer because the process of 'off-shoring' lowers costs. Workers in the American finance industry are better off because they are able to pinpoint the investment opportunities that will benefit the owners of capital. Chinese manufacturing workers are better off because they get access to superior capital. American manufacturing workers are worse off because they are now competing with Chinese workers who are prepared to work for much lower wages.

Because resources are now allocated more efficiently than before, global output is higher. The price of manufactured goods comes down. Other prices may rise. Reflecting higher activity, the most obvious price to go up is that of oil. Because Chinese manufacturing workers are now experiencing rapid income gains, reflecting their now heightened productivity, food prices may also rise. The new affluence increases the demand for protein-based meals which may be tastier but which require far more crops to produce. The resulting rise in crop prices leaves those in China who are still on subsistence incomes worse off.

Now think about this story from a consumer's point of view. If you're a US consumer, are you better off? The answer isn't at all obvious. If you're in financial services, you're probably doing fine, but if you're in manufacturing you have reason to worry. If you own shares in a company that is now choosing to relocate to China, you may make a substantial capital gain, but what if you also happen to work for that company on the production line? If you're on a low income, and food and energy costs make up a big part of your weekly spending, you may find yourself considerably worse off because, while the price of flat-screen televisions is declining, it's the rising price of essentials that is likely to have the biggest impact on your living standards. If you're a Chinese consumer, you may be enjoying a rapid rise in living standards if you happen to be working in a factory in an urban area (or have managed to move to California), but if you're still stuck in a rural occupation you may now be worse off because you can no longer afford basic items of food. Meanwhile, the higher oil price has seemingly left Saudi Arabia better off. Rising incomes associated with the higher oil price, however, make Saudis uncompetitive in other areas of economic endeavour: the kingdom remains, economically, a one-trick pony unable to diversify from its core – and potentially volatile – competence.

WINNERS AND LOSERS

This scenario is no more than a description of likely events based on simple microeconomic theory. It fits, however, with the historical record. Ultimately, globalization has always been associated with a tension between winners and losers, whether the process of globalization has been market-led or otherwise. The Roman Empire had plenty of winners, but the vast number of slaves brought in to build cities and power ships would not count themselves among that happy throng. The Silk Road, sustained by China's Tang dynasty and then by the Mongols under Genghis Khan and Kublai Khan, proved to be a most effective trading route for silk, spices, Arabic horses and religion (Buddhism found its way from India to China along the Silk Road). It was also a murderous road, with the ruling Mongols and a growing numbers of opportunistic bandits happy to indulge in death and destruction in pursuit of material gains (if the Mongols didn't kill you off, the bubonic plague served the same purpose). And, as we saw in Chapter 2, globalization under the British Empire was hardly good news for all concerned. It was no great surprise, then, that the end of the nineteenth century marked a huge increase in nationalism. The Industrial Revolution delivered huge amounts of economic progress, but only a fool would argue that everyone benefited. Nationalism, in part, was a protest against an empire that had unfairly kept the benefits of economic progress residing with a privileged minority.

EMERGING NATIONS AND THE RISE OF INCOME INEQUALITY IN THE DEVELOPED WORLD

According to the World Bank's World Development Indicators, the US and China have roughly equivalent income distributions, as measured by Gini coefficients. (The Gini coefficient is typically expressed as a ratio between 0 and 1, where 0 represents a precisely

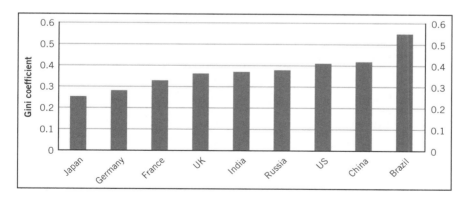

Figure 6.1: Gini coefficients
Source: World Development Indicators 2009, World Bank

equal income distribution and a figure of 1 implies that one person has made off with all the income. It's no great surprise that countries ruled by despots tend to have very high Gini coefficients.) By Western European or Japanese standards, both the US and China are very unequal societies. This is an intriguing result given that the US is regarded as the arch-capitalist economy whereas China still, publicly, hangs on to its communist credentials.

There are three key problems with this data, at least for the purposes of my argument. First, there may be no statistical consistency across countries, leading to an apples and pears problem. Second, the source years for the data vary enormously, from 1993 in Japan to 2007 in Brazil. Third, because the World Bank offers no consistent time series, it's difficult to work out how globalization may have affected income inequality over time.

Nevertheless, other sources are very much consistent with the idea that both the US and China have seen big increases in income inequality in recent decades. The US Census Bureau calculates that, between 1967 and 2007, the Gini coefficient for American household income rose from 0.397 to 0.463. The share of household income delivered to the highest quintile rose over the same period from around 43 per cent to 50 per cent. Meanwhile, the ratio between the richest 5 per cent of households and the poorest 10 per cent jumped from 11.7 to 14.6.

Chinese data are far more difficult to obtain and offer nothing like the wealth of information provided by the US statisticians. However, a paper by Ximing Wu and Jeffrey M. Perloff published in 2004 provided the first consistent set of estimates of China's Gini coefficient.[4] Their numbers suggest the coefficient rose from 0.31 in 1985 to 0.415 in 2001 (the corresponding figures for the US were 0.419 and 0.466).

While the evidence is consistent with my globalization narrative, consistency alone proves nothing. In the US, there are plenty of competing – and complementary – explanations for widening income inequality. One obvious explanation for the limited progress of those at the bottom of the income distribution is that many of those in that segment may be immigrants: while they may be low paid by American standards, they might still be doing well compared with those who 'stayed at home'. Moreover, as with my Romanian cab driver's offspring, second-generation immigrants might be able to leap up the income ladder. That, after all, is part of the American dream.

The problem with this explanation, however, is not just that some household segments in the US have remained very poor but, also, that a huge proportion of the benefits of economic growth have gone to segments that already were very rich. The big story in the US in recent decades has been the failure of the vast majority of people to benefit from sustained economic growth. Overall income levels may have risen, but very few have become significantly better off. The very rich have become fabulously rich. This looks like a rent-seeking story. Is there a connection with China or, indeed, the emerging economies more generally?

EDUCATION, EDUCATION, EDUCATION

There are plenty of nationally based explanations for the widening income gap. One of the more popular is the impact of education on income distribution over time. The idea is that, just like any other investment, investment in education will produce higher returns. Thus those who receive better or more education will tend, over a number of years, to earn more income than those who chose to leave school or college earlier. Given that the numbers in tertiary education in the US increased dramatically in the decades following the Second Wold War, this human capital theory points directly to a rise in income inequality.[5]

To take a simple example, imagine identical twins, one of whom goes to college while the other decides to head into the big wide world. Clearly, the former takes a pay cut in the short term, both through salary foregone and payment of college fees. For the sake of simplicity, I'll ignore this loss and assume that, on leaving college, the student commands a starting salary identical to her sister of, say, $10,000. Now imagine that the salary of the college graduate rises at 5 per cent per year while that of the school leaver rises at 2 per cent per year. Ten years later, the college graduate is earning well over $16,000 while the school leaver is languishing on a little over $12,000. Another ten years go by and the college graduate is enjoying an income of over $26,000 while the school leaver is stuck under $15,000. Ten years further on and, by the time middle age makes its mark, the college graduate is on $43,000 while her sister brings home just $18,000.

If we repeat that experiment at the national level, if the proportion of college graduates in the workforce rises over time, and if their incomes typically grow more quickly because they have the right kinds of skills, it's more than likely that income inequality will increase. It is merely a long-term consequence of market forces rewarding those who have the appropriate skills. On this argument, globalization is largely irrelevant.

NOT GETTING JUST REWARDS

While it might be true that college graduates can look forward to higher returns, that's not the whole story. A paper by Frank Levy and Peter Temin demonstrates that the vast majority of Americans, whether or not they've received a college education, have seen their incomes rise much more slowly than the rate of productivity growth.[6] In other words, although output has been rising, most people in the US have received only very modest benefits. The authors note, 'In the quarter century between 1980 and 2005, business sector productivity increased by 71 per cent. Over the same quarter century, median weekly earnings of full-time workers rose from $613 to $705, a gain of only 14 per cent (figures in 2000 dollars).' They also attempt to gauge the extent to which the 'skills' of graduates in relation to high-school leavers may have led to growing income inequality. In their words, 'For all groups of men – both BA's and high school graduates – the median worker's compensation grows roughly in line with productivity until some date between 1970 and 1980. After that date (which varies by group) the median worker's compensation lags increasingly behind productivity growth.'

The truth is that, while the US economy has shown impressive growth in recent decades, certainly when compared with some of its main industrial rivals like Germany and Japan, most Americans – educated or not – have experienced only modest benefits. This is a totally different experience from the 1950s and 1960s, when the benefits of productivity growth were spread much more evenly.

Levy and Temin argue that the primary reason behind the shift in income distribution is the demise of institutions created during the Great Depression that were designed to spread the benefits of prosperity more widely. These included unions, centralized bargaining frameworks for businesses, workers and government and a protected minimum wage, all of which were dismantled as the economic failures of the 1970s gave way to the laissez-faire Washington Consensus of the 1980s and beyond.

Perhaps not surprisingly, others have disputed these claims. For example, Stephen N. Kaplan and Joshua Rauh suggest that institutional arrangements played only a minor role in the huge income gains for those in the top echelons of the earnings spectrum.[7] They also dismiss so-called trade-based theories, which argue that higher incomes accrue to those who can exploit comparative advantage while lower incomes come to those in the wrong industries at the wrong time ('it seems difficult for trade [theories] to explain the increase in the top end of venture capital investors, private equity investors and, particularly, lawyers and professional athletes'). For them, the key explanations are (i) so-called superstar theories (there is only one Jack Nicholson and only a handful of truly successful hedge fund superstars); (ii) greater scale, particularly on Wall Street, where the amount of capital traders can play with is much greater than in the past; and (iii) technological advances that allow traders and the like to make more informed bets and allow David Beckham to be admired all over the world.[8]

TOO MUCH DOMESTICITY

I struggle with these 'domestic' conclusions for three reasons. First, as already noted, the rise in income inequality in the US has been matched by a similar rise in China. There are good reasons, in my view, to make a connection. While there are numerous reasons for rising income inequality in China (according to Wu and Perloff, inequality is on the rise within both rural and urban areas), the most obvious reason is the growth of urban populations (where incomes are higher) at the expense of rural populations (where incomes are still mediaeval). The growth in urban populations, in part, reflects the investment that has poured into the coastal regions of China in recent decades. As we saw in Chapter 3, some of that investment has been the direct result of the decisions made by multinationals to relocate to China. Other investment has stemmed from the ability of Chinese firms to make inroads into the Japanese *keiretsu* system since the 1990s.

Additionally, there has been a sizeable increase in the number of Chinese students benefiting from tertiary education. According to the World Bank, the percentage of Chinese students enrolling into tertiary education rose from a mere 6 per cent of school leavers in 1999 to 22 per cent in 2006. These numbers are still tiny compared with percentages seen elsewhere: in the US, for example, the equivalent figure is 82 per cent while, for the UK, it's 59 per cent. However, given that China's population is four times the size of America's and twenty times the size of the UK's, the increase that has taken place in just a handful of years is remarkable. Through investment in both physical and human capital, the rapid urbanization of China appears to have global implications that are poorly captured in the largely domestically driven explanations of growing inequality elsewhere in the world.

Second, while the arrival of Ronald Reagan (and, before him, Margaret Thatcher) led to a profound shift in beliefs about free markets, political parties of all colours increasingly felt constrained by global economic realities, whether or not they necessarily sympathized with the views of free-market fundamentalists. The fear of capital or labour exodus plays a bigger and bigger role in government attempts to make economies 'business friendly'. Seen this way, we may not like the consequences of increasingly skewed income distributions, but, with mobile labour and capital, political leaders have been unwilling to stem the tide. Put another way, the institutions created in the 1930s and applauded by Levy and Temin may no longer be tenable in the modern world and, at the very least, could lead to accusations of protectionism.

Third, I am not at all convinced that Wall Street – or, indeed, any other financial centre – is in some sense disconnected from the rest of the world in a way that makes trade-based comparative advantage arguments irrelevant. Rather, we fail to measure trade properly.

Take, for example, a typical month in the life of a Wall Street or City analyst. It might involve some meetings with companies or policymakers. A couple of research papers might be produced. There may be some conference calls with pension funds or hedge funds and, perhaps, a trip to Frankfurt or Hong Kong to meet directly with some of these funds. The cost of the analyst will almost certainly be picked up locally and statisticians will count the analyst's work as being locally produced. The analyst is, apparently, not engaged in the business of exporting his wares to other parts of the world. Nevertheless, the result of his engagement with the rest of the world is that the Wall Street firm's outposts elsewhere in the world are able to conduct trades and earn commission on the back of the analyst's endeavours.

Now imagine the analyst decides to leave the Wall Street firm and set up a consultancy. He now sells his research on the open market. Those who want to receive his research reports will have to pay for them directly. Those who want to have meetings with him will have to pay especially fat consultancy fees (or so the analyst hopes). And many of his customers, as before, are dotted across the world. Suddenly, as a result of the shift from Wall Street to consultancy, the analyst is producing business that will be recorded as an export. This reflected the true position all along, but it wasn't recorded in that way.[9]

THE UK: SHADOWING THE AMERICAN EXPERIENCE

Support for the influence of international finance on income distribution comes from the UK where, like the US, income inequality has increased dramatically since the 1980s. The feature common to both countries – and not shared to anything like the same degree by other developed nations – is the role of financial services. New York and London are the two epicentres of global finance and, in both cases, financial activities have played a significant role in widening income inequality.

According to the Office for National Statistics,[10] the biggest shift in the UK's income distribution occurred between 1977 and 1991, long before the emerging economies mattered for the UK or had any kind of major influence on global economic conditions. Between 1992 and 2007 there was comparatively little change in income distribution, judged by income quintiles. At first sight, then, the UK's experience seems to be very different from America's. But once the top income quintile is prised open, the same results apply. Income for the top 10 per cent of income earners rose quickly throughout the entire thirty-year period and income for the top 1 per cent, as with the US, rose particularly rapidly. Meanwhile, incomes at the very lowest end of the distribution have struggled to keep pace. As in the US, the gains in income at the top end of the distribution appear, once again, to be closely linked to developments in financial services. And, as in the US, the result has been a gradual rise in the Gini coefficient which, according to the Institute for Fiscal Studies, in 2007–08 'increased . . . to the highest level seen over our consistent time series going back to 1961. Over the period since 2004–05, the incomes of the poorest fifth of households have fallen by 2.6 per cent, after inflation, while the incomes of the richest fifth rose nearly 3.3 per cent on the same basis.' All this after a decade of rule by a Labour government that, historically, would happily have burnished its redistributional credentials.

THE EMERGING GAP

As we have seen, growing income inequality is not confined to parts of the developed world. China has witnessed a widening gap between a growing middle class and the majority of people who still remain wrapped in poverty. Other emerging economies have also seen a growing divide between rich and poor.[11] These developments are consistent with the thoughts of Simon Kuznets (1901–85), arguably the father of modern national accounts, who described the changes in the distribution of income as economies shifted from agrarian to urban societies.[12] The argument is straightforward. Urban workers are more productive than their inefficient rural counterparts. As urban development lifts off, so the nation as a whole becomes more productive. The benefits initially accrue almost entirely to the urban workers. Thus, income inequality inevitably increases in the early stages of development because some members of the population become richer while the rest remain as they were. When the numbers in urban areas exceed roughly half the population, income inequality will slowly decline: the majority will now be on the higher income level and it may be easier for the government to compensate the remaining poor through the tax and benefit system.

Yet there is a major problem with this argument: it's related to size. If one small country alone is engaged in this kind of economic development, there may be no significant impact on global economic conditions because global prices of basic commodities such as food and energy are largely unchanged. Even if the country is large, it may still be possible to develop in this way if the shift from rural to urban living is accompanied by a significant rise in agrarian productivity, so that the remaining rural workers are able to meet the basic needs of a rapidly growing aspirant urban population (India's green revolution in the 1970s is a case in point).

If, however, many countries are rapidly developing simultaneously, the global impact of their behaviour is likely to be of significant consequence for income distribution. In Chapters 1 and 5, I referred to the effect on global energy prices of China's rapid economic development. Energy, however, is not the only issue. Food shortages are likely to become increasingly problematic in the years ahead in response to increased affluence within the emerging world.

A MEATY ISSUE

As urbanization has taken hold, the quantity of land used for harvesting cereal crops has steadily declined, notably in China. Crop yields have, in some cases, risen to offset the reduction in land available for agricultural use. However, not all these crops are being used for the purposes of food production. With energy prices driven up partly in response to growing emerging-market affluence, and with growing concerns about the impact on climate change of the use of fossil fuels, land that had been used for cereal production is now increasingly being used for the production of bio-fuels. In Brazil, for example, land used for the cultivation of sugar cane (from which ethanol fuel is created) increased by almost 40 per cent between 1995 and 2007.[13] Climate change is likely to cause further disruptions. Water shortages will inevitably reduce crop yields in various parts of the world, adding to the upward pressure on prices.

While supply constraints are, thus, a major concern, demand factors may ultimately prove to be more important. Members of China's rural population survive on diets heavily dependent on grains. The urban population has much less interest in grains, instead preferring a diet focused around vegetables, meat, poultry and, increasingly, dairy produce (in Chapter 1, I called this the 'Starbucks effect'). More generally, populations in middle- and high-income countries choose diets heavily dependent on meat, fruit and vegetables, whereas those in low-income countries have to make do with cereals, roots and tubers. For people in the rich developed world, vegetarianism is generally a lifestyle choice, linked to concerns over animal cruelty or their own health. For those in low-income countries, vegetarianism is the only option available. The evidence overwhelmingly shows that, as they move up the income scale, most people succumb to eating animals. McDonalds, the fast-food chain, has benefited from this high income elasticity of demand for meat products. In 1987, there were 951 branches of McDonalds in the Asia-Pacific region. Fifteen years later, that number had increased to 7,135.[14] For some, meat is murder but, for the majority, meat is tasty.

This shift to meat-based diets is, ultimately, a costly business. In the words of the United Nations Environment Programme (UNEP) 'taking the energy value of . . . meat produced into consideration, the loss of calories by feeding . . . cereals to animals instead of using the cereals directly as human food represents the annual calorie need for more than 3.5 billion people'.[15] The cost is most obviously likely to show up in the form of higher prices for food which, in turn, will leave the poorest in societies in all parts of the world worse off. There is also likely to be a longer-term environmental cost. Livestock production accounts for a high amount of CO_2-equivalent greenhouse-gas emissions, not least because animals tend to suffer from flatulence (in total, livestock production is estimated to produce more greenhouse gases than transportation). Animals also need a lot of water (directly or virtually through the water content in feed). And global warming means that the amount of land available to produce either crops or animals is likely to decline over the next fifty years.

This all sounds distinctly Malthusian. Admittedly, further advances in agricultural technology may, once again, increase crop yields. Higher prices may well encourage such changes. Perhaps we'll find ourselves forgoing meat and dairy products. Maybe, instead, we'll choose to live on nut cutlets.[16] The mechanism to deliver such changes, though, is likely to be the market and, in particular, increases in world food prices. Those increases, in turn, will be felt more harshly by the poor.

A good deal of the pain will be felt within the emerging economies themselves, where spending on food is a high proportion of aggregate spending. Those who are not part of the aspirant urban population and who work on farms rather than own them are likely to prove the most vulnerable. Within commonly defined consumer price baskets, food as a proportion of total spending is around 10 per cent in the UK and Germany, 14 per cent in the US, 15 per cent in France and 23 per cent in Japan. People in emerging economies are typically poorer and a much greater proportion of their incomes is spent on food. The equivalent shares are 21 per cent in Brazil, 33 per cent in China, 40 per cent in Russia and a staggering 60 per cent in India.

The poor within Western societies are not so vulnerable – social safety nets exist and, in some cases, work reasonably effectively – but, nevertheless, a world of rising food and energy prices would leave poor people increasingly exposed to Malthusian constraints. The UK provides an interesting example. On the basis of IFS calculations,[17] 17.3 per cent of total spending by pensioners goes on food, with a further 7.4 per cent spent on fuel and light. For the non-pensioner population, the figures are 12.4 per cent and 4.3 per cent respectively. The Office for National Statistics uses an alternative approach which focuses not on age but, instead, on the gap between rich and poor.[18] For those in the bottom decile of average household weekly expenditure, around 30 per cent of spending is on food, fuel and light and petrol. For the top decile, the number is only 15 per cent.

Admittedly, these comparisons cannot be taken too far. Since the 1970s, differences in inflation rates across income cohorts and across age groups in the UK have tended to average out. This, in part, reflects the volatility of food and energy prices from year to year without a sustained underlying increase in these prices. Moreover, as economies have become more 'flexible' (or, put another way, the probability of losing your job in any given year has gone up), credit markets have expanded to provide protection against transitory income shocks, in line with the predictions of Milton Friedman's *Permanent Income Hypothesis*.[19] Evidence in the US, for example, suggests that consumption inequality is lower than income inequality (if, in any given year, more people lose their jobs, face temporarily reduced hours or discover their bonuses have been slashed, there will be an increase in income inequality, but if credit markets allow people to carry on spending until a new job is found or the bonus improves, consumption inequality will rise by less).

These arguments assume that income losses are only temporary and that people are therefore able to 'bounce back' from temporary setbacks. The growth in incomes of the rich and the increases in the prices of staples as emerging economies catch up with the developed world suggest, however, that income inequality is increasing not just because the volatility of income is increasing through a person's lifetime but, also, because we are in the midst of some major secular trends that, so far, have either been ignored by policymakers or have proved difficult to control.

Indeed, the easiest way to mask the problem of modest income gains for large swathes of the population has been to encourage a culture of debt dependency. Why worry if income growth is not particularly strong when consumer spending can be fuelled through the exorbitant use of plastic? It's easy to keep the masses happy in the short term through big increases in debt. If, however, GDP growth does not easily translate into household income growth – as has been the case for the vast majority of the US population – the short-term fix will lead to long-term problems. Even if, in a world of low nominal interest rates, debt is easy to service, the truth of the matter is that, eventually, the outstanding debt will have to be repaid (or, alternatively, the debtor will have to default). Repayment is much more difficult if income gains are depressed or if, as discussed in Chapter 4, wealth gains turn out to be transitory.

LIVING WITH INCOME INEQUALITY

Longer term, the education route appears to be attractive, but I cannot help feel there are immense limitations. We're back to the population numbers game. As already noted, US evidence suggests that graduates are not getting their rewards for increases in productivity in recent years. In the UK, the picture is, so far, more encouraging.[20] Yet, for all the additional investment that might be made in education in the US, the UK and elsewhere, the likelihood is that, in the international jobs market, increased competition will be coming from Chinese and Indian graduates who are willing to work for wages significantly lower than those now being paid to the educated elites in the developed world.

The rise of the emerging world is coinciding with the ageing of societies in the developed world. The implications of this will be discussed more fully in Chapter 8. For the purposes of this chapter, the important point is that, with the baby-boomer generation heading into retirement, vulnerability to sustained increases in food and energy prices will increase: living on unearned income in a world of secular price increases may not be much fun. Policymakers in developed countries already worry about the cost of ageing societies – through the provision of pensions and medical support – but they may also have to give consideration to the costs associated with a growing Malthusian constraint.

And then there's the potential for a political backlash. There may be a rising global economic tide, but Jack Kennedy's hopes are in danger of being washed away. Not everyone's boats are being lifted and those who feel vulnerable are becoming easy prey for populist politicians who, in turn, will attempt to turn the debate towards protectionism, nationalism and blatant xenophobia. Even mainstream politicians find the temptation to pander to the worst instincts of society overwhelming, as the quote from Gordon Brown at the beginning of this chapter highlights. In May 2009, President Obama, newly installed in the White House, offered similar sentiments: 'It's a tax code that says you should pay lower taxes if you create a job in Bangalore, India, than if you create one in Buffalo, New York.'[21]

For those in the developed world who wish to carry on consuming regardless of the constraints on their incomes, there is another way. Harold Macmillan, Britain's Conservative prime minister in the late 1950s and early 1960s, launched a now famous assault on Margaret Thatcher's Conservatives in the 1980s, when he likened the privatization policies at that time to 'selling the family silver'.

If the developed world is not ready for the income-redistribution implications of the rise of the emerging economies, an easy short-term solution is to sell Western assets to those who have the money to buy them. The money raised could be used to carry on consuming, at least for a while, even as the ownership and control of capital heads elsewhere. This is the subject of my next chapter. Many people in the West have forgotten about the importance of state capitalism as a source of their economic success. Emerging nations have not. The philosophies of the British East India Company are beginning to return, but, this time, they're being embraced by the emerging world. This is economics at its most political.

CHAPTER SEVEN

WHO CONTROLS WHAT?
THE RISE OF STATE CAPITALISM

OVERRULING THE MARKET

Globalization creates winners and losers. The benefits and costs of globalization are randomly distributed by the market's invisible hand across and within sovereign states. State capitalism, arguably, can be seen as an attempt to overrule this process. It offers a chance to exert government control over resources that might otherwise be lost through market forces to higher bidders elsewhere. State capitalism can be used to ensure resources are either retained for domestic consumption or used as bargaining chips in the exertion of global economic and political power. Whether to guard against income inequality or to pursue geopolitical objectives, almost all governments have an incentive to override the market. Capital is then owned and controlled not by millions of investors keen to maximize profits but, instead, by a limited number of governments and state agencies keen to maximize their political clout.

All the major sovereign players in the world economy are involved in the game today. One of the more visible signs of state capitalism is the emergence of sovereign wealth funds, a response to the large imbalances that have arisen in the global economy since the 1980s. Countries running balance of payments current-account surpluses have built up huge holdings of foreign assets that need to be invested somewhere. As we saw in Chapter 4, some of these assets are held in the form of foreign-exchange reserves, typically invested in a very narrow range of government and quasi-government paper. As these reserves have multiplied, however, the desire to diversify into a wider range of assets has increased enormously. To diversify in this way, more and more nations have resorted to the creation of sovereign wealth funds.[1]

While sovereign wealth funds have undoubtedly received the lion's share of media attention, the rise in state capitalism is not just a question of the ownership of assets, whether through sovereign wealth funds or other investment vehicles. State capitalism is ultimately a story about economic nationalism and global power politics, especially when it comes to energy, food and logistics. The increased gravitational pull of the emerging nations is having a huge impact on relative prices across goods, labour and capital markets. The redistributional consequences of these price changes provide an increasingly strong incentive for governments to intervene in an attempt to bypass or distort the market.

EXCESS SAVINGS AND COMMAND OVER ASSETS

The increased economic clout of sovereign states partly reflects the global savings glut we first came across in Chapter 4. If the emerging economies carry on saving more than they're spending and countries in the developed world – at least the US and the UK – carry on borrowing more than they're earning, there are huge implications for ownership of almost every conceivable asset, from bonds to stocks and from companies to residential real estate.

For every year the US runs a balance of payments current-account deficit – implying an inflow of capital – it increases its liabilities to the rest of the world. For every year the emerging economies run balance of payments current-account surpluses – implying the need to invest abroad – they increase their holdings of foreign assets. Logically, should the US run a current-account deficit for ever, all US assets would be sold off to foreign investors. There would no longer be a USA Inc.

Already, the US is by far the world's biggest debtor nation. Despite all this borrowing, however, US interest rates have, for the most part, been remarkably low. As debts to the rest of the world have risen, so interest rates have declined. The reason is simple: it's not so much that the US has deliberately set out to borrow too much. Instead, people in the emerging economies are collectively saving excessively.

They're saving for all sorts of sensible reasons. They don't have the credit markets that fuel consumer spending in the developed world. If an American wants to buy a car, he can do so today merely by borrowing against projected future income. If a Chinese citizen wants to buy a car, the chances are he'll have to save for many years. Nor do the people in emerging nations have the social-insurance safety nets available in the West, an innovation stemming from the economic crises of the 1930s. If the state won't look after you during periods of sickness or unemployment, you'll have to make the savings yourself. People living in emerging economies don't have the easy access to education enjoyed in the developed world. Despite the millions now going to university in China, India, Brazil and else-where, tertiary education is still very much a luxury that requires a lot of scrimping and saving. And, following the late 1990s Asian crisis, which is seen by many to be a response to excessive emerging-country borrowing, policymakers in the emerging world concluded that saving more and borrowing less was a good idea, at least from the perspective of delivering greater short-term economic stability. No longer did they want to be dependent on 'hot money' inflows from the developed world that could turn tail at any moment.

THE DYNAMICS OF EXCESS SAVING

The dynamics of this process are potentially explosive. An easy way to think about this is to consider a two-country world, involving just the US and China. Imagine that the US economy expands at a rate of around 5 per cent per year, split between 3 per cent of volume gains and 2 per cent of inflation. China, meanwhile, expands at a rate of 12 per cent per year, split between 8 per cent of volume gains and 4 per cent of inflation. For the sake of simplicity, there is no exchange rate: both countries use dollars.[2] Assume, also, that the US has a very well-developed domestic capital market while China's is rudimentary at best. In particular, whereas US citizens can easily borrow on the back of future incomes, Chinese citizens cannot.

Imagine, also, that Chinese excess savings (in other words, the current-account surplus) are a fixed proportion of the value of Chinese national income. This is not a particularly far-fetched assumption: the vast majority of G7 countries found themselves with high household savings rates during the 1950s and 1960s, before the advent of financial deregulation.[3] With this assumption, it's easy enough to show that the US current-account deficit has to get bigger and bigger over time.

In my two-country model, the Chinese and US current-account positions must cancel each other out (there are only two countries, so there is no trade with the UK, Germany or Mars because these additional countries and planets don't exist). If Chinese excess savings are a fixed proportion of Chinese national income, and Chinese national income is rising more quickly than US national income, it must follow that Chinese excess savings are rising as a share of US national income. But as Chinese excess savings must equal US excess borrowing, it follows that US excess borrowing must be rising as a share of US national income. In other words, a combination of strong Chinese growth and a stubbornly high saving ratio will inevitably deliver a rising US current-account deficit as a share of US national income. And, if Americans need to be persuaded to borrow (and often they appear not to require too much persuasion), the most obvious influence is likely to be the impact of Chinese excess saving on US interest rates, which end up lower than would otherwise have been the case. Meanwhile, as this process continues, so China's holdings of US assets climb as a share of US national income and, hence, America's liabilities to China climb as a share of US national income.

WHO OWNS WHAT? SO WHAT?

The end game for this story, with particular emphasis on the US dollar's reserve currency status, will be explored more fully in Chapter 9. For now, I want to focus on one particular aspect of the story. If China's rapid growth and excess savings imply that, over time, China owns a greater and greater proportion of US assets, which particular assets will the Chinese choose to hold and which assets will the Americans let them hold? More generally, if we're living in a world where people in the emerging economies are unable or unwilling to focus purely on domestic investment opportunities, how do things change as a result of their investment in assets which, hitherto, have been seen to be irredeemably American, British or German?

Until now, the vast majority of the surplus savings held by the emerging markets have been invested in foreign-exchange reserves, mostly US dollar government paper. The rising demand for this paper keeps the price high and, hence, the interest rate unusually low. The advantage for emerging-market investors is primarily that US Treasuries are liquid. In other words, with lots of people in the market, Treasuries can be bought and sold very easily. There are also disadvantages. Because interest rates are low, returns are low. With the supply of Treasuries ultimately controlled by the US authorities, there's always the danger that supply will increase very rapidly, driving prices lower, perhaps as a result of a large increase in the budget deficit. And with Treasuries priced in dollars, a big increase in the supply of dollars, leading to surging US inflation or a collapse in the dollar's value against other currencies (or perhaps both), would leave emerging investors nursing potentially big losses in domestic currency terms. Treasuries may be liquid, then, but they are not necessarily safe.

Given this, policymakers in emerging economies have three options. First, they can carry on buying Treasuries, while recognizing that the safety of their investments is not guaranteed, at least in their own currencies. Second, they can choose not to acquire foreign assets, a decision that would require a sustained reduction in their current-account surpluses over many years, primarily through the encouragement of a higher level of domestic consumption and investment. Third, they can choose to diversify their holdings of foreign assets out of Treasuries and into something else.

The first of these options would leave US long-term interest rates unusually low and would, in all likelihood, contribute to further instability of the kind associated with the global credit crunch that kicked off in 2007.

The second option is not likely to be achieved overnight. Indeed, any attempt to do so would probably end in disaster. One mechanism by which smaller current-account surpluses and hence lower capital outflows could be achieved is to allow a surplus country's currency to appreciate rapidly; but, as we observed in Chapter 4, Japan's experience with currency appreciation has not been particularly successful: Japan's surplus has increased, not decreased. Another mechanism might be to cut domestic interest rates rapidly to boost domestic spending, but that might threaten a repeat of Japan's experience in the late 1980s, when a domestic boom driven by remarkably low interest rates was partly responsible for the decades of stagnation that then followed. A more sensible mechanism – the only one that has a realistic chance of working – is for lasting reforms to reduce domestic saving (or increase domestic borrowing). That will take a long time. After all, only after half a century of development in social-security systems and credit markets did Western economies deliver lower levels of household saving and higher levels of debt against a background of incomes per capita far higher than those in the emerging world. Short cuts have been tried before, but, for the most part, they have failed, collapsing under the weight of balance of payments crises or inflation.

The third option, diversification, therefore has significant attractions, at least until there's a radical change in domestic savings behaviour within emerging economies. Diversification implies, at the very least, a change in ownership; but it may also imply a change in control. We are back to political economy. Is the West happy to allow investors from emerging economies to cherry-pick their favourite trophy assets? If not, who decides which assets can and cannot be purchased? And is there a difference between ownership and control?

OWNERSHIP VERSUS CONTROL: WHY THE WEST DOESN'T HAVE TO WORRY ABOUT STUPID DEALS

A canny investor might not be unduly concerned about ownership alone: what matters is the ability to buy assets at a low price and sell them at a high price, not who owns the assets. Under the heroically unrealistic assumption that all investors in the developed world are canny while those in the emerging world are naive, ownership might turn out to be completely irrelevant. The developed world could carry on borrowing cheaply from the emerging world, using the money raised to buy emerging assets on the cheap, the sort of behaviour banks indulge in on a daily basis. Alternatively, the developed world could offload some unwanted domestic assets at ludicrously inflated prices to the emerging innocents, who might be too interested in 'trophy assets' to recognize they're being swindled. Over time, this approach would leave the market value of assets owned by developed market investors in the emerging world rising rapidly, while the value of assets held in the developed world by emerging investors might be in decline.

This has happened before and, doubtless, will happen again. On 31 October 1989, the *New York Times* reported:

> The Rockefeller Group, the owner of Rockefeller Center, Radio City Music Hall and other mid-Manhattan office buildings, said yesterday that it had sold control of the company to Mitsubishi Estate Company of Tokyo, one of the world's biggest real estate developers . . . The proceeds will go into the family trusts established by John D. Rockefeller Jr. in 1934 and be used to diversify the family's holdings.

At the time, the sale of the Rockefeller Center was seen as the beginning of the end for the American way. Over the previous ten years, as rustbelt industries had declined and as the Savings and Loans crisis had swollen, the US economy seemed to have lost direction while Japan, meanwhile, was enjoying a period of extraordinary success. As a symbol of American decline, the Rockefeller Center's transfer to Japanese ownership was hard to beat.

Six years later, on 12 September 1995, the *New York Times* offered a new story:

The Mitsubishi Estate Company of Japan plans to walk away from its almost $2billion investment in Rockefeller Center ... [its] decision ... is the most striking in a string of recent retreats from the trophy properties stretching from New York to Honolulu that Japanese companies acquired during a real estate binge in the 1980s.

No one, as far as I can tell, bothered to ask how the Rockefeller family's trust funds had been diversified. It's quite possible that the money made through the initial sale of the Center was invested somewhere else in the US or, instead, in some attractive opportunity elsewhere in the world. Either way, the returns may have been more attractive than those received by the Mitsubishi Estate Company following its buccaneering adventure in US real estate. If so, the deal was attractive for the Rockefellers and, possibly, for Americans more generally.

Trophy assets are not linked solely to buildings. They are also linked to sport (the typical businessman may not have the physique, but, in the gladiatorial confines of the boardroom, he may have the competitive spirit). For the Japanese in the late 1980s and early 1990s, golf courses were the favoured investment. Minoru Isutani purchased Pebble Beach in California for $841 million in 1990. His company then went bankrupt, forcing the sale of the course for only two-thirds of the original purchase price two years later.[4] With the arrival of the new millennium, soccer clubs replaced golf courses as the trophy assets of choice. Clubs in the English Premier League began to fall into the hands of rich foreign investors: Manchester United and Liverpool were bought by Americans, Manchester City and Portsmouth by investors from the United Arab Emirates,[5] West Ham by an Icelandic businessman who subsequently went bust, and Chelsea by Roman Abramovich, the quintessential Russian oligarch.

But these investments are no more than the playthings of the very rich. Whether they make any money for the sporting billionaire doesn't really matter very much (although, should a wealthy bene-factor end up in financial trouble, the fans would be none too happy).[6] The very rich, however, increasingly come from the emerging markets. According to Forbes.com, the number of billion-aires hailing from the emerging world has been on the increase. In 2000, only two of the world's twenty-five richest billionaires came from the emerging world (one from Saudi Arabia and the other from Hong Kong, which some might think is sufficiently wealthy not to be an emerging market). By 2007, nine hailed from emerging economies, with a further increase to fifteen in 2008. By 2009 the number had fallen back to five, suggesting that the global financial crisis was not good news for emerging-market billionaires. Nevertheless, consistent with the emerging economies' rising share of global income, emerging-market billionaires have become steadily richer and more influential on the world stage. They are symbols of growing emerging-market power.[7] But, as the experience of some English soccer clubs suggests, they are also symbols of murkiness.

TRANSPARENCY, OPACITY AND HYPOCRISY: THE RISE OF SOVEREIGN WEALTH FUNDS

Markets supposedly work best when those involved are driven purely by 'commercial' considerations. Assets are purchased and sold for commercial profit, not for political influence. For Adam Smith, the invisible hand is represented by the market, not shady deals struck in smoke-filled rooms. Yet, as the emerging economies have increased their savings and, therefore, increased their purchasing power over Western assets, so non-market outcomes become more likely. This is not just an issue regarding the activities of sometimes shady billion-aires: governments are also flexing their muscles in ways that threaten to upset the laws of the commercial jungle.

Sovereign wealth funds have been around for decades. The first, in Kuwait, was founded in 1953 and called the Reserve Fund for Future Generations. Others with a respectable longevity include the Abu Dhabi Investment Authority (ADIA) and, in Singapore, the Government Investment Corporation and Temasek. The really big changes, though, have occurred since the beginning of the new millennium, with the emergence of major funds in China and Russia. Most of these funds are state-run institutions investing money on behalf of their populations: because they are state run, it's not obvious they will always pursue a purely commercial agenda.

The growth of these funds is really not surprising. They are ultimately a reflection of three key developments: (i) as we have seen, some emerging economies have excess savings as a result of poorly developed domestic credit markets; (ii) other emerging economies have excess savings because they happen to be major producers of raw materials and, therefore, have benefited from higher commodity prices; (iii) many emerging economies have been unwilling to allow their exchange rates to rise in response to growing foreign demand for their products and, as a result, they have ended up with big increases in foreign-exchange reserves.

The aims of the various SWFs vary, but, in my view, there are three prime objectives.[8] First, where a country is a major producer of a basic commodity with a volatile price history, a fund can be used for stabilization purposes, exemplified by Joseph's desire to put grain aside to protect Egypt from future famine. Second, the funds can be used for savings purposes to protect a country when non-renewable assets – oil, for example – run out. Third, for countries experiencing big increases in foreign-exchange reserves, SWFs can be used for diversification purposes to increase yield and, perhaps, lower risk (in that sense, foreign-exchange reserves should be counted as highly liquid SWFs).

Their growth raises all sorts of issues about the operation of inter-national capital markets. It's frankly anybody's guess how large these funds are because many of them lack any kind of transparency. In 2008, the IMF stated that 'estimates of foreign assets held by sovereigns include about $7 trillion in international reserves (including gold) and an additional $2–3 trillion in SWFs'.[9] As international reserves are, in effect, very liquid SWFs, it's reasonable to conclude that the total amount of funds held by sovereigns stood at almost $10 trillion – 5 per cent of the global total – in 2008 or, put another way, about five times the amount of assets held by the international hedge fund community at that time (the hedge funds' market clout is actually considerably higher than these numbers suggest because, unlike SWFs and foreign-exchange reserve managers, they are heavy users of leverage to increase their power in financial markets).

With size comes potential influence. It's at this point that leaders in the developed world cry foul. The reasons are obvious. SWFs are government-run funds. They're not very transparent. Many of them don't have well-defined investment strategies or, indeed, any investment strategies. It's not clear whether they choose to invest purely on the basis of profit or whether they are pursuing political objectives. And because SWFs are no longer restricted to a few city-states in the Middle East and Asia, the political stakes are much higher. Singapore is not a democracy but it is very small. China isn't a democracy but it is very large. And Russia's democratic credentials are weaker than they once seemed.

The response from international organizations has been to come up with codes of conduct both for the SWFs themselves and for the recipient countries in the developed world who find their assets being snapped up by others. It's difficult to take these codes of conduct seriously. Different countries vary in their attitudes towards sales of assets to emerging investors. The UK, for example, has been rather laissez-faire in its approach whereas Germany and France have been more cautious. The bigger difficulties, however, lie with hypocrisy and a blinkered view of how state capitalism operates.

Demanding, for example, that SWFs should be transparent is all very well (Norway's Government Pension Fund is often cited as the 'model citizen' when it comes to transparency), but hedge funds are no better. Of course, it can then be argued – and often is – that hedge funds are 'pure' funds because they are motivated by profit (or greed, depending on your point of view). However, the argument quickly collapses because hedge funds manage other investors' money – and those other investors include SWFs.

Arguing, meanwhile, that the ambitions of SWFs should be restricted because the involvement of government inevitably distorts market signals is nonsense for the simple reason that Western governments do it all the time, whether through defence contracts, bank bailouts (as happened in 2008 and 2009) or through mixing commercial interests with military muscle (Halliburton, the oil-services giant once led by former US vice-president Dick Cheney, did rather well in the initial stages of the second Iraq War, perhaps modelling itself on the earlier success of the East India Company). The case for restriction, then, rests not on transparency, nor on government involvement, but on the fact that the developed world doesn't trust leaderships in emerging economies.

The lack of trust extends far beyond any specific issues with regard to sovereign wealth funds. If sovereign wealth funds merely hold non-controlling shares in a range of developed-world companies, it's difficult to know why anyone should be overly worried. Moreover, to the extent that all companies have to abide by the laws and regulations of the land, ownership alone is not enough to provide a threat to national security. At the extreme, the assets of a sovereign wealth fund that decided to flex its financial muscles in an undesirable way from the host country's perspective could always be seized. Sovereign wealth funds have to tread carefully.

FULL OF ENERGY: THE RISE OF RUSSIAN POWER POLITICS

In the high-stakes world of energy, raw materials and logistics, it's a different matter. The issue here is not so much one of ownership as of control.

Imagine this. A government brimming with free-market principles decides to privatize its electricity industry. Being a wise government, it chooses to separate the generating companies from the distributors in an attempt to avoid any semblance of monopoly power. For a while, the new companies are owned by a group of pension funds and insurance companies who are intent on earning acceptable returns for their policyholders. Then the fund managers receive an offer too good to refuse from a government-owned foreign corporation, which wants to buy a couple of the electricity distributors. The investors sell out. In effect, the domestic power companies have been renationalized through a foreign government, leaving the privatization process seemingly in tatters. A little later, the government-owned foreign corporation decides it wants not just the distributors but also a slice of the generation business. Given its own background, it's particularly interested in nuclear energy and so makes a successful bid for the nuclear power stations. Suddenly, the country's power supplies, and its nuclear reactors, are in foreign hands, raising all sorts of issues for competitive markets and national security.

While this might seem a decidedly implausible scenario, it is, in fact, a reasonably precise description of events surrounding the UK electricity industry. On 29 January 1999, the Commission of the European Union cleared the acquisition of London Electricity plc, the distributor of electricity to the UK's capital, by EdF International SA, a wholly owned subsidiary of Électricité de France (EdF). On 1 October 2008, EdF acquired British Energy plc, which happens to operate eight out of the UK's ten nuclear power stations. According to EdF's 2008 Annual Report, 84.66 per cent of

EdF's share capital is owned by the French state. Fortunately for the UK, the Entente Cordiale signed in 1904, which brought to an end almost a thousand years of fighting between the British and French, is still in place. And, whereas EdF owns British energy assets, the ultimate control, through law and regulation, is in the hands of the UK government.

Not all ententes last very long, though. The 1907 Anglo-Russian Entente, signed by Count Alexander Izvolsky, foreign minister of the Russian Empire, and Sir Arthur Nicolson, the British ambassador to Russia, was torn up relatively quickly. Designed to carve up Persia (now Iran), Afghanistan and Tibet, this Entente, together with the Entente Cordiale, led to the creation of the Triple Entente which, among other things, drew France, Russia and the UK into the First World War. Following the 1917 Bolshevik Revolution, Lenin's Russia was no longer interested in any kind of entente with the UK and France (and, given their support for the White Russians in the Russian Civil War that followed, the UK and France were not very enthusiastic either). No amount of glasnost and perestroika more recently has made any significant difference. This matters, because Russia is now a giant in the world of energy.

Russia is the world's biggest producer of oil and natural gas.[10] In 2008, it was responsible for 12.4 per cent of global oil production, just behind Saudi Arabia, which accounted for 13.1 per cent. It is natural gas, however, where Russia really counts. In 2008, Russia was responsible for a remarkable 19.6 per cent of global natural gas production, putting it slightly ahead of the US, which was responsible for 19.3 per cent. Unlike the US, which consumes more natural gas than it produces and, thus, is a net gas importer, Russia produces far more natural gas than it needs for domestic purposes. Also, unlike the US, Russia has plenty of natural gas in reserve. At current production rates, US natural gas reserves will run out in a handful of years whereas Russia could keep producing for another eighty years or so: it has over 23 per cent of proved gas reserves globally whereas the US has only 3.6 per cent.

With all this gas, Russia has turned itself into an energy superpower. It's by far the biggest exporter of natural gas in the world. In 2008, for example, Russia exported over 150 billion cubic metres of natural gas, half as much again as the amount exported by Canada, the second-biggest player. For the developed world, this matters because the top five net importers of natural gas globally are the US, Japan, Germany, Italy and France.

Admittedly, neither the US nor Japan has any direct dependence on Russia for its natural gas supplies (Canada is the dominant supplier to the US while Japan gets its natural gas from a wide range of Middle Eastern and Asian producers). For Europe, it's a completely different story.

Russian gas is produced and distributed by Gazprom, the world's largest natural gas company, which is 50.002 per cent owned by the Russian state. Dimitry Medvedev, who became the president of the Russian Federation in 2008, was Gazprom's chairman earlier in the decade. The Russian leadership makes no secret of its desire to use Gazprom as an instrument of international diplomacy. It can do so not just because of Gazprom's huge production of natural gas but also because of the ways in which natural gas is transported to Russia's foreign markets. Russia's economic muscle rests not with its domestic economy nor with its ownership of assets abroad through the growth of its sovereign wealth fund, but, instead, with the threat that, at some point, the pipelines that distribute natural gas throughout Europe might be switched off.

Russia hopes to extend its pipeline network into Europe through the construction of Nord Stream, a pipeline constructed under the Baltic Sea to link Vyborg in Russia with Greifswald in Germany, and South Stream, a pipeline from Dzhugba in Russia underneath the Black Sea to connect with Varna in Bulgaria and then on to Italy and, possibly, Austria. These proposed pipeline connections are significant for three key reasons.

First, their construction will allow Russia increasingly to deal with European countries on a bilateral basis, thereby weakening the role of the European Union in energy negotiations.[11] Some countries are already highly dependent on Russian oil, notably those in Central and Eastern Europe where imports from Russia in some cases account for 100 per cent of domestic natural gas consumption. Countries further west, which managed to avoid being trapped behind the Iron Curtain, now also find themselves in thrall to Russian energy diplomacy: imports from Russia account for almost 50 per cent of German natural gas consumption, virtually 30 per cent of Italian gas consumption, 75 per cent of Austrian gas consumption and around 80 per cent of Finnish gas consumption. This dependency is likely to rise and to spread to other countries such as the UK which, to date, are not heavily dependent on imports of gas from Russia.[12]

Second, following their completion, Russia will no longer have to rely on natural gas flowing through, for example, Ukrainian networks to reach customers further west. At a stroke, then, Russia will be able not only to control supplies to Western Europe but also to the Ukraine and other near neighbours. The importance of this is twofold. Russia will be able to raise the price of gas to the Ukraine by restricting supply. This matters because Ukraine pays well below market prices for its Russian gas, a legacy of the Soviet era, and can happily resist supply restrictions imposed by Russia by cutting off the flows of gas leaving the Ukraine for countries further west. And, by making any threats to cut gas supplies to the Ukraine and other former Soviet States credible, Russia may be able to discourage the tide of NATO membership sweeping in from the west. Indeed, when Nord and South Stream are up and running, the Ukraine will become strategically less important to Western European nations, making it easier for Russia to exert influence on its neighbour without fear of retaliation (see Chapter 10 for more details on this issue).

Third, the companies building the pipelines, Nord Stream AG and South Stream AG are, respectively, 51 per cent and 50 per cent owned by Gazprom and, thus, by the Russian state. Even if the distributors in individual countries are not owned by Gazprom, they are still totally dependent on Gazprom's goodwill to stay in business. Intriguingly, Gerhard Schröder, Germany's chancellor between 1998 and 2005, is chairman of the Nord Stream shareholder committee. Smoke-filled rooms spring to mind.

HEADING EAST

Meanwhile, Russia has ambitions to widen its customer base to the east and south. An oil pipeline between Taishet in Eastern Siberia and Nakhodka on the Pacific Coast near the Chinese border will open up the Asian energy market to Russia. A tributary pipeline will feed directly into Daqing in northern China. Europe will no longer be the sole buyer of Russian energy, dramatically transforming Russia's bargaining power not just economically but also politically.

The creation of the Shanghai Co-operation Organization (SCO) – comprising China, Russia, Kazakhstan, Kyrgyzstan, Tajikistan and Uzbekistan, with India, Iran, Mongolia and Pakistan as observers – is a case in point. Founded in 2001, its main purposes, according to China's foreign ministry, are (take a deep breath):

> strengthening mutual trust and good-neighbourliness and friend-
> ship among member states; developing their effective cooperation
> in political affairs, the economy and trade, science and technology,
> culture, education, energy, transportation, environmental protec-
> tion and other fields; working together to maintain regional peace,

security and stability; and promoting the creation of a new international political and economic order featuring democracy, justice and rationality.

From this long list of ambitions, it's not too difficult to imagine the creation of a new energy cartel involving both producers and consumers, particularly if Iran were to become a full member at some point. This has the potential to become a modern-day, energy-driven equivalent of the Silk Road.

It's also relatively easy to see how these countries, in combination, could pursue an international economic agenda at odds with US interests. As Dimitry Medvedev, the Russian president, said in St Petersburg in June 2009:

> the artificially maintained uni-polar system and preservation of monopolies in key global economic sectors are root causes of the [financial and economic] crisis. One big centre of consumption, financed by a growing deficit, and thus growing debts, one formerly strong reserve currency, and one dominant system of assessing assets and risks . . . there was no avoiding a global crisis . . . what we need are financial institutions of a completely new type, where particular political issues and motives, and particular countries, will not dominate.[13]

Russia is not the only country capable of flexing its economic and financial muscle. China has similar capabilities, stemming in large part from its excess savings and, therefore, its potential buying power over assets elsewhere in the world. The Industrial and Commercial Bank of China Ltd (ICBC) has a 20 per cent stake in Standard Bank, the South African-headquartered bank first established in 1862. Standard Bank has operations in seventeen African countries. For a nation like China, thirsty for natural resources, the ICBC stake in

Standard Bank provides important links across the African continent. China also has strong interests in the Middle East, reflected in a £4.8bn bid made by Sinopec in June 2009 for Addax Petroleum, a London-listed oil explorer with fields in Iraqi Kurdistan and Nigeria. Meanwhile, China has used its financial clout to influence long-standing international allegiances: Chinese purchases of Costa Rican government bonds, for example, were closely linked with Costa Rica's decision to switch allegiance from Taipei to Beijing as the legitimate representative of the Chinese people.

UNWILLING SELLERS

While it has proved relatively easy to buy influence and curry favour in other emerging economies, China and other savings-surplus countries have found acquisitions more difficult in the developed world. In one sense, this is odd given that the US, in particular, is heavily indebted to China, Russia and the Middle East. Yet the US is not very keen on selling its prized assets. Selling the Rockefeller Center was bad enough, but selling California's major energy provider to the Chinese was a step too far. And, unlike the French with their sale of Louisiana and surrounding areas to the Americans at the beginning of the nineteenth century, it's unlikely that the Americans will be selling California or Alaska to the Chinese any time soon, even though both disposals might make economic sense.

Under the leadership of Fu Chengyu, the China National Offshore Oil Corporation (CNOOC) made an audacious bid in 2005 to buy Unocal (the Union Oil Company of California). CNOOC, a listed company, was 70.6 per cent owned by its state parent, also headed up by Fu Chengyu. Was he merely acting on a commercial basis or, as some suggested, on behalf of the Communist Party? In the light of a media frenzy, the US House of Representatives decided the takeover was a national security issue and referred the bid to President George W. Bush. At that point, CNOOC withdrew. Unocal was bought by Chevron, a US oil company. While the British government is content to have its energy supplied by the French, the Americans are not happy to see their energy supplies falling into Chinese hands.

It's not just the Chinese who raise suspicion in Washington DC. Following its acquisition of the UK's P&O in 2006, Dubai Ports World agreed, under intense pressure, to sell its US port operations (including those in New York, New Jersey, Philadelphia, Baltimore, New Orleans and Miami) to American International Group (which subsequently imploded in 2008 as the credit crunch took its toll). DP World knew full well that its takeover of P&O might otherwise have been blocked by US lawmakers, notwithstanding clearance from the Committee on Foreign Investment in the United States (CFIUS). Despite the arrival of Middle Eastern money a couple of years later to bail out US banks, there are clearly some areas that are off limits. As House Representative Barney Frank put it, seemingly echoing the thoughts of David Hume, 'They're Arabs . . . I wish that wasn't the case but it's one thing if you're an Arab and it's another thing if you're Dutch and it's another thing if you're Malaysian. We're not in a good mood towards Arabs. Worse than we should be – I regret that – but that's the reality.'[14]

A RENEWED HUNGER

I am not suggesting that mutual antipathy is confined to relations between the developed and emerging worlds. Energy and logistics may be the biggest flashpoints between, say, the US, China and the Middle East but, within the emerging world, food plays a much bigger role, as we saw in Chapter 6. The big increases in food prices in 2007 and 2008 provided ample evidence of the difficulties associated with food shortages. Within emerging economies, there is a growing gap between the 'urban rich' and the 'rural poor'. In a world of rising food prices, the rural poor are in danger of becoming poorer still, given that a huge proportion of their incomes is devoted to food consumption. Ideally, the best way to resolve this problem is to use a tax and benefit system to redistribute resources from the 'haves' to the 'have-nots', but, within emerging economies, the tax and benefit system is often rather rudimentary and, thus, unreliable. An alternative approach is to drive a wedge between the global and domestic price of food. For food-producing nations, this is relatively easy. It's a matter of restricting exports though the imposition of tariffs, quotas and outright bans. Limiting exports increases domestic supply at the expense of a reduction in supply elsewhere. Domestic food prices therefore decline in relation to global food prices.

There are significant problems with this approach. Smuggling and other cross-border criminal activities will rise. The domestic suppliers may not receive the higher global price for their endeavours, reducing their incentive to produce more food. And other countries can easily retaliate. Nevertheless, as with energy supplies, the producers of food – particularly basics such as grain – may increasingly have the upper hand. That's good news for major emerging-market rice exporters such as Thailand, India, Vietnam, Pakistan and China but not quite so encouraging for major rice importers such as Indonesia, the Philippines, Nigeria and Bangladesh.[15] Could the food-producing nations unleash their own brand of state capitalism on the food-consuming nations? With climate change, might food wars also develop into water wars? And could this provide the opportunity for Western powers to adopt a 'divide and rule' strategy towards the emerging world? With the US willing to share its nuclear technologies with the Arab Gulf States (which are not short of energy) and India (to provide a counterweight to China), one can envisage the development of series of regional 'Cold Wars' sponsored by the West in a bid to maintain the status quo.

SLEEPING GIANTS NO MORE

State capitalism is on the rise because sleeping giants are awakening. Those sleeping giants have hitherto been unable to make a major claim on the world's raw materials because they have been too poor, too disconnected or too dogmatically attached to a defunct political philosophy. Yet all this is now changing. Russia has its gas, China and India have their cheap labour and Brazil has its commodities. They increasingly have incentives to strike deals with each other. They hope, after all, to continue to grow rapidly in the years ahead. They know that energy and food may be increasingly in short supply as the Malthusian calculus threatens to catch up with earlier productivity gains. And they also know that the economic success of the developed world over the last few hundred years depended not just on the triumph of the market but also on the protection of infant industries, the exploitation of virgin lands and the willingness to use military intervention to safeguard economic interests. The British East India Company paved the way for all that followed. We're not really seeing the rise of state capitalism but, instead, its return. And, as it returns, so the developed world's hold on the levers of economic power is slipping away year by year.

CHAPTER EIGHT

RUNNING OUT OF WORKERS

DEMOGRAPHIC DYNAMICS

The developed world is running out of workers. Most of the emerging world is not in the same position, at least not yet. The baby boomers who flooded Western and Japanese labour markets in the 1970s and 1980s are now heading into retirement. They're expecting someone, somewhere, to look after them. People in the developed world are about to become economically dependent on workers in the emerging world.

We've been here before, of course. As I argued in Chapter 2, Europe and its offshoots in the Americas and Australia would never have made so much progress over the last five hundred years without the use of an 'emerging' labour supply. This, however, was a world of slavery and indentured servitude which, one hopes, will not be making a comeback any time soon.[1]

The developed world finds itself, once again, relying on the efforts of other, poorer, people. This time, coercion of individual workers is unacceptable (or, at the very least, is hidden from view). If people in the developed world are to live happily in their retirements, they will have to stake a credible claim on the world's scarce resources through market mechanisms or through the power of their nation states to influence regimes elsewhere.

Population numbers ebb and flow through three main biological influences: the fertility rate (the number of children per woman), the infant mortality rate and adult life expectancy.[2] Population 'explosions' typically occur when there is a decline in infant mortality and a rise in adult life expectancy and only a lagged reduction in fertility.

ALBERT'S MEMORIAL

Infant mortality rates in the UK dropped significantly from the middle of the nineteenth century onwards, helped by public-health programmes such as the Vaccination Act of 1871. Life expectancy for British males rose from around forty in the mid-nineteenth century to about fifty by the time of Queen Victoria's death in 1901. Fertility rates adjusted much more slowly. In the first half of the nineteenth century, a typical Englishwoman would have five children. Queen Victoria herself managed nine (she might have had more had Prince Albert not succumbed to typhoid fever in 1861). Over the following fifty years, the fertility rate declined only modestly. With the arrival of Edwardian England, the typical woman of childbearing age was still giving birth to four children. Only by the middle of the twentieth century had the fertility rate dropped to around two, a number recognizable today. Shortly afterwards, there was a temporary boost back up to about 2.7 as post-war baby boomers popped out, apparently in response to a surge in optimism in the 1950s and early 1960s.[3]

According to the 1801 census, the population of England at the beginning of the nineteenth century stood at 8.3 million. By 1851, the population had risen to 16.8 million, before doubling again to 30.5

million in 1901, a rise of 267 per cent in a single century, implying an average annual growth rate of 1.3 per cent. A hundred years later, in 2001, the population of England had risen to 49.1 million, a further 61 per cent increase at an annual rate of increase of 0.5 per cent. Population growth slowed in the twentieth century primarily because of a more sustained fall in the fertility rate: life expectancy continued to rise and infant mortality rates carried on dropping.

England's experience in the nineteenth century was matched by countries in East Asia in the second half of the twentieth century, although the transformation in China, Japan and Korea was much quicker. From the 1950s through to the end of the 1960s, the East Asian fertility rate averaged around five. Life expectancy, however, rose rapidly, from a remarkably low forty-three in the early 1950s to sixty-four in the early 1970s and around seventy-five in the early years of the twenty-first century. Linked to this was an extraordinary reduction in infant mortality rates: infant deaths per 1,000 live births dropped from 182 in the early 1950s to below 60 by the beginning of the 1970s and around 20 at the beginning of the new millennium, all of which was linked to improved sanitation and water supplies and much better medical treatment, including the widespread use of antibiotics (indeed, this is a positive example of the technology replication I discussed at the end of Chapter 1). Even though the fertility rate has dropped rapidly since the 1970s – partly a reflection of China's one-child policy and the much wider use of contraception across the region as a whole – the decline has not been fast enough to prevent a population explosion. In the early 1950s, East Asia had a population of fewer than 700 million. Half a century later, the population had more than doubled.

DEMOGRAPHIC DIVIDENDS AND DEFICITS

These numbers, although impressive, say little about the *economic* consequences of demographic change. Ever since Thomas Malthus first wrote his *Essay on the Principle of Population*, there has been a heated debate over whether changes in population size are bad for welfare (the Malthusian subsistence argument), good for welfare (what might be termed the human ingenuity argument) or entirely neutral for welfare (the income per capita rather than total income argument). Yet each of these positions misses the main economic point. Demographic change is significant because age structures change. In any one country, it's possible to experience both a demographic dividend and a demographic deficit.

The dividend occurs when the population of working age is large in relation to the population of non-working age. Those of non-working age include children, teenagers and the elderly. The arithmetic is straightforward. If there are lots of 'producers' but not many 'dependants', the burden on the producers is relatively light. If, on the other hand, there are not many producers but plenty of dependants, the burden on the producers is rather heavy.

Population explosions can, therefore, be good news for an economy because, at some point, the proportion of those in work will rise in relation to those doing other things. In these circumstances, it's relatively easy for those in work to support those at either end of the age spectrum. Such was the case in the UK in the nineteenth century and in East Asia over the last fifty years. High rates of economic growth per capita were partly led by productivity, but also supported by the demographic dividend.

The demographic dividend is like a surfer's wave. The wave lifts the surfer high up, it provides a moment of excitement in the surfer's life but, eventually, it fades away. Demographic dividends don't occur quite so frequently as the surfer's wave but they have a similar effect: they temporarily raise the growth rate of an economy. Unlike surfers' waves, though, they can persist for many decades. If handled well, they can help create a virtuous economic circle. Improved healthcare for infants increases their chances of survival and, as a result, women choose to have fewer babies. Families can invest in their children's education, knowing the investment is worthwhile. As women become better educated, and are more knowledgeable about contraception, they can spend more time working and less time having children. The opportunity cost of childbirth rises, thereby placing downward pressure on the fertility rate. The size of the workforce increases because of both the increased number of infants surviving to adulthood and the higher participation of women in the workforce. With an expanded workforce, the volume of savings increases, allowing funds to be channelled to investment projects, which lift incomes even further. And, with a more educated workforce, human ingenuity can lift productivity, allowing more outputs for given inputs of raw materials.

Like a surfer, it's not always easy to jump onto these demographic waves. Sub-Saharan Africa has by far the greatest struggles. Improved medical provision has significantly reduced the rate of infant mortality, but prospects in adulthood remain poor – too many wars, too many diseases for those of working age (most obviously AIDS and malaria) and too little protection of property rights. What is the point of investing in education if the educated die early? For many years, Latin American nations also struggled. Some attribute their misfortunes to the prevalence of military *juntas* and dictators and, thus, the absence of democracy; but there is no shortage of non-democratic regimes in Asia, many of which have delivered rapidly rising living standards. A more likely explanation, in my view, is that Latin American economies had major problems with property rights, inflation and openness, thereby reducing incentives both to save and to trade.[4]

For the developed world, the problem is not so much the inability to jump onto a demographic wave but, instead, working out what to do when it's time to jump off. No longer are these nations benefiting from a demographic dividend. Instead, their leaders should be worrying about a demographic deficit.

The quandary is best expressed through the use of 'dependency ratios', defined as the ratio of the sum of the population aged between zero and fourteen (below working age) and that aged sixty-five and above (retirees) to the population aged between fifteen and sixty-four. While the demographic dividend is at work, the dependency ratio declines. As the wave crests, the ratio begins to rise, signalling the threat of a demographic deficit. Figure 8.1 shows movements in dependency ratios for nations and regions within the developed world compared with the global average. From the 1970s through to the early 1990s, the developed world was riding the demographic wave. Dependency ratios fell rapidly. The baby boomers, ensconced in nurseries and schools in the 1950s and 1960s, entered the workforce, swelling the numbers employed. Those same boomers are now approaching the end of their working lives with the result that dependency ratios are now rising. Meanwhile, fertility rates in some countries – notably Japan, Germany and Italy – are now so low that populations are in the process of shrinking. By the middle of the twenty-first century, according to the United Nations'

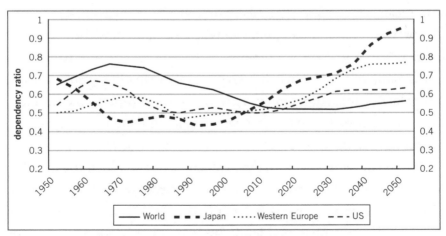

Figure 8.1: The Western world is approaching old age. . .

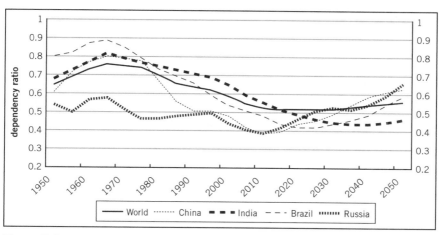

Figure 8.2: . . . but the emerging world is only in middle age
Source: United Nations World Population Prospects: The 2008 Revision

'medium variant' calculations, Italy's population will have declined by 3 million, Germany's by 10 million and Japan's by 26 million. Given that the population of the world as a whole is expected to rise by 3 billion over the same period, this is a remarkable shift in demographic fortunes.

Admittedly, populations in the emerging world are also, on average, getting older. Figure 8.2 shows dependency ratios for some of the largest emerging economies in the world. In the 1950s and 1960s, when life expectancy was low and fertility rates high, dependency ratios were elevated because there were lots of children and not so many workers. That pattern changed in the 1970s and 1980s when dependency ratios began to decline: youths, in plentiful supply, entered the workforce and contraception became increasingly prevalent, lowering fertility rates. Populations in the emerging world will eventually age. The United Nations currently estimates that dependency ratios will rise first in Russia and China, from around 2020, with others following suit over the following thirty years. These increases present major challenges – China, famously, will be the first country to grow old before it grows rich – but they do not alter the underlying fact that the ageing process in the developed world is much more advanced – in fact, thirty years earlier – than in most other countries.[5]

An alternative approach is to consider the changing supply of workers (aged fifteen to sixty-five) by region over time. In 1950, the population of working age in the developed nations stood at 494 million out of a global total of 1.4 billion, a share of 33.8 per cent. In 2000, the working-age population in the developed nations had increased to 743 million but the global total had increased much more, reaching 3.7 billion, leaving the developed nation share down at 20.3 per cent. By 2050, the UN estimates the working-age population in the developed world will have declined to just 662 million, a share of only 12.4 per cent in a global total which, by then, may be as high as 5.3 billion, a reflection of continued population increases in the emerging world and a rapid population acceleration in the world's most impoverished nations. This is a stunning transformation. For the developed world, population ageing is not just a story about providing pensions and healthcare for the elderly: it's also a reflection of shifting global economic power and influence. The rich nations really are running out of workers.

FUNDED PENSIONS AND HEALTHCARE PROVISION ARE NOT THE ANSWER

There is a rather tedious debate that suggests population ageing matters for some countries in the developed world but not for others. Those countries that depend on 'pay-as-you-go' pensions and health-care provision are supposedly more vulnerable, as they rely on current taxpayers to fund the elderly. If the old-age dependency ratio is rapidly rising, the burden on current taxpayers – especially people of working age – threatens to become too painful. Higher tax rates might leave them disinclined to work or tempted to emigrate to countries with more favourable tax regimes, in which case a vicious downward spiral ensues. As the young begin to leave, the nightclubs close and the schools are converted to old people's homes, encouraging a further youthful exodus. The associated loss of tax revenues undermines the government's ability to support the elderly, leading to a further hike in taxes on remaining taxpayers. The cycle is repeated. Many of the continental European countries fit this description. Meanwhile, those countries with funded pension schemes, where money in previous years had been deliberately set aside and invested to support future pension and healthcare needs, will supposedly be better off. This second category includes the US, the UK and the Netherlands.

It's an enticing distinction, but it's largely false. Ultimately, the elderly need access to real resources – doctors, nurses, nursing homes, cruise ships and bowling greens – but, to ensure these resources are put in place, savings need to be invested in the right areas. There is absolutely no reason to believe that this actually happens. The demographic deficit is decidedly not just a problem for nations with pay-as-you-go pension systems. It's also a major difficulty for those who chose, at the outset, to be thrifty.

To understand why, consider two forms of saving. The risk-averse baby boomers of country A decide to deposit their savings in a bank and leave them there, earning a modest amount of interest per year. The buccaneering baby boomers of country B choose to invest their money in real estate and equities, hoping for significant capital returns. The boomers in both countries then reach retirement age. Awash with savings, they decide to go on a spending spree.

The boomers in country A withdraw their piles of cash from the bank and head off to the plastic surgeons and the stair-lift manufacturers. They soon discover that not enough doctors and purveyors of stair-lifts exist, because the younger working generation is now fewer in number than the retired boomers. As the boomers spend their cash, surgery and stair-lift prices start to rise. An unpleasant dose of inflation follows, eroding the real spending power of their hard-earned savings (the plastic surgeons, of course, will end up with more money in their pockets but, as this is spent, other prices will also begin to rise).[6]

The boomers in country B believe they have been much wiser than those in country A. They, after all, have built up impressive portfolios of property and stocks. In retirement, all they have to do is sell their portfolios to the younger generation because, ultimately, they need to have cash in their pockets before they can buy their matinee theatre tickets or book their place in the nursing home. To get the cash, they need someone to buy their assets. If the younger working generation is smaller in size, the process of selling assets will prompt asset prices to fall. The boomers may discover, in fact, that they have been unconsciously involved in a giant scam. From the 1980s through to the early years of the twenty-first century, conventional wisdom suggested that people should invest in equities and property for the long term. Large numbers of boomers followed that advice. Their surplus incomes were invested in all manner of risky assets, creating a self-fulfilling asset price boom. Yet there was no particular reason to argue that long-run returns on these assets were rising. Prices went up because more and more boomers chose to buy risky assets, not because the risky assets suddenly offered better returns. Put another way, as boomers choose to offload assets upon reaching retirement, asset prices are likely to come back down again. The pot of gold at the end of the rainbow may be much smaller than commonly believed.

JAPAN: AN EARLY LESSON IN AGEING

The evidence to support this view is striking. In 1989, Japanese boomers believed they had made a killing. The stock market had risen dramatically through the 1980s and rising land prices seemed to be a one-way bet. Shortly afterwards, however, equity prices and then land prices began to fall, marking the beginning of a twenty-year period of persistent asset-price declines. Ten years later, at the height of the technology bubble in 1999, American and European boomers found themselves in a similar state of fervour. Even when stock prices slumped in 2000, house prices carried on rising, creating the false impression that people genuinely owned assets that would support them in their impending retirements. Other, more esoteric, assets became increasingly popular. Pension funds loaded up on asset-backed securities, which too often were linked to poor-quality loans in the US housing market. Ten years later, with equity markets still hobbled and with house prices having persistently declined for the first time in US post-war history, it turned out that the boomers were not so wealthy after all. Even worse, many Americans and British citizens had borrowed heavily against inflated asset values, leaving them awash with debt at precisely the wrong demographic moment. In the absence of sufficient funds, pay-as-you-go problems, supposedly banished, are making a comeback.

COMMAND OVER LIMITED RESOURCES

The underlying problem, ultimately, is command over limited resources. The risk of inflation or of asset-price declines stems from the process of retirement itself and the creation of a large number of elderly dependants. When pension systems were first created, life expectancy and retirement age were roughly the same. Pensions were designed to provide protection for those who were lucky enough to

183

live beyond the average age of death. There weren't many; the majority of people worked and then died. With improvements in sanitation, healthcare and nutrition, life expectancy has gradually risen. A bigger and bigger gap has opened up between the age of retirement and the average age at which a person dies. Most Americans, for example, plan to retire at around the age of sixty, but life expectancy at birth is now seventy-eight and rising. Meanwhile, those who reach the age of sixty-five can reasonably expect to live another nineteen years. At the beginning of the twentieth century, life expectancy at birth was only forty-seven, while those lucky survivors who managed to hang on to sixty-five could expect to live only another fourteen years.[7]

The numbers reaching retirement age are, therefore, much higher than they used to be. For a while, this demographic reality didn't have much of an economic impact because, while the numbers in retirement were rising, the numbers in work, thanks to the baby boomers, were rising even faster. The tables are now being turned. As the boomers retire, there are fewer workers left to support a large dependant elderly population: the population pyramid is being inverted. Workers can only produce so much, but there are now many more dependant mouths to feed. This is a true issue of economic scarcity.

At the individual country level, markets can adjust. A shortage of workers will push up real wages. Potential retirees may, as a result, choose to delay their retirement. Other workers may choose to work longer hours. Perhaps policymakers will deliver more flexible labour markets by encouraging more part-time work, increasing the provision of crèches and by adopting a more explicit 'hire and fire' mentality (the risk to a company of hiring a worker is reduced if workers can more easily be fired, thereby increasing the demand for workers and, hence, lowering the structural rate of unemployment). Workers in company pension schemes may find themselves having to take on board greater pension risk as defined-benefit pension schemes are shut down. In theory, capital-market reforms might boost investment returns and, hence, lift productivity. (In practice, the law of unintended consequences can sometimes work rather too well. Before the sub-prime crisis of 2007, it was generally believed that securitization was a source of stability in financial markets whereas, in the immediate aftermath of the crisis, securitization received a sizeable proportion of the blame.)

Yet the scope for domestic action is ultimately limited because, with an ageing population, domestic resources are limited. Domestic policies can slice the cake up in different ways but cannot so easily provide a bigger cake, even if people do end up working for longer. If countries want access to additional resources, they have to go global. The security and well-being of the developed world's elderly increasingly depends on the co-operation of workers from other parts of the world, in emerging markets and, increasingly, in some of the world's poorest countries. On UN projections, the population of working age in the developed world started to shrink between 2005 and 2010. By 2030, the population of working age in the least developed countries will surpass that of the developed nations for the first time since records began.

The mechanisms to allow adjustment to this new demographic reality involve the cross-border movement of labour and capital. First, the elderly can move to parts of the world where workers are more plentiful and, hence, living costs are lower. That, though, is easier said than done. Laws and customs vary and the elderly may want to spend time with their children rather than head off to a strange new land.

Second, capital in the developed world can move elsewhere to take advantage of the availability of more plentiful workers. This, in effect, has been the model pursued by Japan and Germany, wealthy countries with ageing populations which, over the years, have run persistent balance of payments current-account surpluses. In other words, domestic savings are higher than domestic investment, implying that savings are being invested abroad. But are these savings being invested on a demographic basis? The evidence is not particularly convincing. From 2005 through to 2008, the biggest recipients of German direct investment included the US, the UK, Italy, Spain, Austria, the Netherlands and Russia, nations not especially known for their youthful demographic disposition.[8]

There is, in fact, a good reason for squeamishness when it comes to investing in the emerging world. It's far more difficult for businesses to thrive. While multinationals are increasingly willing to invest in China and India, as we saw in Chapter 3, it's still heavy going. According to *Doing Business 2009*, the US and the UK are ranked third and sixth in the list of favoured economies as places to get business done. Japan is twelfth, Germany twenty-fifth, France thirty-first and Italy sixty-fifth. While a handful of emerging economies rank well – Thailand is thirteenth, Saudi Arabia is sixteenth and Malaysia is twentieth – the emerging powerhouses score a lot less favourably. China ranks eighty-third, with particular difficulties in business start-ups, employment and construction permits. Russia, India and Brazil sit at positions 120, 122 and 125 respectively, held back by problems in starting up and closing down businesses and paying taxes. In any case, investing abroad will not create doctors and nurses at home. Outsourcing and off-shoring might help bring down the price of iPods and flat-screen televisions, but they're unlikely to have so much impact on the provision of healthcare for the elderly and infirm.

Third, workers in emerging nations can emigrate to developed nations, thereby swelling the ranks of the employed in relation to the retired.

A RENEWED LOOK AT MIGRATION

Throughout human history, people have migrated across lands and countries, whether because of coercion, conflict or the search for a better way of life. After all, US superpower status did not come about by accident. It depended, instead, on both coercive and voluntary immigration. Before the 1820s, over three-quarters of the 11.3 million migrants who went to the Americas were slaves from Africa.[9] Thereafter, however, there was a huge increase in voluntary immigration. Initially immigrants came mostly from the UK (including, at that time, Ireland) and Germany. As the nineteenth century progressed, Scandinavians joined the exodus from Europe. With the twentieth century looming ever larger, southern and eastern Europeans joined in too.

Visitors to the Tenement Museum in New York can get a real sense of these waves of immigration. Located on Orchard Street, the Tenement Museum is tiny – it's a collection of little apartments – but it provides a fascinating insight into the changing ethnic mix of the Lower East Side in the late nineteenth century. In the 1860s, the most common voices were German. Through the 1880s and 1890s, with the onset of the pogroms in Russia against the Jews, Yiddish accents became commonplace. For a while, Italians also made the Lower East Side their home. Many immigrants came directly to the Lower East Side from Ellis Island, the first stopping point for those hoping to embrace the American Dream. More recently, the area has taken on a Chinese and Latin American tone.

Hostility towards immigrants began to rise in the late nineteenth century. Tuberculosis became known as 'the Jewish disease', even though it was hardly the Jews' fault that they had to live in such cramped and unsanitary conditions. Chinese immigrants were banned with the introduction of the Chinese Exclusion Act of 1882. Suspicions about Asians more generally were incorporated fully into

Congressional legislation with the Immigration Act of 1917, otherwise known as the Asiatic Barred Zone Act, which also introduced a literacy test (had this been in operation in the nineteenth century, I suspect many would-be immigrants to the US would have been sent back home). Quotas on immigrants were toughened up throughout the 1920s.

The US wasn't the only nation beginning to worry about immigration. The UK government, which had previously been happy to issue passports to people of any nationality (the idea was to provide the holder with a British government guarantee of safe passage across borders), decided in 1858 to restrict passport issuance to UK nationals alone (ironically, over the previous eighty-six years, British passports had been written in French). In 1914, the government of the day passed the British Nationality and Status Aliens Act which marked the beginnings of border controls around the world, using methods recognizable today.

It is just about possible to argue that the imposition of immigration controls reflected changing economic realities. The argument runs as follows. In the early to mid-nineteenth century, travelling across oceans was both hideously expensive and not for the faint-hearted. The spreading Industrial Revolution, however, both lowered transportation costs and increased the spending power of those who, previously, didn't have the money to fund a move to a foreign land. When transport costs were high and wages low, potential migrants had to jump over a particularly high hurdle to arrive in the Promised Land. Only the economically most resilient or most promising were likely to make the journey. In the nineteenth century, that generally meant young male workers who had the confidence to believe they could make something of the new opportunities presented to them.

At the beginning of the twenty-first century, immigration doesn't necessarily follow the same pattern. Transportation costs are considerably lower, so lower-productivity migrants can more easily travel across borders. Social-security systems in the developed world are much more generous, attracting migrants who perhaps have little economic benefit to add to their new nation. Immigration controls have, therefore, merely recreated the hurdle previously imposed by high transportation costs.

Certainly, patterns of immigration have changed as a result of the imposition and lifting of controls. From the 1920s through to the early 1960s, immigration into the US slowed from a flood to a trickle. Then, in 1965, the Immigration and Naturalization Act was passed, creating a huge new wave of immigrants.[10] These people came from Mexico, the Philippines, Korea, the Dominican Republic, India, Cuba and Vietnam, in some cases reflecting a desire to escape the shackles of communism. If Europe was the source of migrants in the nineteenth century, the late twentieth century saw a shift to Asia and Latin America.

In 1960, US immigrant males earned slightly more than native-born males but, by 1990s, were earning much less. Meanwhile, although there was a gradual improvement in the educational attainment of immigrant workers, the improvement was dwarfed by the progress made by domestic workers.

Some have used this evidence to suggest that, with lower hurdle rates, immigration is no longer providing the economic benefits it did in the nineteenth century. I find this remarkably difficult to believe. In the late nineteenth century, many immigrants from southern, Central and Eastern Europe would have had only modest educational attainments and certainly their command of English was often poor, to say the least. Meanwhile, immigrants' motives varied hugely. Some, of course, made the journey in the expectation of better economic opportunity which, in turn, may have contributed to a 'positive selection' effect. Others made the journey in order to escape repression and violence at home. Ukrainian Jews arrived on Ellis Island not in search of economic opportunity but because, otherwise, they'd have been slaughtered in the late nineteenth-century Russian pogroms. Yet they, and their families, made a huge contribution to the US economy in the twentieth century.

Whether or not the hurdle rate for immigration to the US is too high or too low, the 1965 Act certainly made a big difference in terms of the volume of immigration in the US. Moreover, because the fertility rate of immigrants to the US in the late twentieth and early twenty-first centuries was higher than that of the indigenous population, the balance between young and old has been favourably shifted, at least compared with other developed nations. Japan's demographic profile is poor in part because Japanese society has been unwilling to tolerate a significant influx of immigrants from elsewhere in the world. Europe's is also poor although, with the collapse of the Berlin Wall in 1989, for a while there seemed to be an opportunity for change. Workers in Central and Eastern Europe who, under Soviet communism, had been denied the economic opportunities available to their close neighbours, could now head west.

There are, though, two limitations. First, populations in Eastern Europe and in former Soviet states are already very old. Low fertility rates mean that, in years to come, these populations will rapidly shrink in size. In the fifty years to 2050, the populations of Belarus, Georgia, the Russian Federation and Ukraine, for example, will fall by between 21 and 31 per cent, according to UN projections. Second, European Union governments and their people are, at best, ambivalent about the potential benefits of immigration.

In principle, citizens of the European Union can happily cross the border between one EU nation and another. Workers, in particular, should be able to work anywhere they wish. Yet, while the UK happily welcomed with open arms workers from the first tranche of EU Accession States in 2004 (Cyprus, the Czech Republic, Estonia, Hungary, Latvia, Lithuania, Malta, Poland, Slovakia and Slovenia), workers from the second tranche in 2007 (Bulgaria and Romania) were treated less favourably as a result of new Home Office regulations. According to the EU, 'at the heart of the new regulations is the restriction of low-skilled [Bulgarian and Romanian] workers to existing quota schemes in the agricultural and food processing sectors'.[11] In effect, this means that any increase in the numbers of low-skilled Bulgarians and Romanians coming into the UK will have to be offset by a reduction in the numbers of non-EU low-skilled workers.

In a sly announcement on 8 April 2009, the UK government declared, first, that 'Strict working restrictions for Eastern Europeans will not be scrapped' and, second, that 'the Government is delivering on its promise to be tougher on European criminals and remove those that cause harm to our communities. From today the deportation referral threshold for European criminals will be cut from twenty-four months imprisonment to twelve months for drugs, violent and sexual offences. This means these offenders will be automatically considered for deportation.' Perhaps the intention was not to be xenophobic, but the juxtaposition of these two statements is, at best, unfortunate.[12]

Meanwhile, it's all too easy for people of influence to warn against migration through the pursuit of cheap xenophobic laughs. A few years ago, I spoke at a conference in Germany on demographics and, in particular, the economic consequences of population ageing. I argued in favour of immigration as a useful mechanism to deal with rising dependency ratios. The speaker who followed me – an academic advisor to the government of Gerhard Schröder in Berlin – asked the audience of predominantly white middle-aged men why Germany should go down this route. Following reunification, he observed, the nation was already awash with prostitutes from East Germany. What possible benefit might there be from bringing in additional prostitutes from Bulgaria? The audience laughed heartily. It would have been better had they walked out.

A World Bank paper, published in April 2009,[13] goes some way to undermining the views of those who believe that immigrants arrive to take advantage of a generous tax and benefits system. Immigrants, whether from elsewhere in the EU or from outside the EU altogether, tend to find themselves at either end of the receiving nation's indigenous educational spectrum: a disproportionate share is either relatively poorly or relatively well educated. Immigrant households, though, are largely 'young' and, therefore, have low dependency ratios: while immigrants tend to have more children than indigenous households, the elderly have a low representation in immigrant households. All in all, the authors concluded that immigrant households typically pay more taxes, and receive fewer benefits, than the indigenous population, hardly a surprising result given their relative youth and, hence, the absence of any need for pension benefits.

Academic papers, though, do not provide a full flavour of the extent to which nations are, slowly, becoming dependent on their immigrant populations. On 22 June 2009, Halmstad in Sweden hosted an Under-21 soccer match between England and Germany. The German team had its fair share of Neuers, Schmelzers and Eberts, but it also had its Castros, Ben-Hatiras, Özils and Dejagahs. Some of these players were born in Germany but all come from immigrant families, hailing from Spain, Tunisia, Turkey and Iran. National sports teams have become increasingly international in flavour. Perhaps unsurprisingly, in his talk, the aforementioned German academic advisor chose not to focus on this aspect of the immigration story. I wonder whether he still supports his national team.

IT'S NOT THE TIME TO CLOSE BORDERS

In the absence of a stunning acceleration in productivity growth, ageing populations create awkward dilemmas. Domestically, the solution lies in arithmetic terms with an increase in the hours worked by the population of working age in relation to retirees. That can be achieved through an increase in the retirement age, a reduction in the structural rate of unemployment, an increase in the average hours worked per day, more flexible working hours to include, for example, those who might otherwise stay away from work to look after their children, and, for currently antediluvian societies, an increase in female labour-market participation.

Domestic policies, however, do little to change the reality of global demographic shifts. People in the developed world will become increasingly dependent on people from the emerging and most impoverished nations in the world. This can happen in one of two ways. Either the developed world opens its borders, allows people in and thus adopts the approach used by the German Under-21 soccer team. Or, alternatively, the developed world invests abroad in the hope that, by doing so, workers in poorer parts of the world will happily work all hours of the day to ensure the comfort of retirees in the developed world.

Long term, the second option is unappealing. The rise in state capitalism, the theme of Chapter 7, suggests the developed world would increasingly be in danger of exposure to economic blackmail. Workers in emerging nations might increasingly choose to work for their own benefit and not for the benefit of corpulent Westerners. Developed market assets in the emerging world would be vulnerable to seizure. And, in time, the ability of the developed world to impose a military solution on potentially hostile countries elsewhere in the world will fade. This is a simple matter of fiscal arithmetic. According to estimates from the OECD, public spending on pensions and healthcare within the G7 nations will rise by around 7 per cent of GDP between 2010 and 2050.[14] Unless tax revenues also rise – difficult if the workers being relied upon to produce the necessary goods and services live abroad – the likely response will be expenditure cutbacks in other areas. Gunboat diplomacy might have worked well for Victorian and Edwardian Britain but, with limited resources, it will be a fading option for the developed world in the twenty-first century.

The first option is, in my view, much better. US history, both in the nineteenth century and in the late twentieth century, shows that it is possible to incorporate into society all colours and creeds. Border controls are a creation of the early twentieth century and, from an economic perspective, should be generally regarded as acts of protectionism. They stifle the free flow of labour across borders and, hence, lead to an inefficient and unfair allocation of global resources. These are not, though, the only arguments in favour of immigration. If the developed world is to become increasingly dependent on workers coming from elsewhere in the world, surely it's better for those workers to be broadly sympathetic to the values of democracy and freedom that are regarded so highly in the US and Europe. That sympathy is likely to be far greater if the developed world not only recognizes its dependency on youthful workers elsewhere in the world but is also happy to welcome those workers across its own borders. Those workers, in turn, are likely to end up earning more than they might do had they stayed at home, providing a stream of remittances to help alleviate poverty in poorer parts of the world.[15]

There are, admittedly, weaknesses in any approach. Higher spending on healthcare in the developed world may take doctors and nurses away from needier patients in poorer parts of the world. Despite the evidence from the World Bank, indigenous populations tend to be suspicious of foreigners and, often wrongly, blame new arrivals for job losses, crime and so on.[16] Social-security safety nets are much more supportive now than they were in the nineteenth century; some immigrants, therefore, may be tempted to head to countries where they can, in effect, live on the efforts of indigenous taxpayers. And, unless immigrants intend not only to stay in their new country but also to have their own families, any increase in the population of working age may prove to be only temporary: immigrants, after all, will also eventually retire.

These are all valid arguments. Yet the big-picture effects of the 1965 Immigration and Naturalization Act appear to have been generally beneficial: the US may have an ageing population, but the time-bomb is nothing like as worrying as is the case in Japan and in many European nations.

The main obstacle to immigration is, of course, a heady mix of nationalism and xenophobia, which has blighted the international mobility of people on and off for centuries. This has not yet gone away. In June 2009, L'Oréal, the French cosmetics company, and Adecco, a temporary recruitment agency, were found guilty of racial discrimination by the Cour de Cassation, the French equivalent of the US Supreme Court, with regard to their hiring of a sales team to promote Fructis Style, a shampoo. Whereas 38.7 per cent of applicants were from ethnic minorities, of those offered a job fewer than 5 per cent were non-white. Perhaps L'Oréal thought they weren't worth it.

The developed world may be increasingly dependent on people from the emerging world and even poorer countries, but it's facing huge challenges coming to terms with this new reality. The choice, though, is stark. Either people work for longer – either more hours per week or more years per lifetime – or borders are made more porous. The nation state was very much an invention of the late nineteenth and twentieth centuries. The concept now desperately needs an overhaul.

PART FOUR

GREAT POWER GAMES

CHAPTER NINE

INDULGING THE US NO MORE

CAPITAL FLOWS AND NATION STATES

Time and again, I have returned to the key issue of cross-border capital flows, whether to explain the growing instability of financial markets (Chapter 4) or the rise of state capitalism (Chapter 7). Indeed, these two themes are connected. After all, the huge expansion of cross-border capital flows alongside the proliferation of nation states have become the defining features of modern-day globalization. The stock of foreign investment, which stood at an already high 20 per cent of global GDP in 1980, rose dramatically to over 100 per cent of global GDP twenty years later, a huge increase that dwarfs anything achieved in the heyday of nineteenth-century globalization. Meanwhile, the number of sovereign states, each with their own legal and regulatory structures, their ever-increasing public-spending commitments and, in many cases, their own currencies, has more than doubled since the late nineteenth century.

For those who believe markets can solve everything, the rise of cross-border capital flows is a remarkable result. The national constraints on capital movements that dominated much of the twentieth century have been removed. In their place, investors have been served a smorgasbord of investment opportunities. Balance of payments surpluses and deficits have ended up much bigger, not necessarily because countries have been pursuing foolish domestic policies, but, instead, because capital has been able to travel in an increasingly unconstrained fashion across borders, eking out the highest returns for the benefit of both savers and borrowers.

The creation of an apparently unconstrained global capital market is, nevertheless, something of an oddity, sitting uneasily with the proliferation of nation states. If both creditors and debtors reside within one nation, it's relatively easy to see how the political process could deliver a resolution in the light of, for example, rising default risk. If, however, creditors and debtors reside in different nations, and include sovereign actors among their number, it's much harder to achieve a meeting of minds. Indeed, the lack of any coherent international approach to capital markets is both a source of potential short-term volatility within capital markets themselves – as argued in Chapter 4 – and a long-term threat to the international economic, financial and political order. That long-term threat stems from three factors: a single global capital market; the participation within that market of an increasing number of sovereign nations as opposed to commercial investors; and the dominance of the dollar on the foreign exchanges.

To understand why, we have to think about a 'perfect world' where distortions to capital markets are minimized. In this world, there would be a single currency issued by a single central bank that would take into account global economic and financial developments and not be swayed by local or regional peculiarities in its pursuit of price stability. The capital market would be made up of many players, none of whom would be large enough to distort prices. All players would, therefore, have to accept the prevailing price: they would all be 'price takers'. Those people investing funds would be doing so purely on the basis of risk and reward, with no consideration given to alternative rent-seeking or political aims. With one currency, there would be no debate over currency manipulation through the accumulation of foreign-exchange reserves. Meanwhile, those choosing to borrow would do so knowing the money would have to be repaid in full, with interest, and that failure to do so would result in the ignominy of default, possible loss of access to capital markets for years to come and, perhaps, the threat of incarceration in the nearest prison.

This, of course, is a fantasy world to be found only in textbooks. The real world is much more complicated. There is more than one currency. Some currencies are more 'liquid' than others. Put simply, people are generally happier to transact their international affairs in US dollars than, say, the Mongolian tögrög. Many countries have yet to establish any real sense of monetary and financial credibility. As noted in Chapters 4 and 5, their leaders end up choosing to shadow popular, liquid currencies like the US dollar or, more recently, the euro. Changes in US or Eurozone monetary policy therefore have an impact which spreads well beyond national or regional borders. The world's big lenders increasingly are made up of public-sector entities in the emerging world and, of the world's biggest borrowers, the US government is the neediest by far. The legal rules of the game vary hugely from one country to the next. It's very difficult, therefore, to argue that international capital markets are really markets in the textbook sense. There are all sorts of incentives for governments to behave badly and, thus, for markets to malfunction.

I am not trying to imply that capital markets are powerless to exert any influence on government behaviour. That clearly is not the case. Rather, I'm suggesting that governments exert a series of distorting influences on capital markets. Governments either pursue their own agendas or, through revolution, *coup d'état*, invasion or the democratic process, are forced to listen to the will of their, or their neighbours', people. Those views may not easily gel with the interests of, say, a government's international creditors. Indeed, why should they?

WHO PICKS UP THE BILL FOR AMERICAN BORROWERS?

In Chapter 8, I referred briefly to the rising costs in the developed world of pensions and healthcare. It's now time to think about the possible long-term consequences for taxpayers, government popularity and the vulnerability of foreign creditors of these growing burdens.

In an insightful paper published in 2003, Jagadeesh Gohkale and Kent Smetters produced deeply disturbing calculations regarding the future tax liability of the American people.[1] Their starting point was to think about future federal spending from the perspective of the long-term payment obligations associated with social security and Medicare. By doing so, they were able to calculate the likely changes in fiscal policy required to make the budgetary numbers add up over time. They offered a series of bleak policy options: a doubling of the tax on US payrolls,[2] an increase of two-thirds in income tax revenues or the permanent elimination of all future federal discretionary spending: no new roads, no new schools and no new bombs.

Since that paper was written, the fiscal situation has rapidly deteriorated on both sides of the Atlantic. As populations have aged, so governments should have been running fiscal surpluses, thereby saving for their nations' futures.[3] Governments chose otherwise. In the first decade of the twenty-first century, the US and UK governments, in particular, allowed their budget deficits to rise even before the sub-prime crisis took hold. Following the crisis, deficits rose to hitherto unimaginable levels, advancing into double digits as a share of national output in both the US and the UK,[4] with associated huge increases in government debt. To put these numbers into context, never before in peacetime has either the US or UK government had to borrow so much. The tax and discretionary spending implications of these fiscal positions are potentially alarming.

But for whom? There is an obvious conflict between the interests of, first, the current domestic taxpayer (or current voter), second, the future domestic taxpayer and, third, foreign creditors. If a country has been living beyond its means for too long, and current taxpayers are unwilling to pick up the bill for their past indiscretions – or, indeed, for their future healthcare and medical 'rights' – the obvious options are either to rob future generations by deferring tax payments to them or to default to a nation's creditors. If those creditors live abroad, the default option is particularly enticing.

The thinking behind emerging-nation purchases of US government paper (in effect, IOUs) has already been explained in earlier chapters. While each of the reasons – protection against capital flight, links to Federal Reserve monetary credibility, mercantilist trade policies, Ricardian comparative advantage – may stem from short-term clear-thinking, the longer-term consequences of these policies are less encouraging. Partly, this reflects a 'merry-go-round' effect. The more US government and quasi-government paper is purchased by emerging nations, the more the price of this paper comes to depend on emerging-nation beneficence. Should a major emerging nation then attempt to sell any of this paper, the signal to the rest of the market would be, to say the least, discouraging. The price of US government paper might collapse in response, leading to much higher American interest rates and huge losses for holders of US paper around the world. To avoid this, emerging nations feel compelled to buy more and more pieces of US paper even though their ultimate exposure to US problems becomes greater by the day. Future US taxpayers may never be able, or willing, to repay their foreign creditors. In the meantime, the merry-go-round spins faster and faster.

INDULGENCES REVISITED

The US appears to have adopted some of the techniques of Catholic priests in mediaeval times, when the sale of indulgences became a lucrative money-raising operation for the construction of cathedrals and churches and the funding of crusades (given the ultimate dependence of the US military machine on foreign creditors, George W. Bush's post 9/11 crusade gaffe as he prepared the world for the Second Gulf War and the war in Afghanistan was historically rather accurate).[5] Indulgences offered the promise of salvation in exchange for a contribution to whichever pet project the priest wanted to support. Priests became bond salesmen for the hereafter. Trading indulgences was, of course, partly an act of faith, but it was also, for a while, a very useful way for the Catholic Church to raise money and, thus, increase its power. Eventually, in 1517, Martin Luther came along with his Ninety-Five Theses, and, allegedly, nailed them to the church door, thus sparking the Protestant Reformation. As Abraham Lincoln said, 'you cannot fool all the people all the time'.

Whereas indulgences were supposedly repaid in the hereafter, the time frame for repayment of US government debt is a little shorter. Nevertheless, the act of faith is still there. Investors elsewhere in the world choose to own US assets because they believe the US has a strong rule of law, excellent protection of investors' rights and a central bank determined to keep inflation under control. They also believe that other investors have the same beliefs: in that sense, each investor benefits from an act of 'groupthink' faith. However, at some point, the merry-go-round may spin out of control, threatening a major financial disaster. Can this be avoided? If so, who picks up the cost of bringing the merry-go-round to a halt? Will there be a financial equivalent of a Protestant Reformation?

A POST-DOLLAR FINANCIAL ORDER

The issue at stake is America's reserve currency status. On a variety of different measures – foreign-exchange transactions, depth and liquidity of financial markets, the rule of law – the US dollar scores very favourably. Everyone is happy to hold dollars. This, in turn, makes it very easy for the US to raise funds in international capital markets. Many countries – notably emerging economies – have to transact with the rest of the world in foreign currencies. It's an expensive business. They have to export and import in dollars, not their own currencies. They have to borrow in dollars and not in their own currencies (although this is now beginning to change). That leaves them cruelly exposed to speculative attack. Should their currencies fall in value, the burden of their own dollar-denominated debt rises in domestic currency terms, thereby increasing default risk and triggering a vicious circle.[6] The US, in contrast, has none of these worries. It's a key reason why the US is easily able to run a persistent balance of payments current-account deficit while many emerging nations choose to run protective surpluses.

This is an unstable, asymmetric, relationship. It cannot easily continue. The US extracts too many benefits and the rest of the world ends up with most of the costs. But what can other countries do about it? It's not possible to create a new reserve currency overnight. Trying to conduct transactions in an alternative currency that is not universally acceptable is no easy business. It's like trying to challenge Microsoft's supremacy in computer software.[7]

Yet the dollar's supremacy may be on the wane. The threat comes not so much from the rise of the euro, even though it, too, now offers deep and liquid currency markets, but, rather, from countries within the emerging world. Speaking at the World Economic Forum in Davos on 28 January 2009, Vladimir Putin, prime minister of Russia, said:

The entire economic growth system, where one regional centre prints money without respite and consumes material wealth, while another regional centre manufactures inexpensive goods and saves money printed by other governments, has suffered a major setback ... excessive dependence on a single reserve currency is dangerous for the global economy. Consequently, it would be sensible to encourage the objective process of creating several strong reserve currencies in the future. It is high time we launched a detailed discussion of methods to facilitate a smooth and irreversible switchover to the new model ... it is important that reserve currency issuers must implement more open monetary policies ... these nations must pledge to abide by internationally recognized rules of macroeconomic and financial discipline.

It may be that Mr Putin, never a man to mince his words, was just trying to antagonize American delegates who, in earlier years, had been more than happy to talk up their own successes. In his Davos remarks, Mr Putin also offered the following pithy reminder:

just a year ago, American delegates speaking from this rostrum emphasized the US economy's fundamental stability and its cloudless prospects. Today, investment banks, the pride of Wall Street, have virtually ceased to exist. In just twelve months, they have posted losses exceeding the profits they made in the last twenty-five years.[8]

In Russia, they call it *zloradstvo*. In Germany, it's *Schadenfreude*. In the US or the UK, there is no precise word. We know, however, what Mr Putin meant.

Russia's concerns about the emerging world's reliance on the dollar are well founded. Because the US borrows from the rest of the world in its own currency, a decline in the dollar's value reduces the amount the creditors receive from the US in their own currencies.

The US has, therefore, a strong incentive to carry on printing dollars so long as investors elsewhere are prepared to snap them up. The merry-go-round suits America's interests very well indeed.

One obvious way to deal with this problem is for emerging investors to buy assets priced in dollars over which the US authorities have no control. Commodity producers, for example, could easily fall into Russian or Chinese hands. Their products are priced in dollars but, in the event of a dollar decline, the price of their products in dollar terms would simply rise – this is one reason why China is so keen to build up relationships in Africa and the Middle East. There are only so many commodity producers up for sale, however. Another option would be for Russia and China to diversify away from US bonds into US equities and company acquisitions, but, as we saw in Chapter 7, this is easier said than done given the climate of mistrust in Washington.

Arguably, then, major emerging nations have no alternative other than to challenge the dollar's pre-eminent reserve currency role. It's not just a case of switching out of dollars into, for example, euros. That might bring diversification benefits but it would not deal with the underlying problem, namely that the emerging economies would still be dependent on foreign currencies to conduct their international business. They need, instead, to create their own reserve currencies. They need to create the financial equivalent of the Protestant Church.

CHINA'S RESERVE CURRENCY

In principle, it's a simple process. Imagine, for example, that China's renminbi became a reserve currency, widely held around the world and used for trade and capital market transactions. Imagine, also, that the use of the renminbi in this way led to a partial displacement of the dollar. How would China fare in these circumstances? The likely appreciation of the renminbi against the dollar would leave China nursing losses on its foreign-exchange reserves. However, the wider use of the renminbi around the world would lower transaction costs for Chinese individuals and businesses. Ultimately, whether China gained or lost overall from this process would be an empirical question. Nevertheless, China's own dependency on a monetary system created in Washington would gradually fade.

In practice, of course, turning the renminbi into a reserve currency poses all sorts of difficulties. Given China's record on property rights and business undertakings more generally, would people elsewhere in the world willingly hold renminbi when they could, instead, choose to hold dollars or euros? Could China easily dispose of the capital controls which, to date, have prevented Chinese citizens from directly owning foreign assets (and have limited foreign ownership of Chinese assets)? How might this fit with the limited political freedoms in China compared with those in, for example, the US? Given a lack of depth and development in China's capital markets, together with continued heavy state involvement, is it realistic to believe that foreign investors will happily hold large amounts of Chinese assets when there are other, more liquid, alternatives available elsewhere in the world?

While these doubts are all perfectly valid, there are, nevertheless, six points that favour the development of the renminbi as a reserve currency. First, China is now the second or third largest economy in the world and, by the middle of the twenty-first century, will probably be the largest. That does not give China any right to impose the renminbi on anyone else, but it increasingly makes it difficult for governments, businesses and individuals in other countries to ignore China's currency. Second, as we saw in Chapter 3, China's share of world trade has risen dramatically over the last thirty years. China doesn't just have a large economy, it also has one of the most successful trading nations on the planet. Third, as China has become economically more powerful, other countries have become increasingly dependent on China's status as a key trading partner. Now it is the world's biggest consumer of metals and the second-biggest consumer of oil, other countries have a strong incentive to strike bilateral deals with this new economic behemoth, an economy that finds itself at the epicentre of expanding emerging-market-to-emerging-market trade. Fourth, even if China did nothing to promote the renminbi as an alternative to the dollar as a reserve currency, the renminbi's status could be elevated by default, merely as a result of growing disenchantment with the dollar. Fifth, many countries that tried but failed with the so-called Washington Consensus might now be content to build economic relationships with a country that at least offers an alternative to US economic hegemony.[9]

Sixth, and politically most interesting, China is now actively promoting the renminbi's role as an alternative reserve currency to the dollar. Admittedly, it's still early days. However, China has seen a blossoming of bilateral currency swap deals with, amongst others, Indonesia, Belarus and Argentina. At the time of writing, these deals were worth a total of $650bn. If similar deals proliferate around the world, China will increasingly be able to conduct trade with other nations – notably those in the emerging world – in its own currency and not in dollars. State capitalism isn't just a matter of the ownership of foreign assets; it can also be used to strike bilateral trade and financial deals between nations and avoid too much concern about market forces. By so doing, it threatens the multilateral arrangements that have increasingly governed the global economic system since the 1950s.

There is a long way to go. China conducts around $2.6trn of annual trade of which around 70 per cent is invoiced in US dollars. China's foreign-exchange reserves, by far the biggest in the world, now stand at over $2trn and cannot be easily diversified. China's capital markets are still mostly shut. They will have to open more fully before the renminbi can be treated as a serious contender for reserve currency status. Importantly, though, these initial steps reflect a slow redrawing of the world financial landscape. Emerging economies, previously in thrall to Washington, now want to stand on their own two feet. They no longer want to be slaves to the dollar.

A FINANCIAL SYSTEM UNDER STRAIN

There is a tendency to believe that only one reserve currency can dominate the international financial system at any point in time. Certainly, the dollar has dominated since the end of the Second World War, thereby supporting this notion. Pre-war, however, it was a different story. As Barry Eichengreen of the University of California at Berkeley notes, 'At the end of 1913, sterling balances accounted for less than half of the total official foreign exchange holdings whose currency of denomination is known, while French francs accounted for about a third and German marks a sixth . . . In the 1920s and 1930s three currencies again shared [the reserve currency] role, although now the dollar supplanted the German mark.'[10] In other words, although the dollar has monopolized the reserve currency role in recent times, sterling wasn't quite so dominant, at least not in the first half of the twentieth century.

Arguably, the existence of rivals to a sterling reserve currency reflected an empire already in decline. Sterling may have accounted for less than half of known foreign-exchange holdings in 1913, but, at the end of the nineteenth century, sterling had accounted for around 64 per cent of holdings. While, therefore, reserve currencies may co-exist, their co-existence may be an indication of a growing malaise with the prevailing *ancien régime*. The dollar's rise in the 1920s was, in part, a reflection of the economic costs of the First World War: the Treaty of Versailles and subsequent hyperinflation put paid to the German mark's reserve currency status, while economic upheavals in both France and the UK (with its General Strike in 1926) made the dollar a more attractive option. These were not happy times for globalization. Similarly, the dollar temporarily lost its way as a reserve currency in the 1970s alongside the collapse of the Bretton Woods exchange-rate system. The Deutsche Mark was suddenly in high demand while globalization was in trouble. Germany, unlike the US, wasn't in the business of creating inflation.

Thus, while it's perfectly possible to have more than one reserve currency circulating simultaneously, it has typically been a sign of weakness rather than strength. Reserve currency rivalry generally reflects unease with the international financial system, whether for economic or political reasons. Mr Putin's comments and Beijing's actions deserve to be taken seriously.

In both the interwar years and the 1970s, the loss of trust in the prevailing reserve currency contributed to huge economic dislocations. This is hardly surprising. A reserve currency acts as a beacon of stability in an otherwise uncertain world. It lubricates the wheels of trade and allows capital more easily to move across borders. Should a reserve currency lose its way, the wheels of international trade and finance are in danger of falling off. The world needs an international means of exchange. Should the prevailing currency be rejected, trade shrivels, cross-border capital flows dry up, exchange rates become increasingly volatile and periodic bouts of price instability become commonplace, as the world saw in both the 1930s (with excessive deflation) and the 1970s (with excessive inflation).

FEAR OF THE PRINTING PRESS

We face similar risks today. In response to the 2007/8 credit crunch and the part-collapse of the Western banking system, the US authorities, alongside those in the UK, chose to adopt so-called unconventional policies, designed to increase the supply of money by, in effect, turning on the printing press. These policies were a response to a perceived shortfall of lending as banks came to terms with earlier losses linked to sub-prime loans. By increasing the supply of dollars, however, the dollar's value on the foreign exchanges dropped. In effect, the pursuit of unconventional policies revealed a schism between the sovereign interests of the US as a nation and the global demands for a stable reserve currency. With a higher world supply of dollars, existing holders of dollar assets – including reserve managers across the emerging economies – suddenly found themselves sitting on potential losses. Moreover, because unconventional policies lower the cost of government borrowing – they operate partly through central-bank purchases of either government or quasi-government debt, thereby increasing the supply of money – there is no great pressure on the US government to put its fiscal house in order. If the long-term costs of the credit crunch are persistently high budget deficits funded through resort to the printing press, holders of dollars elsewhere in the world have every right to be very worried indeed.

US PROBLEMS AND SIXTEENTH-CENTURY SPAIN

The US response to the credit crunch may be the last throw of the dice for a country that, for too long, has been able to live beyond its means. To understand what's at stake, it's worth going all the way back to the sixteenth century when, for a while, Spain was, like the US today, an all-conquering nation.

If 1492 marked a seismic geopolitical shock, 1519 arguably marked the beginnings of a seismic economic shock. In February of that year, Hernando Cortés landed in the Yucatan peninsular in Mayan territory (in what is modern-day Mexico) with eleven ships, five hundred men, thirteen horses and assorted cannon. In time, he and his fellow conquistadors destroyed the Aztec, Inca and Mayan civilizations through a mixture of supreme violence, noxious pathogens and naked greed. Cortés' ambition was nicely focused. It wasn't long before the conquistadors discovered silver in huge quantities (notably at the Andean 'silver mountain' of Potosí, in modern-day Bolivia). They had uncovered a printing press for the sixteenth century's version of a reserve currency. Everyone wanted silver. The Spanish had more of this precious metal than they could possibly imagine. Faced with a choice between spending and investing, they chose the former. With so much silver, they could pay others to do all the hard work. Not all Spaniards lived a life of luxury – it was no fun being on the wrong side of the Inquisition – but those who could, did.

They imported high-quality consumer goods from elsewhere in Europe. The hardest-working people in Spain itself were a mixture of foreigners (particularly the French) and despised local minorities, most obviously Jews and Muslims. The Spanish forgot how to struggle. They became increasingly dependent on the efforts of other nations. And, as those nations made more effort, they began to challenge the earlier Spanish economic and military supremacy. While bad weather is a convenient excuse for the Spanish Armada's failure in 1588, in reality Spanish defeat owed much to the superior shipbuilding skills the English had acquired over the previous fifty years. Silver made sixteenth-century Spain wealthy, but it confined the Spanish nation to relative poverty in the centuries that followed. Whereas other nations expanded their economic horizons, in some cases through an unholy alliance between sugar and slavery, the Spanish happily lived off their precious metal while fighting wasteful wars.

There is no doubt that the arrival of huge quantities of silver fuelled global trade in the sixteenth century, in much the same way that huge quantities of dollars have helped fuel world trade since the end of the Second World War. Silver spread from west to east, across the Atlantic to Europe, overland to the Levant and beyond and around the African

Cape to India, Indonesia and other, to European eyes, exotic locations. Spices, silks and cottons came back the other way. Silver also headed west, across the Pacific to Manila in the Philippines. It then went onwards to China, where high demand for silver reflected the collapse of the paper currency system of the Ming Dynasty (a case of good money driving out bad). In fact, rising silver supplies had different effects in different parts of the world. In Europe, the increase in the supply of silver led to a decline in its price and, hence, an increase in inflation. In China, the increase in the supply of silver was a response to rising demand – reflecting the monetary failures of the Ming Dynasty – and left no imprint on inflation.

Increased silver supplies were thus abused by the Spanish, a source of inflation elsewhere in Europe and a welcome financial lubricant in China and other parts of Asia. They were instrumental in creating a sixteenth- and seventeenth-century world of outsourcing and off-shoring where, for a while, the Spanish were able to live on the efforts of others. But the Spanish ultimately lost out.

There is no particular reason why such distant history should repeat itself. The US is a highly productive economy where there is no shortage of work ethic. Nevertheless, like the Spanish of the sixteenth century, Americans have lived beyond their considerable means, taking full advantage of the rest of the world's willingness to hold dollars, in much the same way that the Spanish benefited from the rest of the world's enthusiasm for silver. Should that willingness begin to fade, the US will no longer be able to conduct trade, or access the world's capital, on the favourable terms it has enjoyed particularly since the end of the Second World War. As already noted, the appetite for dollars may already be fading. Will the US economy also fade?

The answer is partly out of America's hands. Yes, heightened immigration could make a difference by providing more taxpayers to fund the elderly. Yes, successive governments could find ways to raise taxes (if the US ever becomes really serious about climate change, it could raise taxes on energy by a substantial amount) to pay for the elderly and infirm. Yes, wishful thinking in favour of another productivity miracle might eventually come true. Yes, households could repay sack-loads of debt, thereby allowing a permanent reduction in the US balance of payments current-account deficit and even, perhaps, a move into surplus to replicate the nineteenth-century British model. If all these were achieved, then the dollar might retain its reserve-currency status. My impression, though, is that the rest of the world – at least those parts with a penchant for state capitalism – is fast running out of patience and, importantly, able to survive without having to depend on the US consumer.

The dollar's reserve-currency status has given Americans an unfair claim on global resources. For a while, the rest of the world was willing to tolerate this unfair claim. After all, other countries didn't go away empty-handed. They were able to trade internationally in a currency that was better than their own. Strong American domestic demand gave those countries with a mercantilist bent an extremely attractive export market. In time, other countries became increasingly skilled in producing goods for a hyper-competitive US market. It is often forgotten that, in the 1970s, few goods destined for the American market were 'made in China'. Yet the system has worked only through rising foreign claims on future US taxpayers. In a world where other countries have been growing more quickly than the US, that aspect of the arithmetic has never really seemed to add up. It was, and remains, an unstable situation.

If political leaders in the emerging world have their way, the dollar's reserve-currency status will slowly dwindle. Trade and capital flows will increasingly take place within the emerging world, creating room for other currencies to play the role hitherto performed by the US dollar alone. The process will lead to significant costs for the US.

As the dollar declines in value, so oil and other commodity prices will rise for Americans. America's ability to access global capital will deteriorate, leading to higher interest rates. A higher cost of capital, in turn, will squeeze American demand and place limits on the size of the capital stock. The long-term growth rate will fall away, making the fiscal situation an even bigger headache than it is today.

America's position in the world economic order is, thus, under threat. Indeed, the Western world as a whole is increasingly vulnerable to the economic revolution taking place within the emerging world. How the Western nations react to this threat is the subject of Chapter 10.

CHAPTER TEN

COPING WITH THE WEST'S DIMINISHED STATUS

For the Western world, major challenges lie ahead. Economic life is increasingly unpredictable and (dare I say it) unfair. Markets cannot easily resolve the key issues – economic instability, income inequality, state capitalism, demographic change – that are now confronting policymakers in both the Western and emerging nations. The choices open to nations vary, however. In this chapter, I spell out some of the good, bad and downright ugly options open to Western policymakers. We are, I believe, living in a highly unstable world where Western policymakers will be tempted to choose options that, while offering short-term political advantages, could be destructive for globalization and, ultimately, destructive for Western prosperity. We have reached a point where the Western world has to recognize and accept its growing dependence on economic and political ties with the emerging world. For the West to reject these ties would ultimately be damaging not just for the emerging nations but for the West as well.

My concern is a return of the complacency exhibited by Keynes's fictional English gentleman, a man I first introduced in Chapter 2.

Here was an individual who failed to see how the political and economic landscape was beginning to change at the beginning of the twentieth century. It wouldn't take much for the gains of the late twentieth century, like those of the late nineteenth century, to evaporate. Our policymakers could just as easily be sleepwalking into another crisis.

There are, of course, plenty of people willing to defend the West's economic superiority. They do so in a number of different ways. For the religious, the West's superiority represents the triumph of Christian values, a view which might be shared, at least in private, by George W. Bush and Tony Blair. For libertarians, the West's superiority represents a triumph of political freedoms. Freedom of speech, freedom of association and the spread of liberal democracies were instrumental in creating a climate conducive to scientific investigation and associated technological breakthroughs, even though many of those freedoms either occurred too early (the Magna Carta in 1215) or too late (Switzerland finally got around to giving women the vote in 1971) to explain satisfactorily the West's progress. For free-marketeers, the growth of legal systems that created and protected property rights allowed people to enter into binding contracts which, in turn, allowed the invisible hand to do its work (even though the state plays a much bigger role in the allocation of resources in the developed world than it did at the end of the nineteenth century). And there are those who embrace the supposed benefits of the post-industrial 'knowledge economy'. For example, in *The Writing on the Wall* Will Hutton says:

> Soft knowledge is becoming as crucial as hard knowledge in the chain of creating value. By hard knowledge I mean the specific scientific, technological and skill inputs into a particular good or service ... soft knowledge refers to the bundle of less tangible production inputs involving leadership, communication, emotional

intelligence, the disposition to innovate and the creation of social capital that harnesses hard knowledge and permits its effective embodiment in goods and services and – crucially – its customization. Their interaction and combination is the heart of the knowledge economy.

There is something rather theological about this approach, in part because it is so intangible. It encapsulates the idea that the West will continue to outperform because (i) it has done so in the past; (ii) its social arrangements are more 'advanced' than in countries elsewhere; and (iii) liberal democracy has triumphed over all other systems. It's easy to imagine nineteenth-century missionaries proselytizing with similar, albeit more religious, zeal, guiding the peoples of other nations to the one true path.

These arguments, however, don't sit very easily with the history of the twentieth century. Should the First and Second World Wars be described as triumphs of Enlightenment thinking? Should the Great Depression be described as a victory for market forces? Should the credit crunch of 2007/8 be described as a success for soft knowledge? And should Asia's relentless rise over the last sixty years – the greatest economic expansion of all time – be simply described as a multi-decade credit-fuelled flash-in-the-pan, a wealth-creating machine that will ultimately be brought to its heels by crony capitalism and silly bank lending?

That, after all, is the argument. The claim that Asia and, indeed, other emerging economies offer no real threat to Western economic superiority strikes me, however, as absurd, for the reasons outlined in this book. Those who take comfort in the idea of the West's destiny point to Japan's stagnation since the 1990s, arguing that while Japan successfully caught up with the US and Western Europe economically, it never surpassed them, despite projections to the contrary. Indeed, in the effort to do so, it stagnated. As noted in

Chapter 3, however, Japan's lost decades should be seen not as a relative triumph for Western economic systems but, instead, as a sign of what may lie ahead for the developed world as a whole.

For me, the issue for the developed world is not so much that China will fail because it refuses to embrace Enlightenment values, or that Russia will collapse because it isn't behaving in the liberal democratic tradition. Rather, the threat is home-grown. Will the rise of the emerging nations lead the developed world to reject its current liberal values, particularly in the international arena? And what sort of dystopian world might then emerge?

The triumph of the second half of the twentieth century was, ultimately, the degree to which the world economy opened up to allow wealth to spread much more widely. In the first half of the twenty-first century, it's easy to imagine the reverse. For Western commentators, seduced by the superiority of the Western model, it's the emerging economies that are most likely to shut up shop. In Beijing's case, the threat is a repeat of the 1400s, not through the destruction of China's ocean-going fleet but, instead, through the obliteration of new forms of communication such as the Internet in an attempt to preserve the political status quo. In Moscow's case, the failure fully to embrace liberal democracy by, for example, limiting press freedoms will leave the Russian economy facing years as a one-trick energy pony, seemingly condemned to wax and wane on the basis of movements in global energy prices and unable to diversify into other areas. If openness matters, these countries are apparently in trouble.

But wait. These countries are still benefiting from openness in other ways. They increasingly trade with the developed world. They increasingly trade with each other. Mutual trade within the emerging world is a supreme example of Ricardian comparative advantage – China with its manufacturing skills, India with its new software technologies, Brazil and Russia with their various raw materials. They are signing bilateral deals with each other. What we're beginning to see, in fact, is the creation of a new, global Silk Road linking emerging nations in Asia, the Middle East, Eastern Europe, Africa and Latin America via land, sea and the electronic ether. It is a new, major and incredibly important artery linking the nations of the emerging world. There may ultimately be political constraints on economic progress, but it's doubtful that those constraints are going to be triggered in the near future: instead, we are witnessing the creation of new emerging economic synapses that will enable non-liberal democratic political regimes to survive more easily.

The biggest threat to economic openness comes less from the emerging nations – who are beginning to enjoy their time in the economic sun – and more from the West. The US and Europe will need to come to terms with their diminished role in the world economy. No longer will their economies determine the price of raw materials. Their workers will be unable to determine the market price for their labour. Their people will not be able to pursue so easily the rent-seeking agendas that allowed returns on all factors of production in the US and Europe to rise far beyond those seen elsewhere in the world. Their pensioners will not be able to look forward to a guaranteed real income. And they will no longer so easily be able to manage their economic destinies.

How will policymakers come to terms with the West's diminished status? The policy options available are, I believe, a mixture of the good, bad and ugly.

THE GOOD . . .

Many words in this book have been devoted to problems associated with inflation and capital markets, notably the arbitrary redistribution of income and wealth both within and between nations. These problems stem in part from a lack of proper regional or global institutions designed to cope with the twin, but conflicting, desires of monetary sovereignty and free cross-border capital flows.

The easy answer for those who wish to satisfy both desires is to have a world of flexible exchange rates. I argued in Chapter 5, however, that this is not always a workable option, as demonstrated through my fictitious account of the monetary problems associated with Lilliput and Blefuscu. In any case, there is something very strange about the call for many separate currencies. The more currencies there are, the less likely it is that the world will continue to enjoy the benefits of a single capital market. Frequent currency crises have become part and parcel of modern international financial shocks, leading to huge volatility in economic activity and inflation.

Dealing with the Paradox of a Single Capital Market and Many Nations

Policymakers have to stop the pretence and confront head-on the conflict between a single global capital market and the proliferation of nation states, many of which have their own currencies. Either nations can attempt to hang on to their financial sovereignty by reintroducing capital controls or, instead, new institutions need to be developed which can pool financial sovereignty effectively.

The idea of dampening down capital markets through capital controls has a long and rich history and was, of course, part of the post-war international financial consensus: if countries wanted to control simultaneously their exchange rates and their domestic inflation rates, they had no choice but to regulate capital inflows and outflows. As that consensus began to unravel in the 1970s with the failure of the Bretton Woods system of fixed but adjustable exchange rates, countries slowly moved away from capital controls to the world we're now living in. In a world of constant financial innovation, it became increasingly difficult to impose capital controls successfully.

Moreover, capital controls allowed countries to pursue bad domestic policies for too long, ultimately to their own detriment.

Nevertheless, the abolition of capital controls has hardly been plain sailing. Some economists foresaw the problems associated with newly liberalized capital markets. James Tobin (1918–2002), for example, suggested in 1972 a (now-eponymous) tax – to be paid on foreign-exchange transactions – to limit speculative cross-border capital flows. He feared that the failures of Bretton Woods would be replaced by anarchy in the capital markets. On occasion, he was proved right.

Enthusiasm for some kind of capital control has recently returned (as I wrote this book, capital controls were making a comeback: Brazil and Taiwan, for example, introduced capital controls in November 2009). In the light of the 2007/8 credit crunch, central banks began to argue the need for two separate policy instruments: short-term interest rates to control inflation and some kind of 'macro-prudential' policy to limit the impact of unstable capital inflows on domestic bank lending. In the macro-prudential world, banks would be forced to put aside extra savings in the form of higher levels of capital during the years of cross-border lending feast as an insurance against the famine that was likely to follow. In other words, there would be an attempt to limit the domestic implications of cross-border capital flows by imposing the equivalent of a variable tax on the banking system.

At the global level, however, these kinds of reforms seem rather messy. If one country alone imposes them, that country might end up with some protection against the volatility induced by currency speculation, for example. In the UK's case, a policy to force banks to raise their capital ratios during cross-border lending booms might limit the extent of speculation in the domestic housing market. If, however, all countries went down this path, it's difficult to see anything other than the financial equivalent of the primordial soup

223

developing: at the very least, cross-border flows of capital would drop and many countries might find themselves cut off from international capital markets altogether; indeed, the world might descend into capital market protectionism, a mirror-image of the infamous Smoot–Hawley trade tariff, enacted by US Congress in 1930. Whatever the problems associated with the disruptive effects of capital flows, it's difficult to avoid the broader conclusion that their huge increase since the 1970s has been instrumental in raising living standards in many parts of the world. As I have reiterated throughout this book, openness matters.

Time for Tea and a Lesson from Europe

There is, however, a far more radical option. It's indirectly linked to tea or, at least, to the international tea crisis of the eighteenth century and the principle of 'no taxation without representation'. A modern-day version might be 'no monetary decisions without representation'. Policymakers could collectively choose to do something about the dollar's dominance in the world's financial system.

As with so many issues in this book, the tea crisis involved the British East India Company. The Company had been granted a monopoly on the importation of tea into the UK. The tea was then auctioned off to wholesalers who could then redistribute the tea to the colonies. The colonies, meanwhile, were allowed to buy their tea only from the UK. The arrangement led to excessively high prices for tea, monopoly rents for the East India Company and bumper tax revenues for the British government.

There was, however, a hitch. The high price of British tea led to an acute problem with smuggling. Dutch tea was considerably cheaper. Some of this tea was smuggled to the UK for illicit domestic consumption. To deal with this problem, the price of tea sold in Britain was lowered, thus reducing both the incentive for smuggling and the government's tax take. The government needed revenue, however, and decided the colonies were a soft target. The colonists of North America, not surprisingly, were less than enthusiastic about this idea. They, after all, were supposed to be taxed only locally and not by the government in London. Their opposition spilled over, alongside crates of tea, with the Boston Tea Party of 1773. The rest, as they say, is history.

Even if the US isn't rigging the international financial system in quite the same way as the East India Company and the British government fixed the international tea market in the eighteenth century, other countries are suffering from what I'll call monetary 'decisions without representation'. US monetary decisions reach far and wide for reasons spelt out earlier. Yet the Federal Reserve has no real duty to worry about the rest of the world. For a heavily indebted US economy, persistent dollar depreciation is an attractive option. It imposes a burden on the rest of the world. Unlike the tea crisis, the burden is carried by America's creditors, not foreign taxpayers. The principle, though, is similar. It is not a good one.

As argued in Chapter 9, we could end up in a world where the dollar is rejected, where nations go their separate ways, where the agenda of globalization is increasingly determined outside the US and where, in the steadfast defence of monetary sovereignty, globalization in all likelihood goes into retreat. There is, however, another option.

The blueprint for radical reform can be found in Europe. It's called the European Central Bank. Its establishment left individual European nations without domestic monetary sovereignty. Germany, France, Italy and others in effect pooled their monetary interests together. This was a logical extension of the European Single Market which, in 1992, had finally put an end to capital controls within the European Union.

The unusual feature of the European Central Bank, at least compared with other central banks, is that it has no fixed geographical jurisdiction. The Federal Reserve has to worry only about the fifty

American states. The Bank of England needs to concern itself only with the so-called home nations (if it ever came to pass, Scottish independence would probably lead to the introduction of the euro north of the border, reducing the Bank of England's responsibilities even further). The European Central Bank, in contrast, cannot easily tell from one year to the next which countries will fall within its remit. When the euro was first formed, it wasn't obvious that, in the years to come, Greece would give up its drachma, Slovenia its tolar, Cyprus its pound, Malta its lira or Slovakia its koruna in favour of the euro.

Widening euro membership presents an interesting antidote to the conflict between a single global capital market and the proliferation of nation states. In effect, it reduces the monetary sovereignty of nation states while allowing them to maintain sovereignty in other areas, at least to the extent allowable under European Union law. Importantly, those who join the euro have voting rights on monetary policy. Unlike other currency arrangements – full-scale dollarizations and the various currency pegs arrangements described in Chapter 5 – membership of the euro gives a country a seat at the policy table. There is a loss of sovereignty, but it is not a complete loss. Meanwhile, the trials and tribulations of currency upheavals are, at least in theory, permanently removed.[1]

To date, euro membership is confined to members of the European Union and is contingent on countries meeting specified 'convergence criteria'. Like any club, therefore, the euro has a strict membership policy. That policy, however, could change. European Union membership could widen further. The convergence criteria might be relaxed (in the case of Italy and Greece they were not imposed rigorously). Or, signalling a much bigger revolution, perhaps a time will come when countries not in the European Union may be able to join the euro.

Imagine, for example, that Turkey joins the European Union. Turkey's membership would signal, once and for all, that the

European Union was not, as some might claim, a specifically Christian union. Would Turkish membership begin to change the nature of Europe? Recognizing this changed nature, would other countries seek to become more closely integrated in the financial aspects of the European project, even if they were geographically detached? In this very different world, it wouldn't be so difficult imagining euro membership extending eastwards to Central Asia and to the Levant and southwards to North Africa. Indeed, such an arrangement would not be unlike the Roman Empire 2,000 years ago, where peoples were connected around the entire Mediterranean Sea. This time, however, the connections would be on a voluntary basis – an empire of equals, if you like.

If this could happen in Europe and its near neighbours, then perhaps similar developments might eventually occur elsewhere. It's unlikely we'll ever see the Chairman of the Federal Reserve and the Governor of the People's Bank of China sitting down in the same room deciding on a common monetary policy for the US and China even though, as an economist, I could probably make a good case for regular Sino–US monetary meetings. Other associations, however, are easier to imagine. Why not, for example, have a single North American currency extending across Canada, the US and Mexico? Eventually, this new currency could spread further south, with countries in Central and Southern America also taking part and, in the process, receiving voting rights. After all, Panama and Ecuador are already 'dollarized', but, unlike my suggested new arrangement, they currently have no voting rights over US dollar monetary policy.

The same process, meanwhile, could happen in Asia. I argued in Chapter 9 that China is already pushing for the renminbi to have a bigger international role. Why not go one step further and create an Asian monetary union? Could China and Japan, for example, bury their differences and end up with a common currency? Might India also want to take part? If these countries did so, would South Korea still hang on to its won? Would the Thai baht, the Philippine peso and the Indonesian rupiah then survive?

Admittedly, many of these ideas are no more than flights of fancy.[2] The euro was created only after many decades of, at times, difficult political integration forced through by the common desire to avoid the conflicts of Europe's past.[3] The US doesn't have the same incentives as far as the Americas are concerned. China and India also have limited incentives from an Asian perspective. Common currencies would, however, help to remove one of the key asymmetries that, today, make the financial world so unstable, namely, the dominant role in international transactions of the dollar.

At the moment, the US Treasury and Federal Reserve seem to hold all the cards, just as the British government and East India Company did in the late eighteenth century. This is not sustainable. Either countries eventually go their separate ways – as happened with the American Revolution – or, instead, they pool together their monetary and financial interests, giving all those involved a seat at the table, subject to the rules of the club.

Domestic Reform: Important but Secondary

More can also be done at the domestic level. In a world of winners and losers, Western governments could spend more time thinking about the redistributional consequences of globalization, particularly through the tax system. This is not a book about tax reform, but the growing inequalities that have developed over the last thirty years cannot, in my view, easily be explained purely through domestic developments. If globalization is to continue, a healthy debate over how the losers from globalization should be compensated is surely necessary. At the moment, there is too much denial, perhaps because politicians think they are impotent to act in the midst of the storm generated by the emerging powerhouses. Nevertheless, the case for maximizing growth with no regard for the distribution of that growth is fading fast: the gains are distributed so narrowly that the majority of Americans, British and others are just not benefiting from apparent national economic success. This, ultimately, is a recipe for conflict and the rise of extremist views.

Domestic reforms are, however, secondary: what matters more than anything else is establishing more stable and sustainable economic relationships between the developed and emerging worlds because, without these, domestic reforms can all too easily turn into protectionism. Improved international economic relationships require the dollar's role to be reappraised, either as part of a grand plan or, alternatively, in the light of its growing rejection by the new economic superpowers.

. . . THE BAD . . .

Since the end of the Second World War, the world has moved, inch by inch, towards a system of multilateral arrangements. Some of these – like the Bretton Woods exchange-rate system – have not survived. Others – such as the United Nations – have persisted even though their strictures have often been ignored. The icing on the cake for multilateralism was, arguably, the fall of the Berlin Wall. The collapse in Soviet communism created freedoms for many countries which had previously been under the Soviet yoke. Some of these countries joined the European Union. Others joined NATO. Some joined both. Russia itself joined the G7, turning it into the G8. And, as we saw at the end of Chapter 2, the G8 is being supplanted by the G20.

These events, however, can equally be described in very different terms. The widening of NATO membership to Central and Eastern Europe is construed by Russia as an attack on its sphere of influence. Discussions about possible membership for Georgia or the Ukraine naturally create anxiety in Moscow (in much the same way that Cuba's willingness to become a base for Russian missiles created anguish in Washington in 1962). As Sir Christopher Meyer, the former British ambassador to Washington, notes, 'The fall of the Soviet Union did not wipe the slate clean. The Russia that we are dealing with today, with its fear of encirclement, its suspicion of foreigners and natural appetite for autocracy, is as old as the hills, long pre-dating communism. It is a Russia that will never be reassured by the West's protestations of pacific intent as it pushes Nato and the EU ever eastwards.'[4] Put another way, the fall of Soviet communism has reopened imperial rivalries and led to the re-emergence of ethnic and religious strains which, for so many decades, had lain dormant. The 1990s conflict in former Yugoslavia underscores this conclusion all too clearly.

China, also, has reason to be suspicious about the new 'multilateral' world. At first sight, China has fewer reasons to worry about organizations such as NATO. However, NATO's operations take place in many different parts of the world. Its active involvement in Afghanistan has an obvious explanation but is, nevertheless, odd from a geographical perspective: on the last occasion I looked at a map, Kabul was a long way from the North Atlantic. Moreover, in the 1995 *Study on Enlargement*, NATO established the following conditions for new members:

> countries seeking NATO membership would have to be able to demonstrate that they have fulfilled certain requirements. These include:
> - a functioning democratic political system based on a market economy;
> - the fair treatment of minority populations;
> - a commitment to the peaceful resolution of conflicts;
> - the ability and willingness to make a military contribution to NATO operations; and

- a commitment to democratic civil-military relations and institutional structures.

NATO is, thus, a military club for like-minded democracies with market economies. China doesn't qualify. This immediately creates room for tensions. If, for example, NATO can operate in Afghanistan, perhaps it will also operate in Sudan or other African 'rogue states' accused of harbouring terrorists. If so, what happens to China's economic interests in Africa, which have expanded so rapidly over the last twenty years as China's appetite for raw materials has expanded at an exponential pace?

We are in danger of returning to the political games of the late nineteenth century, focused on the 'enabling resources' of land and fuel. The spike in food prices in 2007 and 2008 led some Asian countries – including China, South Korea and India – to strike deals with leaders of African states to provide access to agricultural land, typically in return for promises regarding the development of infrastructure and logistics, both of which are severely lacking in many African nations. Whether these deals work for all involved – most obviously the local smallholders with poorly defined property rights – is another matter. Nevertheless, they can be regarded as a mechanism to safeguard food supplies for rapidly advancing Asian nations which, themselves, are facing increasing problems associated with growing water shortages and shifting dietary preferences.

Even though these deals are routinely described as land grabs, they are, in reality, no more than a minor version of the activities pursued by European nations before the twentieth century. They reveal, however, an underlying truth about twenty-first-century economic development. Countries will continue to prosper only if they can gain access to food and fuel supplies. Increasingly, nations are beginning to believe that the market, alone, cannot safeguard ongoing prosperity. Bilateral deals are becoming commonplace, creating for some countries privileged access to resources which may, as a consequence, be in short supply for others. If this is a new colonialism, it comes as no surprise: it's merely a response to economies bumping into domestic resource constraints. It also suggests we can expect an increase in non-market outcomes when it comes to the allocation of scarce resources. Adam Smith's invisible hand may no longer be acceptable.

Of course, it's quite possible that bilateral deals will lead to productivity advances which, in turn, will have a hugely positive effect on, for example, agricultural production, boosting supplies to such a degree that food prices will fall rather than rise. In those circumstances, worries about food security would surely begin to fade. Equally, technologies which, in the past, were seen as too closely linked to Dr Frankenstein may be rehabilitated if food prices rise too far. Genetically modified crops will, I suspect, become increasingly acceptable in the same way that nuclear energy is now seen as an increasingly effective antidote to climate change. Nevertheless, the language with regard to food supplies is changing for the worse. Countries increasingly talk about the need for food 'self-sufficiency'. Although this debate is sometimes bundled together with concerns regarding the environment – it's better to grow food locally than to fly it in from the other side of the world – it's increasingly clear that securing food supplies has become, for many governments, a strategic security issue.

Thus we may be heading towards a world outlined in Chapter 7 full of smoke-filled rooms and questionable deals behind closed doors. Marking a departure from the international free-market principles that have dominated economic life since the 1980s, this world would surely represent the renewed rise of economic nationalism and, possibly, a return to the economic values that dominated the interwar period.

One counter-argument is that the US and China are now so dependent on one another economically that it is impossible to imagine a breakdown in relations without severely damaging consequences for both sides and, indeed, for the rest of the world. But we know from history – and from Keynes's English gentleman – that arrangements of mutual economic benefit all too often hang from gossamer threads, ready to snap at any moment. In fact, I suspect China would emerge from any collapsed Sino–US relationship in a relatively stronger position.

It is commonly assumed that China's exports have grown in line with US consumer spending and that China, therefore, is ultimately a satellite of the US economy. The annual rate of growth of China's exports has, in fact, been three times faster than the growth rate of US consumer spending. The revolution in economic affairs that has taken place since the 1980s has not been driven by the demands of US consumers but rather by the increased efficiency of the Chinese and other emerging economic producers. Their enhanced production capacities are one of the key reasons why Asia's share of global output – and, hence, global demand – is set to rise so rapidly in the years ahead.

In a world of bilateral deals, Asia's voice will, therefore, become much louder. Why should Russia sell its gas only to Europe when it will also benefit from a rapidly expanding market to its east? Why should Brazil worry too much about US demand for its metals when the key marginal consumers will be coming not from the North Atlantic but on the other side of the Pacific? How will the US continue to exert influence in the Middle East if some of the key players – such as Iran – are able to become increasingly cosy with China, Russia and other countries to the East, for example by means of the Shanghai Cooperation Organization? For much of the twentieth century, countries have had to define themselves economically primarily in terms of their relationship with the US or Europe. That may no longer be true in the twenty-first century. Indeed, there are already signs of change. Brazil is now far more dependent on China as a destination for its exports. Russia is much more interested in trade with Europe, the Near East, Central Asia and China and has no strong link with the US. India and China still depend on the US but they now increasingly trade with each other. The US still dominates, but, as a trading partner, it is facing relative decline. European nations are already in decline.

Whether or not we see a return to bilateral deals, it's likely that patterns of trade will continue to change, with the US and Europe increasingly squeezed out of the equation. Asia's progress reflects both political openness and the benefits of new technologies, without which capital could not swirl around the world in ever-increasing volumes. Is it too much to suggest that the ease with which capital can cross borders and time zones represents a revolution as great as that triggered by the pioneering explorers who discovered the New World and rounded the Cape of Good Hope, in the process undermining the Silk Road and the economic and political power of Islam? If so, does the rise of Asia in the twenty-first century mirror the rise of Europe in the sixteenth century and beyond? And what then happens to the future of Western values?

. . . AND THE UGLY

Can the Western powers manage to maintain control? Yes, but at a significant price. The developed world would have to disengage from the emerging world. The frameworks to do so already exist. The North American Free Trade Association and the European Union could quite easily become aggressive, inward-looking customs unions, maintaining openness for the privileged few while ignoring relations with the rest of the world. There is no shortage of supporters. Congress is full of people with their pet protectionist projects. And, a few years ago, I was quizzed by a former finance minister from an EU country who wanted to know why Europe bothered to trade with the rest of the world: 'Surely', he said, 'we can produce all we need here in Europe.' It's as if the second half of the twentieth century never happened. Then again, politicians have always preferred to listen to their constituents than to a group of economists: the Smoot–Hawley tariff contributed to the massive increase in economic nationalism in the 1930s even though it was opposed at the time by, amongst others, 1,028 US economists.

Even today, not all our markets are open, despite the oft-repeated claim that the West supports free trade. In some industries, we're still living in a mediaeval world of workers' guilds protected by metaphorical city walls designed to keep foreigners out. The European Union's Common Agricultural Policy is a case in point. As a result of excessive subsidies, European farmers produce more than the international market can take. Market prices are forced lower, pushing farmers in poorer parts of the world out of business (in mediaeval times, it was a matter of routine to venture occasionally beyond the city walls to destroy any fledgling cottage industries: modern-day subsidies achieve much the same result).

Trade protectionism is bad enough but, as already noted, there's also the risk of capital-market protectionism. Governments could enact legislation to ensure that savings were invested at home rather than abroad. As with Dubai Ports World, they could refuse to sell assets to 'untrustworthy' foreigners. The rise of state capitalism is an obvious trigger for a newly 'national' approach to the balance between savings and investment, thereby reducing the chances of allocating capital efficiently on a global basis. Another trigger is the 2007/8 credit crunch: if cross-border capital flows are deemed to have disruptive economic effects, either cyclically or because of the burden on future taxpayers, why not restrict banks merely to domestic financial activities, thereby reversing the massive opening of capital flows that has taken place since the 1980s?

Imagine the consequences. The West wouldn't so easily be able to invest in the emerging world, which would lead to a reduction in returns on capital and, thus, lower savings for its pensioners. Resources wouldn't be allocated so efficiently, which would reduce global output. Trade barriers would restrict cross-border specializations. The price of tradeable goods would rise. American Treasury yields would spike higher as China and others disengaged from the world's bond markets. Economic autarky would replace the freedoms we have grown accustomed to over the last thirty years. We'd head back to a world last seen in the first half of the twentieth century, when economic and political crises on the grandest of scales occurred with monotonous and frightening regularity.

In the midst of this protectionist endeavour, there would probably be a series of currency crises, offering a repeat of some of the conditions seen in the 1970s. With the US retreating from the world economy, the rest of the world would surely retreat from the US dollar. China would push harder to turn the renminbi into a new reserve currency, in the process accepting losses on its holdings of US Treasuries. Faced with a declining dollar, the US would suffer both an increase in import prices and much higher interest rates. Retreat from the global economy comes at a very high price.

The rise in economic nationalism would, in all likelihood, be linked to a descent into ethnic rivalry. The first half of the twentieth century was characterized not just by a collapse of the international economic order but by the growth of racism in parts of the world that had, supposedly, benefited from the peak of Enlightenment thinking. The *Clash of Civilizations* offers a large-scale threat to a more integrated world.[5] The rise of casual racism – growing support for the xenophobic British National Party in the UK is just one example – provides a small-scale threat. It's not difficult to imagine Gordon Brown's promise of 'British jobs for British workers' becoming a clarion call for a new anti-immigration and anti-foreigner approach to policymaking.[6] With the developed world running out of workers, this would surely create conditions in which the time bomb of demographic ageing would go off with a particularly big bang.

And then there's the possibility of war. As the emerging world becomes economically stronger, so in time it will also become militarily more powerful.[7] One possible response from the West is to develop a 'divide and rule' strategy, selling weapons and technologies to 'friendly' emerging nations to counter aggression coming from more obvious foes. This, however, can easily backfire, as the US discovered with its backing of Saddam Hussein's Iraq against Iran in the 1980s. More generally, the West needs to address awkward questions regarding political ideas and property rights. As NATO and European Union membership spreads eastwards, will there come a point where the self-determination of individual nations in Eastern Europe and Central Asia clashes with, for example, Russia's domestic security concerns? The Crimean War (1853–6) provides a nineteenth-century example. The war was indirectly the consequence of a dispute between France and Russia about protection of Christians in the Holy Land in the light of the diminishing powers of the Ottoman Empire; but it was ultimately a battle about spheres of influence.

What happens if the property rights surrounding investments by the developed world in the emerging nations prove to be inadequate? Investors in the developed world are expecting more youthful populations in the emerging world to work hard for them in their retirement: is this really an economic match made in heaven? And, in the attempt to secure food and fuel supplies, will nations find themselves fighting each other for access to scarce resources? That, after all, was one of the sources of conflict between Japan and the West in the Second World War. Japan's decision to attack Pearl Harbor in 1941 was partly prompted by its military government's response to the embargo placed on Japan by the Americans, British, Dutch (in exile) and Australians. The aim of the embargo was, of course, to curb Japan's aggression, particularly in China, by starving it of much-needed steel and fuel. Instead, Japan's rulers became even more aggressive, believing that a successful conclusion of its war with China could only be reached by a Japanese move into Malaya and the Dutch East Indies alongside a pre-emptive attack on the US fleet to prevent the US from siding with the UK in the event of a Japanese pre-emptive strike.

The history of the world is full of strategic miscalculations. There's no reason to believe the future will be any different. The West can play its part in ensuring the smooth progression of globalization, but it can also throw the whole process into reverse.

CONCLUSION

EVERYONE'S A WINNER?

For many people, the collapse of Soviet-style communism and the reform of Chinese communism signalled the triumph of free market thinking. An economic and political nirvana beckoned. Liberal markets were the secret behind the West's economic success over the last few hundred years. It seemed to follow that, with the spread of market capitalism far and wide, other nations and their people could look forward to a future of Western-style economic progress. The West, meanwhile, would continue to advance, making profits from its investments in the emerging world while delivering continued productivity advances inspired by the enlightened values of liberal democracy: freedom of speech and freedom of association.

These arguments, however, are unsound. Western progress did not depend solely on free market capitalism. Nation states, and the empires they created, frequently intervened to protect 'commercial' interests. Sometimes, these interventions were supportive of free markets. An effective legal system, after all, is a necessary condition of free market success: without property rights, there is no incentive to save, borrow or invest. At other times, however, these interventions were deliberately designed to uphold one nation's interests against another's. Ironically, market forces appeared to work well within the Western world, in part because they were not allowed to work elsewhere. In the nineteenth century, Western nations rigged market rules to suit themselves, whether through acts of protectionism, drug trafficking or the law of the gunboat. Through much of the twentieth century, experiments with Marxist-Leninism kept many nations in the economic deep-freeze, even as the developed nations flourished.

Market-led solutions are profoundly amoral and, thus, fail to address many of the key issues of political economy. Market forces may lead to more efficient outcomes, but efficiency says nothing about whether the rewards are fairly distributed. For markets to provide widespread benefits, property rights and the rule of law are most certainly required, but they may not be enough. As Adam Smith wrote in *The Wealth of Nations*, 'Wherever there is great property, there is great inequality . . . the affluence of the rich excites the indignation of the poor, who are often driven by want, and prompted by envy, to invade his possessions . . . The acquisition of valuable and extensive property, therefore, necessarily requires the establishment of civil government.' This view can be taken in one of two ways, depending on which side of the political spectrum you sit. Either the rich need the protection of civil government or the government has to intervene to calm the poor through an official 'invasion' – by redistributive taxation – of the possessions of the rich.[1]

As markets open up all over the world, so the West's ability to rig those markets to suit its own interests is on the wane. As a result, for many in the West, the market's amorality threatens to become a significant problem, increasingly reshaping attitudes towards globalization. The world economy is growing quickly and, as a result, many millions of people are being pulled out of poverty. The gap between rich and poor (but not very poor) nations is narrowing. Yet the gap between rich and poor within nations is widening. In relative terms, at least, globalization appears to be creating a world of winners and losers. The unleashing of market forces around the world and the contemporaneous, if paradoxical, rise of state capitalism have had surprising effects which, in my view, policymakers in the developed world have not fully understood.

The barometers by which policymakers assess economic weather conditions have started to give false readings. Trade flows between the developed and emerging worlds have flourished, but this isn't purely the Ricardian trade of comparative advantage. Japan's experience suggests that outsourcing and off-shoring can lead to domestic economic stagnation. Pretending that Japan is 'different' and therefore carries no immediate relevance for the US or the UK may be comforting but probably isn't right. Capital can cross borders more easily. In the process, the economic rents earned by some Western workers – in the form of high wages, healthcare benefits, lucrative pensions and employment rights – are under threat.

Long-term interest rates – the rates that matter for savers and for businesses – have fallen victim to the savings behaviour of emerging nations, most obviously China. As a result, it's become increasingly difficult for investors to work out the 'right' price for all sorts of assets, ranging from equities to housing and from commodities to asset-backed securities. As uncertainty has increased, the volatility of asset prices has risen sharply. After many decades in which the easy answer to pension saving was 'buy equities', there are no longer any hard-and-fast rules. In fact, the only hard rule now is that most Western savers will not be able to accumulate sufficient assets to allow a comfortable retirement. The rise of state capitalism provides a threat to cross-border property rights for ageing Western populations.

Meanwhile, the growing emerging-nation demand for raw materials will reduce the real value of Western wealth because of higher energy and food prices.

There is no pot of gold at the end of the rainbow of investment opportunities. As the emerging economies expand, so their own claims on global resources will rise. In the absence of a productivity boost in the world economy the likes of which have never before been seen, this will inevitably lead to a redistribution of global income and wealth. There are investment opportunities in the emerging world, but it's also important to learn the lessons of the gold rush: everyone can dream of being rich, but a lot of people may become poor in the pursuit of their dreams.

If inflation is low and stable, economic weather conditions are supposed to be set fair. This conclusion, however, is no longer safe. Low inflation may be more a result of good luck than of good judgement, a reflection of external forces beyond the control or influence of a central bank. Emerging economies have become the key players in commodity markets while their own monetary decisions increasingly have an impact on financial conditions in the developed world.

Policymakers, however, are human: they like to take the credit for economic success, even where no credit is due. And, in doing so, they keep interest rates either too low or too high, accepting near-term success on inflation at the cost of longer-term economic instability. Put another way, the achievement of price stability may inadvertently lead to the creation of deeper economic imbalances of the kind which contributed to the 2007/8 credit crunch.

Our economic barometers tell us more today about income distribution than they do about macroeconomic stability. Domestic explanations for the growing gap between haves and have-nots work up to a point, but the most compelling reason for widening income inequality is the arrival on the world stage of the emerging nations. There are plenty of benefits from globalization, but those benefits are either going to the many in the emerging world or the very few in the developed world. A big chunk of the developed world's population has derived little direct benefit from globalization.

The rise of state capitalism can be understood more easily given this background of rising income inequality. Nation states will increasingly be interested in subverting market mechanisms to ensure domestic social stability. There's nothing new about this process: from the East India Company to Halliburton, the West has successfully played this game for centuries. The difference this time around, however, is that China and Russia, in particular, can also play this big boys' game. Indeed, the growing links between emerging nations suggest the rise of new alliances that will ultimately threaten Western interests. Imagine, for example, that emerging nations are increasingly able to rig food and energy markets to suit their own purposes.

Meanwhile, the global financial system is increasingly unstable on a systemic basis, a reflection of moves towards a single capital market, multiple (and multiplying) nation states and, at the heart of the issue, a US dollar that can no longer easily serve the interests of the world economy very well. It is possible to piece together policies that would allow a smooth evolution away from a dollar-based financial system – notably through the creation of major currency 'blocs' in which individual nations would all enjoy monetary voting rights – but what is possible isn't always probable. The alternative, from a Chinese point of view, is to bolster the renminbi's reserve currency status. This will be many years in the making. Meanwhile, the dollar's demise as a reserve currency will inject greater volatility into the world's financial system and, for US citizens, will doubtless hugely raise the cost of imports, making US consumers worse off. It's another way of saying that, for too long, the US has been living beyond its means.

Globalization is not one-way traffic. Over the centuries, there have been many reversals and many shifts in economic and political tectonic plates. At least some of those reversals have come about because of the political rejection of the forces of globalization. Markets work because nations allow them to: nations can just as easily stop them working if they wish to. The big mistake in this latest wave of globalization has been the developed world's collective failure to think about globalization's evolution from the perspective of both winners and losers. Pretending that everyone is automatically a winner both raises expectations and sows the seeds of future disenchantment.

LOSING BIG OR LOSING SMALL?

A few years ago, I asked a German friend how his nation had coped with the economic backlash that followed reunification. West Germany, after all, had been an economic powerhouse in the 1970s and 1980s, yet its performance had withered in the mid-1990s. Growth had ebbed away, taxes had gone up, property prices had fallen and unemployment had risen.

The answer was simple. West Germans knew that the integration of the East would be economically expensive. They knew there would be severe adjustment costs. They knew sacrifices would have to be made. They also knew, however, that the sacrifices were worth it. The German people had been separated by a physical and economic wall for too long.

The developed world as a whole, however, doesn't feel the collective warmth towards the emerging world that West Germans felt for East Germans. Globalization delivers tremendous benefits, but for the developed world comes with a big bill attached. The risk is that, in time, the developed world refuses to pay up. At that point, globalization disintegrates, whether through protectionism, financial collapse, ethnic and religious rivalry or war. The developed world needs to decide whether it wants the emerging nations to enjoy the economic opportunities that, for so long, had been enjoyed only by the privileged Western few, or, instead, whether it wants to retreat into a bunker that will only leave the world as a whole facing political and economic catastrophe.

If the developed world goes down the first path, it will have to accept a smaller role in world affairs. The emergence of the G20 marks only the beginning of a major shift in global economic and political power. Western workers may still benefit from income gains, but those gains will be smaller than in the past. Pensioners will find life increasingly difficult: a mixture of low interest rates and high commodity prices will reduce both their incomes and their spending power. Ageing Western populations will be forced to sell assets – increasingly to new owners in the emerging nations – and, in the process, will lose control of the 'commanding heights' of the global economy. Our children will have to compete with graduates from the emerging world for the best jobs. They will also have to pay the taxes to repay the huge debts of the current generation. Lower US growth will shrink military muscle, reducing the global reach of today's most powerful military machine. Governments will have to think far more seriously about income and wealth redistribution. Otherwise, they will find that popular support for globalization begins to wane.

This might sound bleak. The alternative, however, is far worse. Severing the links altogether between the developed and emerging worlds would make life much more difficult: no cheap access to Chinese savings, a collapse in the dollar, a drying-up of world trade, a meltdown in global capital markets, a string of government debt defaults, a massive increase in unemployment and the possibility of war. The world economy has flourished since the Second World War and, in particular, since the end of the Cold War. To throw openness away in an attempt to defend Western interests might be a vote-winner, but it would ultimately be a job-loser: the Depression tells you all you need to know about what happens when economies disengage from one another. It is surely better for the West to lose relatively than it is for the world as a whole to lose absolutely. As its population ages, I hope the West gains the wisdom to make the right choice.

NOTES

PREFACE

1. See, for example, J. Campbell Gibson and Emily Lennon, *Historical Census Statistics on the Foreign-born Population of the United States: 1850–1990*, Population Division, US Bureau of the Census, Washington, DC, 20233-8800, February 1999, Population Division Working Paper No. 29. The number of immigrants coming into the US today is higher than it was in the nineteenth century but that is a function of the much bigger global population. In relation to the size of the indigenous population, the proportion of foreign-born citizens is now a lot lower: in the second half of the nineteenth century the proportion stood at between 13 and 14 per cent whereas, over the last fifty years, it has oscillated between 4 and 8 per cent. The proportionate economic impact of immigration has, thus, faded over the last half-century.
2. Source: US Census Bureau.
3. The range of arguments is vast. Supporters of globalization include Martin Wolf with his *Why Globalization Works* (Yale University Press, New Haven, 2004) and Thomas Friedman's *The World is Flat: A Brief History of the 21st Century* (Farrar, Strauss, Giroux, New York, 2005). Its detractors – using varying arguments – include Joseph Stiglitz (*Globalization and its Discontents* [Penguin, London, 2003]), Naomi Klein (*No Logo* [Fourth Estate, New York, 1999]) and Noreena Hertz (*The Silent Takeover* [The Free Press, New York, 2002]). My sense, however, is that many of these books are written as if the West is still pulling the strings – either governments or corporations. This book suggests otherwise.

CHAPTER 1: WIMBLEDON, THE OLYMPICS AND SCARCITY

1. Source: *Washington Post*, 23 January 2007.
2. Given on 6 December 2006, the full speech is available at <http://www.hm-treasury gov.uk/prebud_pbr06_speech.htm>. In Mr Brown's reference to the 'major

economies', he conveniently forgot to mention China, India, Brazil and other emerging nations.

3. Source: International Olympic Committee at <http://www.olympic.org>

4. Owens won four gold medals.

5. A case of 'No we can't' rather than 'Yes we can'.

6. Source: International Olympic Committee. The US achieved a haul of eighty-three medals in Los Angeles in 1984 but the Soviet Union chose not to turn up for those Games after the US had boycotted the 1980 Moscow Olympics in protest at the Soviet invasion of Afghanistan. To put China's gold medal haul into context, the Middle Kingdom managed to win only five gold medals in the Seoul Olympics in 1988.

7. For an informed discussion of the client state problem, see Tony Judt's *Post War: A History of Europe since 1945* (William Heinemann, London, 2005).

8. *An Inquiry into the Nature and Causes of the Wealth of Nations*, first published in 1776. As it turned out, this was a remarkably auspicious year for political and economic developments.

9. See, for example, 'The market for lemons: quality uncertainty and the market mechanism', the groundbreaking paper by George A. Akerlof, *Quarterly Journal of Economics*, 84.3 (1970), pp. 488–500.

10. For an interesting modern discussion of the role of 'good government', see Timothy Besley's ' 'Principled Agents?' The Political Economy of Good Government', The Lindahl Lectures (Oxford, 2006). The case for government in general is famously well expressed in Thomas Hobbes's *Leviathan,* where the 'state of nature' gives rise to continuous wars leaving human lives 'solitary, poor, nasty, brutish and short'. Even the best of governments, however, have difficulties coming up with policies that work in the international arena.

11. Thomas Malthus (ed. G. Gilbert), *An Essay on the Principle of Population* (Oxford University Press, Oxford, 1993), p. 18.

12. For an attempt to rehabilitate Thomas Malthus, read Gregory Clark's *A Farewell to Alms: A Brief Economic History of the World* (Princeton University Press, Princeton, 2007).

13. From *The Communist Manifesto*, by Karl Marx and Friedrich Engels. For an update on Marx and globalization, see Meghnad Desai's *Marx's Revenge: The Resurgence of Capitalism and the Death of Statist Socialism* (Verso, London, 2002).

14. Smith is justly famous for his *Wealth of Nations,* but his earlier *Theory of Moral Sentiments* (1759) provides the moral and legal foundations for all that followed.

15. Booms and busts were also a common feature of late nineteenth-century economic progress.

16. Although, with polonium poisonings in London, the presence of Russian spooks cannot be ruled out. See, for example, Edward Lucas's *The New Cold War: How the Kremlin Menaces both Russia and the West* (Bloomsbury, London, 2008).

17. Source: Vodafone.

18. The Oxford University website states the following: 'Oxford's university community is truly international. Students currently come from 138 countries around the world and study a wide range of subjects. They make up one third of our student body, including 14 percent of our full-time undergraduate students and 63 percent of our full-time postgraduates.'

19. Purchasing power parity basis.

20. In 1980, only 15 per cent of urban Chinese families owned a colour television and a refrigerator. In 2004, 70 per cent of families owned a home, mobile phone and a DVD player. Source: Qu Hongbin, *The Great Migration*, HSBC Research, October 2005.

CHAPTER 2: THE SECRETS OF WESTERN SUCCESS

1. The arguments were outlined in *On the Principles of Political Economy and Taxation* (1817).

2. The first 'modern' stock market was established in Amsterdam to trade shares in the Dutch East India Company in 1602.

3. For those who believe the Enlightenment really was a triumph of free markets and liberal thought, it's worth reflecting on the views of David Hume (1711–76), one of Britain's greatest philosophers, on racial differences: 'the Jews in Europe, and the Armenians in the east, have a peculiar character; and the former are as much noted for fraud, as the latter for probity' or 'You may obtain any thing of the negroes by offering them strong drink; and may easily prevail with them to sell, not only their children, but their wives and mistresses, for a cask of brandy.' See Hume's essay '*Of National Characters*' in his *Political Essays*, ed. Knud Haakonssen, Cambridge Texts in the History of Political Thought, Cambridge University Press, Cambridge, 1994, pp 78–92.

4. Protectionist tariffs were unusually high in the US in the late nineteenth century, prompting development economists such as Ha-Joon Chang to argue that 'tariff protection was critical in the development of certain key industries, such as the textile industry in the early nineteenth century and the iron and steel industries in the second half of the nineteenth century' (from *Kicking Away the Ladder: Development Strategy in Historical Perspective* [Anthem, London, 2002]). British wool-makers became increasingly concerned at the end of the seventeenth century about the competition coming from cottons produced in India and elsewhere in Asia. Their agitation led to a ban on cotton imports from the East, which simply prompted the establishment of the Lancashire cotton industry. The Indian cotton industry lost out, unable to compete with the remarkable innovations in spinning, weaving and dyeing that followed and which became key stages in the Industrial Revolution. Ironically, the British wool industry also lost out. Economic advance in particular parts of the world, or in particular industries, has not always been synonymous with rewards for everyone.

5. As Bernard Lewis points out in *What Went Wrong? Western Impact and Middle East Response* (Weidenfeld & Nicolson, London, 2002), the Ottomans were largely uninterested in events taking place on the periphery of the Islamic world.

6. Maddison's *Contours of the World Economy 1–2030 AD: Essays in Macro-economic History* (Oxford University Press, Oxford, 2007) is essential reading.

7. A Malthusian view of the world suggests that the initial gains in per-capita incomes in Europe were related to the outbreaks of plague, which left workers in short supply and therefore pushed up their wages.

8. Keynes wrote the *Consequences* in 1919. He offered a brilliant analysis of the implications of the Treaty of Versailles.

9. Source: D. R. Headrick, *Tools of Empire: Technology and European Imperialism in the Nineteenth Century* (Oxford University Press, Oxford, 1981).

10. British sea power was immortalized in 'Rule Britannia', first heard in 1740, and now sung at the Last Night of the Proms every year in a fit of Union Jack-waving nostalgia for times past. One verse sums it all up: 'The nations, not so blest as thee, must, in their turns, to tyrants fall; while thou shalt flourish great and free, the dread and envy of them all.' The Chinese, for good reason, certainly dreaded the British: the *Nemesis*, a British warship, could operate in just five feet of water, and could therefore be used to impose Britain's will on a technologically backward China during the Opium Wars in the mid-nineteenth century.

11. See *Global Capital Markets: Integration, Crisis and Growth* (Cambridge University Press, Cambridge, 2004).

12. The UK ran a trade deficit, but surpluses in services and in net income from abroad more than offset the shortfall of merchandise exports. The US current account of the balance of payments offers the same mix, but the deficit on trade completely swamps the surpluses elsewhere.

13. Source: OECD *Economic Outlook*, June 2009.

14. The G20 includes the G8 members – the US, Japan, Germany, France, the UK, Italy, Canada and Russia – alongside Argentina, Australia, Brazil, China, India, Indonesia, Mexico, Saudi Arabia, South Africa, South Korea and Turkey and the European Union as a whole. At the time of writing, pressure was mounting for the creation of a G4 including the US, the Eurozone, China and Japan, thereby leaving out in the cold the UK, Russia, Canada, Brazil and India, amongst others.

15. T. Fleming, *The Louisiana Purchase* (John Wiley & Sons, New Jersey, 2003).

CHAPTER 3: THE PLEASURES AND PERILS OF TRADE

1. Audi's UK strapline, '*Vorsprung durch Technik*', literally means 'Advancement through technology'.

2. In the words of the Volkswagen Corporate History Department, 'As far as we can say, there was no official possibility to sell or buy an Audi Quattro in the former GDR before the opening of the Berlin Wall in 1989. But as a GDR citizen could receive such a car as a present from someone in West Germany it is possible that such a car was used in former GDR, although we think this might have happened – if at all – only in very rare cases.'

3. As I wrote this, plans were announced to launch a new eco-friendly Trabant for the twenty-first century.

4. The irony was that British-built cars were, in many cases, as uncompetitive as those manufactured in Soviet Eastern Europe.

5. In 1542, the Portuguese navigator Juan Rodríguez Cabrillo set sail from Mexico on behalf of the Spanish and came across what he thought was an island. He named it California after a sixteenth-century Spanish novel (*The Exploits of Explanadian*) in which there was a reference to a mythical island of that name ruled by Calafía, a pagan queen. California properly fell into Spanish hands in 1769 following the establishment of a number of missions up and down the land. Mexico gained its independence from the Spanish in 1821.

6. See, for example, Paul Samuelson's article 'Where Ricardo and Mill rebut and confirm arguments of mainstream economists supporting globalization', *Journal of Economic Perspectives*, 18.3 (2004), pp. 135–46.

7. See, for example, Alan G. Ahearne; Joseph E. Gagnon; Jane Haltmaier; Steven B. Kamin, *Preventing Deflation: Lessons From Japan's Experience in the 1990s.* published by the Federal Reserve in 2002 and available at <http://www.federalreserve.gov/pubs/ifdp/2002/729/ifdp729.pdf>.

8. According to the 2009 WIR, the top ten non-financial multinationals ranked on the basis of foreign assets were General Electric, Vodafone Group plc, Royal Dutch/Shell, British Petroleum plc, ExxonMobil, Toyota Motor Corporation, Total, Electricité de France, Ford Motor Company and E.ON AG.

9. Source: World Bank, *World Development Indicators*.

10. The calculation is remarkably simple: $(X_{(n,t)} - X_{(n,t-1)})*100/X_{(g,t-1)}$ where $X_{(n,t)}$ denotes exports to country n at time t and where $X_{(g,t-1)}$ represents total exports a year earlier. Adding up all the percentage point contributions in any one year provides total export growth in that year.

11. A press statement released by US Senators Charles Schumer and Lindsey Graham on 17 May 2005 said, 'By rigging its currency between 15 and 40 percent below its appropriate

value, China is giving a subsidy to its imports to the United States and imposing a direct cost on U.S. exporters to China. This unfair advantage has hurt U.S. manufacturers, workers, and farmers and contributed to the U.S. trade imbalance with China growing by 50 per cent since 2001, to a record $120 billion.' See <http://schumer.senate.gov/new_website/record.cfm?id=261020>.

12. The US bilateral trade deficit with Japan has persistently expanded in dollar terms although, since Japan's stagnation in the 1990s, there has been a gradual narrowing of the deficit as a share of US GDP, largely because Japan's economy as a whole has been shrinking as a share of US GDP reflecting Japan's ongoing economic stagnation.

13. Nominal GDP basis.

14. China and other Asian economies fit this pattern very well, but not all emerging economies do so: some, like Russia, are dependent on a limited number of commodities while others, like India, have bypassed manufacturing altogether and have moved straight to the provision of services. In general, though, the picture is correct.

CHAPTER 4: INTERNATIONAL ROULETTE: ANARCHY IN CAPITAL MARKETS

1. Plenty has been written on this period of international financial history. Barry Eichengreen, *Globalizing Capital: A History of the International Monetary System* (Princeton University Press, Princeton, 1996) contains a useful summary.

2. The speech can be found at <http://www.federalreserve.gov/boarddocs/speeches/2005/200503102/>.

3. In every year since 2000, the consensus forecast for US Treasury yields has been too high, suggesting that the link between domestic economic performance and interest rate levels has altered. Source: Consensus Economics and HSBC.

4. That, at least, was the conclusion reached at the time. The sub-prime crisis and credit crunch that followed ten years later suggests this was not solely an issue for Asia specifically or, indeed, for emerging economies more generally.

5. In its semi-annual *Report to Congress on International Economic and Exchange Rate Policies*, the US Treasury typically berates China for its exchange-rate policies, even though at the time of writing it had yet to make the charge that China was a 'currency manipulator'. The October 2009 version of the report can be found at <http://www.treasury.gov/offices/international-affairs/economic-exchange-rates/pdf/FX%20Report%20FINAL%20October%2015%202009.pdf>.

6. Source: HSBC global currency research.

7. The yield on Ukrainian debt had dropped back to around 14.3 per cent by the summer of 2009, but this still implied a big loss in relation to the halcyon pre-credit crunch days.

CHAPTER 5: PRICE STABILITY BRINGS ECONOMIC INSTABILITY

1. It's not easy for policymakers to 're-think' policy. In 1999, at the annual central bankers' symposium organized by the Kansas City Federal Reserve at Jackson Hole in Wyoming, leading central bankers discussed the merits of targeting asset prices under the umbrella title of 'New Challenges for Monetary Policy'. The broad conclusion was that a focus on inflation as conventionally measured was good enough for ongoing economic stability. Economic events in the following decade suggested otherwise. The proceedings of the symposium can be found at <http://www.kc.frb.org/publicat/sympos/1999/sym99prg.htm>.

2. Despite the focus on macroeconomic 'demand management', the key source of friction between Keynesians and Friedmanite monetarists ultimately focused on the extent of market 'failures' and the likely success of any state intervention to prevent or offset these failures.

3. Labour Party Conference, 1976. These words were probably written by Peter Jay.
4. The UK Office for National Statistics has a webpage that allows people to calculate a 'personal' inflation rate. The details can be found at <http://www.statistics.gov.uk/pic/>. In my view, it is an unhelpful idea: if inflation is seen to define the value of money, a personal inflation calculator suggests that the value of money varies from person to person, which is a ridiculous proposition. That people become richer or poorer as a result of changes in relative prices says nothing about the value of money itself: the same effects could happen in a barter economy where money did not exist.
5. In homage to Jonathan Swift.
6. In the modern era, the first country to adopt an explicit inflation target was New Zealand in 1989–90.
7. From 'The Federal Reserve System: Purposes and Functions'.
8. The letter, dated 22 April 2009, can be found at <http://www.bankofengland.co.uk/monetarypolicy/pdf/chancellorletter090422.pdf>.
9. The first reference to the 'Great Moderation' was in James H. Stock and Mark W. Watson's *Has the Business Cycle Changed and Why?*, Research Working Paper No. W9127, National Bureau of Economic Research, Cambridge, MA, 2002. The term was popularized by Ben Bernanke in a speech in February 2004 when he was a Governor at the Federal Reserve. His speech is available at <http://www.federalreserve.gov/BOARD-DOCS/SPEECHES/2004/20040220/default.htm>.
10. Purchasing power parity assumes the cost of a non-tradable service is the same in all parts of the world. The opportunity cost of providing a haircut in Beverly Hills, however, is likely to be higher than in, say, Kunming in China. The American hair-dresser might have foregone a career as a movie star whereas the Kunming barber might only have had the option of being an underemployed rural worker. A haircut is, therefore, more expensive in Beverly Hills, even in the absence of highlights.
11. See <http://www.imf.org/external/pubs/ft/weo/2006/02/pdf/c5.pdf>.
12. See 'The Challenge of Central Banking in a Democratic Society', December 1996, available at <http://www.federalreserve.gov/boarddocs/speeches/1996/19961205.htm>.
13. The comment comes from John Maynard Keynes's *Economic Consequences of the Peace* (Macmillan, London, 1919). 'Lenin is said to have declared that the best way to destroy the Capitalist System was to debauch the currency . . . Lenin was certainly right. There is no subtler, no surer means of overturning the existing basis of society than to debauch the currency. The process engages all the hidden forces of economic law on the side of destruction, and does it in a manner which not one man in a million is able to diagnose.' (pp 220–1) No one can be sure that Lenin actually said anything of the sort, but Keynes, a member of the British Peace Delegation at Versailles, may well have heard stories about the Soviets saying such things and was happy to make the claim that the words had come from Lenin's lips.
14. Of the largest countries in the emerging world, both China and Russia have managed exchange rates against other currencies. China's renminbi is no longer linked to the dollar alone but, instead, to a basket of currencies which, in my view, appears to mimic the performance of the European monetary snake of the 1970s, retaining a heavy bias towards the US dollar. Plenty of other emerging economies follow similar models. Russia's currency regime is explicitly linked to a US dollar and euro basket. Countries and regions that, at the time of writing, still had an explicit dollar peg included the Caribbean nations, Cuba, the Democratic Republic of Congo, Ecuador, Equatorial Guinea, Hong Kong, Liberia, Malaysia, Nigeria, Oman, Panama, Saudi Arabia, Singapore, Syria and the United Arab Emirates (source: Bloomberg).

15. Bela Balassa, 'The purchasing power parity doctrine: a reappraisal', *Journal of Political Economy*, 72 (1964), pp. 584–96; Paul Samuelson, 'Theoretical notes on trade problems', *Review of Economics and Statistics*, 23 (1964), pp. 145–54.
16. The minutes and transcripts of FOMC meetings can be found at <http://www.federal-reserve.gov/monetarypolicy/fomccalendars.htm>.

CHAPTER 6: HAVES AND HAVE-NOTS

1. Remarks made in Heber Springs, Arkansas, at the dedication of Greers Ferry Dam, 3 October 1963
2. From speech given to the GMB Union on 5 June 2007
3. In *The Bottom Billion* Paul Collier discusses four traps which leave nations facing abject poverty: the conflict trap, the natural resource trap, the 'landlocked with bad neighbours' trap and the 'bad governance in a small country' trap.
4. *China's Income Distribution Over Time: Reasons for Rising Income Inequality.* Department of Agriculture and Resource Economics Paper 977, University of California, Berkeley.
5. The US Census Bureau calculates that the percentage of the US population with a bachelor's degree or above stood at 4.6 per cent in 1940, rose to 7.7 per cent by 1960, was at 16.2 per cent by 1980 and by 2000 had risen to 24.2 per cent. See <http://www.census.gov/population/socdemo/education/phct41/table2.csv>.
6. *Inequality and Institutions in 20th Century America* (MIT Press, Boston, 2007).
7. *Wall Street and Main Street: What Contributes to the Rise in the Highest Incomes?* (Center for Research in Security Prices, University of Chicago Graduate School of Business, July 2007).
8. In an earlier draft of this book, Tiger Woods was my chosen example. As Mr Woods discovered in November 2009, global admiration can quickly evaporate.
9. In strict balance of payments terms, the increase in recorded exports from the analyst would be offset by lower profits made by the overseas affiliate of the company which would now be paying for the analyst's consultancy services. If – and it's a big 'if' – the profits of this affiliate were routinely brought home, the overall impact on the balance of payments would be neutral. Nevertheless, the point of my argument is simply that activities considered to be domestic are, in reality, often international.
10. Francis Jones, Daniel Annan and Saef Shah, 'The distribution of household income 1977 to 2006/07', Office for National Statistics, *Economic and Labour Market Review*, 2.12 (2008), pp. 18–31.
11. Some emerging economies, notably those in Latin America, have always had high levels of income inequality: political systems have allowed the middle classes to extract reasonable incomes even though rates of economic growth have often been poor.
12. Simon Kuznets, 'Toward a theory of economic growth'. in Robert Lekachman, *National Policy for Economic Welfare at Home and Abroad* (Doubleday, Garden City, NY, 1955).
13. Source: UN Food and Agriculture Organization.
14. Source: Prabhu Pingali, *Westernization of Asian Diets and the Transformation of Food Systems: Implications for Research and Policy*, ESA Working Paper No. 04–17, Rome, September 2004.
15. United Nations Environment Programme, 'The Environmental Food Crisis: The Environment's Role in Averting Future Food Crisis', Norway (February 2009), p. 27.
16. I personally won't be: I suffer from a nut allergy. More seriously, scientists have been investigating the possibility of creating synthetic meats. See, for example, <http://www.timesonline.co.uk/tol/news/science/article6936352.ece>.
17. Andrew Leicester, Cormac O'Dea and Zoë Oldfield, *The Inflation Experience of Older Households*, IFS Commentary No.106, London, October 2008.

18. Rob Pike, Catherine Marks and Darren Morgan, 'Measuring UK inflation', *Economic and Labour Market Review*, 2.9 (2008), pp. 18–25.
19. Milton Friedman, *A Theory of the Consumption Function* (Princeton University Press, Princeton, 1957).
20. See, for example, Ian Walker and Yu Zhu, *The College Wage Premium and the Expansion of Higher Education in the UK*, UCD Geary Institute Discussion Paper July 2008.
21. Remarks by President Obama on international tax policy reform, the White House, Washington DC, 4 May 2009.

CHAPTER 7: WHO CONTROLS WHAT? THE RISE OF STATE CAPITALISM

1. Not all of these funds reside in emerging nations and not all of them are controlled by nation states. Norway and Alaska, for example, both have sizeable funds.
2. The difference in inflation rates is a token gesture towards the Balassa–Samuelson condition outlined in Chapter 5.
3. Household savings ratios – the ratios of the gap between income and consumption, divided by income, in any one year – in the developed world were generally much higher in the 1960s than they are today.
4. Source: Bloomberg.
5. Manchester City was previously owned by Thaksin Shinawatra, the former prime minister of Thailand, who was deposed in a coup while out of the country and then sentenced *in absentia* to two years in jail.
6. Many of the Premiership club purchases were funded through short-term debt, an unfortunate process given the arrival of the credit crunch shortly afterwards. These leveraged deals leave the ownership of clubs in doubt and also raise questions about the motivations of the billionaires regarding the purchase of these clubs: in some cases, it's not the love of soccer that is driving the deal but, instead, the desire to curry favour and to shift assets across borders.
7. In a chance conversation with a real-estate agent who specialized in sales in Cap Ferrat, one of the most exclusive areas in the Côte d'Azur, I was reliably told, 'The English can no longer afford properties here: it's all Russians and Turks.'
8. For a detailed description of the aims, objectives and risks associated with SWFs, see *Sovereign Wealth Funds – A Work Agenda* by the IMF, Washington DC, 29 February 2008.
9. IMF. *Sovereign Wealth Funds – A Work Agenda*, Washington DC, 2008.
10. All figures quoted in this section come from the *BP Statistical Review of World Energy*, June 2009.
11. South Stream's competitor project, Nabucco, was favoured by the European Union but may not be able to guarantee sufficient gas supplies running through its network. The Russian leadership may still be able to adopt a 'divide and rule' approach to supplying energy to Western European powers: indeed, although Turkey signed up for Nabucco in July 2009, causing much EU rejoicing, Vladimir Putin was still able to get Turkey to agree on South Stream in August, helped along by promises regarding oil pipelines and nuclear power.
12. Gazprom bought Pennine Natural Gas in 2006, its first UK acquisition. At the time, Vitaly Vasiliev, chief executive of Gazprom's UK arm Gazprom Marketing & Trading (GMT), said: 'Gazprom has always intended to enter the UK gas supply market and this deal offers us an excellent base from which to grow our supply business.' (Source: *Daily Telegraph*, 23 June 2006)
13. Remarks made at St Petersburg Economic Forum, June 2009.
14. Alan Beattie, Stephanie Kirchgaessner and Raphael Minder, 'Left in the cold: foreign bidders find themselves out of favour', FT.com, 24 April 2008. It's unclear whether

Frank's comments were an attack on Islam: if they were, they were remarkably ill-informed given that around 60 per cent of Malaysia's population is Muslim.

15. The US Department of Agriculture publishes a wealth of detail on food production and trade around the world. 'Food wars' are, in fact, 'water wars' because, in effect, the export of grain is, indirectly, the export of water: grains cannot grow without water. Climate change will lead to further disruptions in this area.

CHAPTER 8: RUNNING OUT OF WORKERS

1. Slavery was abolished in the UK and its empire through the Acts of 1807 and 1833. Slavery remained in force in parts of the US until the addition of the Thirteenth Amendment to the US Constitution in 1865. Nazi Germany and the Soviet Union used slavery. Saudi Arabia only abolished slavery in 1962. Today, although slavery is illegal more or less everywhere, the practice hasn't stopped. A common modern-day version is human trafficking.

2. For individual countries and regions, net migration rates are a very important influence to be discussed later in the chapter.

3. I have to admit that the 'surge in optimism' argument is rather unconvincing; to my mind, it sounds like an *ex post* rationalization. The study of demographics seems to be rather full of these kinds of arguments.

4. See, for example, David E Bloom, David Canning and Jaypee Sevilla, *Economic Growth and the Demographic Transition* (National Bureau of Economic Research, Cambridge, MA, 2001).

5. There are, of course, exceptions to this general rule. Birth rates in Russia, Belarus, the Ukraine and Georgia are remarkably low: their populations are ageing through an absence of youth rather than a huge increase in the elderly.

6. For those familiar with simple monetary economics, the increase in spending represents an increase in the velocity of money supply.

7. Source: US Department of Health and Human Services.

8. Source: Deutsche Bundesbank.

9. Source: Jeffrey G. Williamson, 'Global migration', *Finance & Development*, 43.3 (2006), IMF, Washington DC.

10. The Immigration and Nationality Act of 1965 was proposed by Emanuel Celler and co-sponsored by Philip Hart. It got rid of the national-origin quotas that had been in operation following the 1924 Immigration Act. A limitation of 170,000 visas was established for immigrants from countries from the Eastern Hemisphere. No more than 20,000 could come from any one country. By 1968, the annual limitation from the Western Hemisphere was set at 120,000 immigrants. Visas were given out on a first-come first-served basis. The number of family reunification visas was unlimited.

11. Source: European Commission EURES website. The specific page is <http://ec.europa.eu/eures/main.jsp?acro=free&lang=en&countryId=UK&fromCountryId=RO&accessing=0&content=1&restrictions=1&step=2>.

12. The relevant article can be found at <http://www.ukba.homeoffice.gov.uk/sitecontent/newsarticles/Government-keeps-work-restrict>.

13. L. Barbone, M. Bontch-Osmolovsky and S. Zaidi, *The Foreign-born Population in the European Union and its Contribution to National Tax and Benefit Systems*, World Bank, Washington, DC, April 2009.

14. OECD *Economic Outlook Interim Report*, March 2009.

15. Higher remittances will tend to lift the exchange rate of the receiving country, thereby limiting other areas of economic endeavour. Overall, though, remittances probably exert a positive economic impact.

16. For an entertaining, if sobering, history of the UK from the perspective of immigration, read Robert Winder's *Bloody Foreigners: The Story of Immigration to Britain* (Little Brown, London, 2004).

CHAPTER 9: INDULGING THE US NO MORE

1. *Fiscal and Generational Imbalances: New Budget Measures for New Budget Priorities*, Policy Discussion Paper No. 5, Federal Reserve Bank of Cleveland, OH, 2003.
2. In the UK, this would be the equivalent of a doubling of National Insurance contributions for both employers and employees.
3. Fiscal surpluses would likely lead to lower interest rates, possibly increasing household and corporate borrowing. The rise in the fiscal surplus would have to more than offset any increase in private-sector borrowing to ensure an overall increase in national saving, which, in turn, would facilitate a move into balance of payments current account surplus.
4. Source: OECD *Economic Outlook*, June 2009.
5. At a White House press conference on 16 September 2001, President Bush said, 'This crusade, this war on terrorism is going to take a while.' See <http://georgewbush-white-house.archives.gov/news/releases/2001/09/20010916-2.html>.
6. Argentina fell into this trap: it devalued and defaulted to its foreign creditors in 2001.
7. At the time of writing, Google was attempting to do exactly that.
8. Source: Office of the Russian Prime Minister.
9. The Washington Consensus was a view driven by the idea that 'the market knows best' and was often imposed by the IMF and others on unsuspecting economies that simply couldn't cope with liberalized markets and small government. Most obviously, it demanded aggressive fiscal consolidation. Funnily enough, this particular stricture has now been forgotten in the light of the huge increases in budget deficits which followed the 2007/8 credit crunch.
10. 'Sterling's Past, Dollar's Future: Historical Perspectives on Reserve Currency Competition', Tawney Lecture delivered to the Economic History Society, Leicester, 10 April 2005.

CHAPTER 10: COPING WITH THE WEST'S DIMINISHED STATUS

1. Not having a currency does not create a free lunch: governments would have to be more fiscally conservative because the printing press option – creating inflation to defraud government creditors – would no longer exist.
2. I could go even further: to limit the risk to future British and American taxpayers of having large international financial institutions based in London and New York, why not turn London and New York into international cities, supported by the taxpayers of all nations? They could then become financial equivalents of the Vatican City: after all, their love of money is sometimes almost religious in its zeal.
3. A single currency does not, of course, guarantee a free lunch. Strains within the euro area began to emerge at the end of 2009 as countries with weak fiscal positions were faced with the prospect of years of miserable austerity, threatening political instability. At the time of writing, it was unclear whether the appetite to take tough fiscal medicine was really there, leading to nervousness in sovereign debt markets.
4. 'A return to 1815 is the way forward for Europe', *The Times*, 2 September 2008.
5. Samuel Huntingdon's influential – and controversial – take on the world's political, social, ethnic and religious divisions.

6. For a detailed discussion of the dangers associated with the narrow-minded labelling of people according to their national, ethnic or religious background, see Amartya Sen's *Identity and Violence: The Illusion of Destiny* (Allen Lane, London, 2006).
7. Paul Kennedy's *The Rise and Fall of the Great Powers* (Random House, New York, 1988) ties together both economic and military influences in explaining shifts in great power tectonics over the centuries.

CONCLUSION

1. The classic modern-day texts on these issues include John Rawls, *A Theory of Justice* (Harvard University Press, Cambridge, MA, 1971) and Robert Nozick, *Anarchy, State and Utopia* (Basic Books, New York, 1974).

SELECT BIBLIOGRAPHY

Aherne, A., Gagnon, J., Haltmaier, J. and Kamin, S., *Preventing Deflation: Lessons from Japan's Experience in the 1990s*, Federal Reserve International Finance Discussion Paper, Washington DC, 2002

Akerlof, G., 'The market for lemons: quality uncertainty and the market mechanism', *Quarterly Journal of Economics*, 84.3 (1970), pp. 488–500

Balassa, B., 'The purchasing power doctrine: a reappraisal', *Journal of Political Economy*, 72 (1964), pp. 584–96

Barbone, L., Bontch-Osmolovssky, M. and Zaidi, S., *The Foreign-born Population in the European Union and its Contribution to National Tax and Benefit Systems*, World Bank, Washington, DC, April 2009

Baumol, W., Litan, R. and Schramm, C., *Good Capitalism, Bad Capitalism and the Economics of Growth and Prosperity*, Yale University Press, New Haven, 2007

Bernanke, B., *The Great Moderation*, Federal Reserve, Washington DC, 2004

————, *The Global Savings Glut*, Federal Reserve, Washington DC, 2005

Besley, T., 'Principled Agents? The Political Economy of Good Government', The Lindahl Lectures, Oxford, 2006

Bloom, D., Canning, D. and Sevilla, J., *Economic Growth and the Demographic Transition*, National Bureau of Economic Research, Cambridge MA, 2001

BP, Statistical Review of World Energy, London, June 2009

Buruma, I. and Margalit, A., *Occidentalism: A Short History of Anti-Westernism*, Penguin Press, New York, 2004

Chang, H.-J., *Kicking Away the Ladder: Development Strategy in Historical Perspective*, Anthem, London, 2002

————, *Bad Samaritans: The Myth of Free Trade and the Secret History of Capitalism*, Bloomsbury, London, 2008

Clark, G., *A Farewell to Alms: A Brief Economic History of the World*, Princeton University Press, Princeton, 2007

Collier, P., *The Bottom Billion: Why the Poorest Countries are Failing and What Can Be Done About It*, Oxford University Press, Oxford, 2006

Davies, N., *Europe: A History*, Oxford University Press, Oxford, 1996

Desai, M., *Marx's Revenge: The Resurgence of Capitalism and the Death of Statist Socialism*, Verso, London, 2002

Eichengreen, B., *Globalizing Capital: A History of the International Monetary System*, Princeton University Press, Princeton, 1996

———, *Sterling's Past, Dollar's Future: Historical Perspectives on Reserve Currency Competition*, Tawney Lecture, Economic History Society, Leicester, April 2005

———, *Global Imbalances and the Lessons from Bretton Woods*, The Cairoli Lectures, MIT Press, Cambridge MA, 2007

Federal Reserve Bank of Kansas, *New Challenges for Monetary Policy*, Proceedings, Jackson Hole, WY, 1999

Ferguson, N., *Colossus: The Rise and Fall of the American Empire*, Allen Lane, London, 2004

———, *The Ascent of Money: A Financial History of the World*, Allen Lane, London, 2008

Findlay, R. and O'Rourke, K., *Power and Plenty: Trade, War, and the World Economy in the Second Millennium*, Princeton University Press, Princeton and Oxford, 2007

Friedman, B., *The Moral Consequences of Economic Growth*, Alfred A. Knopf, New York, 2005

Friedman, M., *A Theory of the Consumption Function*, Princeton University Press, Princeton, 1957

Friedman, T., *The Lexus and the Olive Tree*, Farrar, Strauss & Giroux, New York, 1999

———, *The World is Flat: A Brief History of the 21st Century*, Farrar, Strauss, Giroux, New York, 2005

Fukuyama, F., *The End of History and the Last Man*, Free Press, New York, 1992

Gibson, C. and Lennon, E., *Historical Census Statistics on the Foreign-born Population of the United States: 1850–1990*, Population Division Working Paper No. 29, US Bureau of the Census, Washington DC, 1999

Gohkale, J. and Smetters, K., *Fiscal and Generational Imbalances: New Budget Measures for New Budget Priorities*, Policy Discussion Paper No. 5, Federal Reserve Bank of Cleveland, OH, 2003

Greenspan, A., *The Challenge of Central Banking in a Democratic Society*, Federal Reserve, Washington DC, 1996

———, *The Age of Turbulence: Adventures in a New World*, Allen Lane, London, 2007

Headrick, D.R., *Tools of Empire: Technology and European Imperialism in the Nineteenth Century*, Oxford University Press, Oxford, 1981

Heilbroner, R., *The Worldly Philosophers: The Lives, Times and Ideas of the Great Economic Thinkers*, 7th edn, Simon & Shuster, New York, 1999

Hertz, N., *The Silent Takeover*, The Free Press, New York, 2002

Hobbes, T., ed Gaskin, J., *Leviathan*, Oxford University Press, Oxford, 2008

House of Commons Treasury Committee, *Globalisation: Prospects and Policy Responses*, Fourteenth Report of Session, London, 2006/7

Hume, D. *"Of National Characters"* in "Hume: Political Essays", ed. Knud Haakonssen, Cambridge Texts in the History of Political Thought, Cambridge University Press, Cambridge, 1994, pp 78–92

Huntingdon, S., *The Clash of Civilisations and the Remaking of World Order*, Simon & Schuster, New York, 1997

Hutton, W., *The Writing on the Wall: China and the West in the 21st Century*, Little Brown, London, 2007

IMF, *World Economic Outlook*, Washington DC, September 2006

———, *Sovereign Wealth Funds – A Work Agenda*, Washington DC, 2008

———, *Currency Composition of Foreign Exchange Reserves*, Washington DC, 2009

Select Bibliography

Jones, F., Annan, D. and Shah, S., 'The distribution of household income 1977 to 2006/07', Office for National Statistics, *Economic and Labour Market Review*, 2.12 (2008), pp. 18–31

Judt, T., *Postwar: A History of Europe since 1945*, William Heinemann, London, 2005

Kaplan, S. and Rauh, J., *Wall Street and Main Street: What Contributes to the Rise in the Highest Incomes?* Center for Research in Security Prices, University of Chicago Graduate School of Business, July 2007

Kay, J., *The Truth About Markets: Why Some Nations are Rich but Most Remain Poor*, Allen Lane, London, 2003

Kennedy, P., *The Rise and Fall of the Great Powers*, Random House, New York, 1988

Keynes, J.M., *The Economic Consequences of the Peace*, Macmillan, London, 1919

Kindleberger, C., *Manias, Panics and Crashes: A History of Financial Crises*, 3rd edn, John Wiley, New York, 1996

King, M., 'The MPC Ten Years On', Lecture given to Society of Business Economists, London, May 2007

King, S., *A Shifting Centre of Gravity*, HSBC Research, January 2007

———, *Money Makes the World Go Round*, HSBC Research, May 2007

King, S. and Green, S., *The Tipping Point*, Global Economics, HSBC Research, Fourth Quarter 2009

King, S. and Henry, J., *The New World Order*, HSBC Research, First Quarter 2006.

Klein, N., *No Logo*, 10th anniversary edn, Fourth Estate, New York, 2009

Kuznets, S., 'Toward a theory of economic growth' in R. Lekachman, *National Policy for Economic Welfare at Home and Abroad*, Doubleday, Garden City, NY, 1955

Kynge, J., *China Shakes the World: The Rise of a Hungry Nation*, Weidenfeld & Nicolson, London, 2006

Landes, D., *The Wealth and Poverty of Nations*, W.W. Norton and Co., New York, 1998

Leicester, A., O'Dea, C. and Oldfield, Z., *The Inflation Experience of Older Households*, IFS Commentary No.106, London, October 2008

Levy, F. and Temin, P., *Inequality and Institutions in 20th Century America*, MIT Press, Boston, 2007

Lewis, B., *What Went Wrong? Western Impact and Middle East Response*, Weidenfeld & Nicolson, London, 2002

Lucas, E., *The New Cold War: How the Kremlin Menaces both Russia and the West*, Bloomsbury, London, 2008

Maddison, A., *Chinese Economic Performance in the Long Run, Second Edition, Revised and Updated, 960–2030 AD*, OECD Development Centre, Paris, 2007

———, *Contours of the World Economy, 1–2030 AD: Essays in Macro-Economic History*, Oxford University Press, Oxford, 2007

Malthus, T., ed. Gilbert, G., *An Essay on the Principle of Population*, Oxford University Press, Oxford, 1993

Marx, K. and Engels, F., *The Communist Manifesto*, Penguin, London, 2005

Meyer, C., 'A return to 1815 is the way forward for Europe', *The Times*, 2 September 2008

Nozick, R., *Anarchy, State and Utopia*, Basic Books, New York, 1974

Obstfeld, M. and Taylor, A., *Global Capital Markets, Integration, Crisis, and Growth*, Cambridge University Press, Cambridge, 2004

OECD, *Economic Outlook Interim Report*, Paris, March 2009

OECD, *Economic Outlook*, Paris, June 2009

Pike, R. Marks, C. and Morgan, D., 'Measuring UK inflation', *Economic and Labour Market Review*, 2.9 (2008), pp. 18–25

Pingali, P., *Westernization of Asian Diets and the Transformation of Food Systems: Implications for Research and Policy*, ESA Working Paper No. 04-17, Rome, September 2004

Qu, Hongbin, *The Great Migration*, HSBC Research, 2005

Rawls, J., *A Theory of Justice*, Harvard University Press, Cambridge, MA, 1971

Ricardo, D., *The Principles of Political Economy and Taxation*, Dover, New York, 2004

Samuelson, P., 'Theoretical notes on trade problems', *Review of Economics and Statistics*, 23 (1964), pp. 145–54

———, 'Where Ricardo and Mill rebut and confirm arguments of mainstream economists supporting globalisation', *Journal of Economic Perspectives*, 18.3 (2004), pp. 135–46

Sandbrook, D., *White Heat: A History of Britain in the Swinging Sixties*, Little Brown, London, 2006

Santiso, J., *Latin America's Political Economy of the Possible: Beyond Good Revolutionaries and Free-Marketeers*, MIT Press, Boston, 2007

Sen, A., *Identity and Violence: The Illusion of Destiny*, Allen Lane, London, 2006

Shiller, R., *Irrational Exuberance*, Princeton University Press, Princeton, 2000

Smith, A., *The Wealth of Nations, Books I–III and Books IV–V*, Penguin, London, 1999

———, *Theory of Moral Sentiments*, Prometheus, London, 2000

Stevenson, D., *1914–1918: The History of the First World War*, Allen Lane, London, 2004

Stiglitz, J., *Globalisation and its Discontents*, Penguin, London, 2003

Stock, J. and Watson, M., *Has the Business Cycle Changed and Why?* Research Working Paper No. W9127, National Bureau of Economic Research, Cambridge, MA, 2002

Stone, N., *World War One: A Short History*, Allen Lane, London, 2007

Sturzenegger, F. and Zettelmeyer, J., *Debt Defaults and Lessons from a Decade of Crises*, MIT Press, Cambridge, MA, 2006

UN, *World Population Prospects*, 2008 Revision, New York

UNCTAD, *World Investment Review*, Geneva, 2008 and 2009

US Treasury, *Report to Congress on International Economic and Exchange Rate Policies*, Washington DC, 2009

Walker, I. and Yu, Z., *The College Wage Premium and the Expansion of Higher Education in the UK*, UCD Geary Institute Discussion Paper, July 2008

Williamson, J., 'Global Migration', *Finance and Development*, 43.3 (2006), IMF, Washington DC

Winder, R., *Bloody Foreigners: The Story of Immigration to Britain*, Little Brown, London, 2004

World Bank, *World Development Indicators*, Washington DC, 2009

Wolf, M., *Why Globalisation Works*, Yale University Press, New Haven, 2004

———, *Fixing Global Finance: How to Curb Financial Crises in the 21st Century*, Yale University Press, New Haven, 2009

Wu, X. and Perloff, J., *China's Income Distribution Over Time: Reasons for Rising Income Inequality*, Department of Agriculture and Resource Economics Paper 977, University of California, Berkeley

INDEX

Index

Index

Index

Index

Index